Calvert's Guide
to
THE BRITISH

British stereotypes in order of social rank

Calvert's Guide
to
THE BRITISH

British stereotypes in order of social rank

Illustrated by

Tim Bulmer

that company called **if**
PUBLISHERS

that company called **if** Publishers,
if House, Thornton Road, Pickering,
North Yorkshire YO18 7JB.

Published by that company called **if** 2012

First Edition

Copyright © John Calvert

Written by John Calvert and Michael Powell
Illustrated by Tim Bulmer
Production by Ned Hoste

A catalogue record for this book is available from the British Library.

ISBN: 978-1-903413-40-1

Printed and bound in the UK by Butler Tanner & Dennis Ltd, Frome

We hope you enjoy it!

Introduction

This book is all about the British People. There isn't another one like it in print in the world and it is essential reading for visitors and residents seeking to understand traditional British stereotypes within the class system. This unique guide aims to provide a contemporary social commentary and capture a snapshot of British folk as they are today.

This country has always been a cosmopolitan blend of sundry influences but despite our best efforts to be individualistic, we are all influenced by our history and surroundings. Our homes, gardens, partners, cars, fashions, accents, attitudes, haircuts, domestic pets and choice of music are all refracted through a nationalistic prism. Collectively these limited choices combine to make us distinctive as a nation but desperately unoriginal as individuals.

Volume One of this exclusive work of reference sets out boldly to identify a wide range of common British stereotypes but also to point up their position in the class system, to highlight the psychological issues that affect them and the social markers they adopt to assert their identity.

The characters appear in ascending order of social status. Rest assured that we reached these strata through extensive independent qualitative research.

Secretly all British people rank themselves against neighbours and strangers. Some scramble to out-do, some doggedly reject the idea of competition or social order and firmly declare equality for all but we all fall predictably into clichés that enable others to accurately categorise and judge us.

Stereotypes do exist, however strenuously political correctness tries to avoid them and they are funny. If you're a woolly liberal you'll probably choke on your blueberry and tahini smoothie as you read this book; if you're a snob or xenophobe you will seek validation of your repellent beliefs within these pages. All three miss the point. The harder we overstate similarity or difference the more we mistrust each other and ignore the truth. So here we tell it how it is and get down and dirty with the Brits in all their eccentricity and colourful crapitude.

Sadly, many of the older and more interesting stereotypes are dwindling and will soon disappear forever to be replaced by a national identity that will fit into a pocket-size edition within twenty years, thanks to the increasing homogeneity of popular culture and the pursuit of instant gratification which will soon reduce a once great nation to a mere handful of stereotypes with which to populate its soil.

Our younger citizens are fast becoming bland and repetitive in the same way that city centres have been infected by globalism – same hair, same clothes, same feeble questioning intonation, same "whatever", same brands, same music, same attitude. Dull, frankly. Three cheers for the Chelsea Pensioner, train spotter and retired miner.

Icons used in this book

The icons in this book are self-explanatory, but here is a brief account of why they were chosen and what makes them such important social predictors.

Life expectancy

The life expectancy for someone living in the UK *at birth* is 77.9 for men and 82 for women, that's eight years longer than in the 1970s so maybe all those terrifying public information films about seatbelts, ponds and electric pylons finally did some good. Life expectancy at birth is calculated using the formula $(e_x = \sum_{t=1}^{\infty} tPx = \sum_{t=0}^{\infty} t\, tPxqx + t) / (y^2)$ where y is the number of Staffordshire Bull Terriers in the extended family and *t* is the average annual expenditure on American style food.

IQ

An intelligence quotient, or IQ, is a score derived from one of several standardized tests designed to measure how intelligent your parents are. Because, let's face it, anecdotally we can all agree that stupid breeders produce dumb kids, but for some reason boffin scientists with high IQs still can't decide to what extent intelligence is inherited. They do at least concede that IQ is linked to many life outcomes such as rates of morbidity, involvement in crime, wealth creation, education and parenting skills.

Television

[Hours per week] The UK has the highest television viewing figures in Europe, equalling the United States with a mean of 28 hours per week. These statistics are even more depressing when you consider the quality of the programs that get the most viewing figures. Although unproven, this guide shows evidence that television habits and program choice are directly linked to life expectancy.

Books

[Read per year] The UK regularly tops the list of the number of new books published each year per country with more than 200,000 titles. This staggering waste of paper is supposed to indicate our high standard of living and education. In fact it merely charts a year on year growth of the three largest reading sectors – women, pensioners and the chronically constipated. Furthermore, one in five people in the UK claim not to have read a single book in the past year.

Alcohol

[Units per week] The unit of alcohol has been a revelation for the political elite in this country. Not only has it made drinking habits and tax revenues measurable, it has given Whitehall demographers a case file of priceless correlative data such as socio-economic background, mental health, domestic violence, underage pregnancy, proximity to Scotland, sales of skimpy outfits and fake tan and the tendency to act like a bit of a twat. Alcohol consumption has become the single most powerful tool to assess and exploit the British population since the introduction of the training shoe.

Smoking

[Cigarettes/cigars/pipes/spliffs per day] In the UK, smoking remains the greatest single cause of defensive superiority. Every year about 100,000 smokers die of a superiority related disease. Many smokers start feeling cooler and more intelligent than non-smokers during their early teens and by adulthood they are addicted. Many develop leathery grey skin and interesting character lines during their thirties and half will at some point be killed by their own self-importance. As with all life-shortening government scams, there is a strong link between smoking and low incomes. The anti-smoking lobby whines about the £5 billion annual burden of smoking on the NHS but it also generates a tax revenue of £11 billion, a net gain of £6 billion or 12,000 cruise missiles to help Britain export peace and democracy around the world.

Domestic pets

You shouldn't judge a person by their pet but we all do even though it's a poor predictor of personality and personal hygiene. Recent figures show that dogs are set to eclipse cats as the nation's favourite pet, mainly due to a steep rise in fashionable handbag breeds such as pugs and Chihuahuas caused by a combination of shrinking incomes and the rampant growth of celebrity culture.

Days spent in jail

[Per lifetime] Days spent in jail is a useful indicator of an individual's injunctive norms but on balance it's probably a better judge of stupidity and incompetence plus it ignores undetected criminality, early release due to jail overcrowding and woolly Liberalism. Days spent electronically tagged or unconscious in police custody are not catered for in this guide neither is deviancy in the corporate, political and judicial branches of British society.

Long Term Unemployed Dad

 62

 61

 58

 75

 21

This Jack Russell owning sponger 'lives with his mum' if anyone asks but spends most of his time watching TV, smoking weed or shopping at the cheapest German food retailers. He claims he wants a job and that being unemployed is tough; he recently had to take out a DWP budgeting loan to pay his X-Box Live and Sky Sports subscriptions.

He blames the migrants that Brown and Blair let in for taking his job and he hates students because he knows many of them will also take his job when they graduate and can't find higher paid work. He claims he's not a racist though because he fancies black girls in porn mags. Really there is no such thing as 'his job' because he hasn't worked for years and he couldn't take one if it was offered to him because he has a bad back, although this doesn't stop him humping like a rabbit. The government should employ him to visit failing schools and tell kids to study hard if they don't want to end up like him.

When he isn't smoking he chews gum with a slack jaw while lurching down the road as though somehow his walking and chewing are interconnected. He has given up on his dreams of forming an obscure rock band no one has heard of so Kate Moss will shag him. He once had a bass guitar with two strings but he never managed to put a plug on the stolen amp a mate left at his house for a while. He could live a better life in a warm country like India or the Caribbean but the idea does not occur to him. He only looks forward to getting his dole money and buying the cheapest black market fags he can lay his hands on.

Characteristics

Reading Material: Daily Express, lottery draw

Favourite TV Programmes and Films: National Lottery Live, Sky Sports, X-Box, Jeremy Kyle – either watching it or on it!

Heroes and Role Models: Premiership footballers, wrestlers and boxers, guitarist with The Kills

Most likely cause of death: Bound to be unpleasant

Favourite Music: Anything on FLAVA

Political Views: Doesn't vote

Ego Issues: He classes himself as a tax payer because some of his handouts return to the treasury as VAT

Fears: Getting a job interview, getting a job, being made to do compulsory manual labour under a Work Activity scheme, introduction of the universal credit

Likes: Taxpayer-funded lifestyle, taking drugs, sitting on his arse, making excuses and blaming circumstances

Dislikes: Work, being labelled as a scrounger, dreaming about his dreams rather than pursuing them

Earnings: Income Support

Offspring: He has four children to two ladies but married neither in the interests of Income Support claims.

Drives: Playstation 3

Most likely to say: "I'm not racist but if I woz a muslim single mother, right, they'd give me a fookin mansion"

Chav

64

50

40

210

6

This bling and junk-food obsessed bottom feeder walks with a swagger and knows he's a lowlife gimp so he blows any dole money not tied up in Big Macs on ludicrous markers of wealth. He wears a Burberry baseball cap and Reebok Classics, shoplifted designer labels, and fakes from the local market. Popular labels used to be Nike, Adidas, Juicy Couture, McKenzie and Lacoste but more recently Abercrombie and Fitch and Holister have also become infested. Sovereign rings and dookie ropes are sourced from Argos or H Samuel and his hair is gelled forward into a straggly fringe. For monthly court appearances he wears a machine washable suit from Ciro Citterio.

He can't land a punch, but likes spitting and kicking and would get the crap kicked out of him if he wasn't backed up by six of his scrawny mates. He drinks between 20 and 40 units of alcohol a day, usually discount cider and lager (mixed).

He pimps his small hatchback with body kits, blue lights, bucket seats, decals and double exhausts from Halfords. He is also attracted to shiny plastic rims and car mats with pieces of electric blue brushed steel glued on. At dusk he drives to McDonalds car park (the chav equivalent of the Royal Society) and plays drum 'n' bass through a 1000W sub woofer to announce his availability to any chavettes in the area who aren't currently shagging behind the roll top wheelie bins. Prior to acquiring his "ride" he rode everywhere on a BMX bike which was blatantly stolen from a small child.

Characteristics

Reading Material: Autotrader (Cars Under £1000), (still asks for News of the World), whatever's tatooed across his girlfriend's bum

Favourite TV Programmes and Films: Shameless, The National Lottery Live and anything with an 18 certificate

Heroes and Role Models: Michael Carroll, Jason Statham

Most likely cause of death: Argument over a Big Mac, rickets

Favourite Music: Trans/Techno, hard core dance

Political Views: Believes the government should bail out JD Sports

Ego Issues: No one yet has managed to take a photo of a chav with mouth closed, because whenever someone points a camera at them they pull a face and make a defiant ghetto gesture with splayed hands and arms spread wide

Fears: Being sober or being made to work

Likes: Fake designer labels, pimping his car, spitting, benefits, shopping at Iceland, hanging pine fresh tree-shaped air freshener from rear view mirror, ASBOs, thick gold chains that turn green in the rain, Lambert & Butler

Dislikes: Goths, speed bumps and coppers

Earnings: Benefits, whatever he can make from selling stolen goods

Offspring: Two or three, he is not sure

Drives: Vauxhall Nova/Citroen Saxo

Most likely to say: "Mint", "well smart", "bruv", "but seriously though"

Chavette

71

48

40

35

She has badly coloured blonde hair scraped back into a tight pony-tail for the classic 'council house facelift', complete with a few strands hanging down in front of her face. Her eyebrows are terminally overplucked and she wears fake designer tops in pink and or white coupled with 'gold' earrings from Argos so huge that a gorilla could swing off them.

She spends so much time texting that when she looks beyond her mobile her vision goes all blurry. The same happens most evenings after she consumes two litres of cider, or drops an 'E'. She's never used family planning, or as the rest of society calls it, crime prevention.

She's been on R&R (Ritalin & duty free Richmonds) since she was eight. She was recently arrested for attempting an illegal termination but claims she only wanted to pierce her baby's ears.

She lives on McDonald's and sausage rolls from Greggs and smells of Big Macs. She has four kids by five different fathers and she has had their names tramp stamped to help her remember them at meetings with her social worker.

Characteristics

Reading Material: Take away burger menus, texts

Favourite TV Programmes and Films: Embarrassing Bodies – either watching it or on it!

Heroes and Role Models: Cheryl Cole, Coleen Rooney, Tulisa from N-Dubz

Most likely cause of death: High Cholesterol or being in the back without a seat belt on

Favourite Music: Tinchy Stryder; beat from baby's foot in stomach, N-dubz

Political Views: Benefits should be increased

Ego Issues: Wishes she looked more orange, being thought of as easy

Fears: Running out of PAYG credit on her mobile, eyebrows – she plucks them all off and draws them back in again with a black Sharpie 'like what David Beckham advertises'

Likes: Drinking very cheap cider to get wasted then having a shag; Chavs with blue neon windscreen-washer jet lights and under-car lighting

Dislikes: Small portions of chips, contraception, school

Earnings: Benefits, free condoms from STD clinics

Offspring: Four(!) and counting

Would like to drive but actually drives: Mini/Pushchair

Most likely to say: "What are you looking at?"

Racist (nasty thug)

He's lived a bland life in an insipid household, and has had a colourless career managing a DVD rental store. He survives on a diet of pies, chips and pastries and never goes out in the sun or touches foreign food. Having never exerted himself in his life, he nevertheless feels like his mediocrity and 'struggle' is in some way the result of a racial conspiracy though he is as yet unclear of the detail.

He gets together once a month with similarly pitiful, indolent specimens in a room above a snooker hall to practice fascist salutes, compare badges and talk in the vaguest of terms about their views on race, women and homosexuality. None of his political ponderings have any basis in fact, nor do they constitute anything like an ideology. In fact, he's just a thick Staffy owner who's been ignored and ignorable all his life and is now looking for an excuse to hide behind a bunch of other guys and kick off.

He irons his own uniform and sews on his badges like a demented scout leader. He's a divisionist who always sees things in terms of two competing sides because he doesn't have the intellectual ability to reason beyond a dialectic view which makes him feel secure; one example of this is his claim that blacks are more racist than whites.

Characteristics

Reading Material: Voice of Freedom, Identity Magazine, The Sport

Favourite TV Programmes and Films: Jim Davidson, Love Thy Neighbour, Bernard Manning, History Channel

Heroes and Role Models: Bernard Manning, Alf Garnett, Churchill, Heinrich Himmler

Most likely cause of death: Type II Diabetes, stroke

Favourite Music: National Anthem, Jerusalem, Johnny Rebel

Political Views: Ban immigration, re-open mines and shipyards

Ego Issues: Three St George's flags and a Union Jack in his back garden.

Fears: Racial conspiracy

Likes: Fish and chips, playing Call of Duty in his underpants

Dislikes: Racial minorities, naming races after primary colours

Earnings: £8,500

Offspring: None – they got savaged to death by his mate's pit bull

Would like to drive but actually drives: Nazi half-track Sd.Kfz. 250/9 Aire leichte Schützenpanzerwagen /Skoda pick-up

Most likely to say: "Them Pakis should get back to Africa"

Rural Pervert (Misunderstood)

As broadband price and connectivity have improved you don't see that many Rural Perverts around any more despite the community care policy. He's the weird loner tramp guy that country kids used to throw stones at and give a nickname like Pervy George, not without some justification because 'a friend of a friend said he saw him in the lane once with his hands in his pockets and a strange grin on his face'.

Little is known about this misanthrope except that he lives in a disused power station in the woods or at the bottom of the Old Quarry. As a kid you were either one of the insensitive stone throwers, or if you were more imaginative you wished you could talk to him, and then maybe you could have lots of adventures together like Stig of the Dump. This fantasy was soon nipped in the bud after your friends said you wanted to be George's batty boy. There's a rumour that he's really rich and has lots of money buried under an oak tree and that he killed his wife and her ghost guards the treasure. His real name is George Brown he's a caring philanthropist and loved by his nieces and nephews, when they're not throwing stones at him.

Characteristics

Reading Material: Old seed catalogues, back copies of Fertiliser Focus

Favourite TV Programmes and Films: 1970s reruns of Open University (in black and white) on VHS

Heroes and Role Models: Simo Hayha (Finnish war hero)

Most likely cause of death: At home in his sleep

Favourite Music: Mahler, Rachmaninov, Lutosławski

Political Views: As long as he got paid at the end of each week he didn't care! Until the farmer had to let him go, of course

Ego Issues: Is aware of his inability to relate to the outside world but doesn't know what to do about it. He tries smiling at the children but it just makes things worse

Fears: Losing the only people who truly understand him

Likes: Being with those who love him, being left alone by everybody else

Dislikes: The local children, dogs, mistrust and prejudice in locals' eyes, stones

Earnings: State pension

Offspring: None

Drives: Prefers to walk

Most likely to say: "Humph!", "Ouch!"

Resurfacing Consultant

This grubby individual is unfeasibly stubbly and drives a battered old truck. He's richer than you will ever be because he mends roofs, tarmacs drives and fells trees for cash in hand and has never paid a penny in tax. He does, however, have a bank account, and regularly walks into his local branch to make a deposit with twenty-thousand pounds stuffed into his trousers.

He can always undercut the best quote you've been given for a job because the day after he's milked you for information he sends one of his cousins round to shave a few quid off the asking price while making you feel that he's doing you a massive favour.

He lives locally in a caravan or a house he has built without planning permission, kept spotless by his sixteen-year-old wife, while several members of his extended family are buried beneath the patio. He feels it is his birthright to exploit the community and keep a wife young enough to be his granddaughter by claiming he is part of a great tradition handed down over the centuries, but he's not a true Romany, he's just a thieving nonce.

His grubby kids invariably have head lice but to avoid any unpleasantness the school tell us that nits prefer clean hair. Even the nits know this is rubbish.

Characteristics

Reading Material: Can't read

Favourite TV Programmes and Films: Look North, Emmerdale

Heroes and Role Models: David Essex, Richard Branson, The Pogues

Most likely cause of death: Liver failure

Favourite Music: Anything involving tambourines and violins

Political Views: Tory, but can't vote because he's not on the electoral register

Ego Issues: He thinks he's a charming nomad, but he's a dishonest lazy sod who lives in a bigger house than you. When the sun's shining he loves to strip topless to show off his grubby body.

Fears: Tea tree oil; being arrested for nasty offences dating back thirty years

Likes: Lying to people about his £1 million of personal liability insurance for tree felling, mending roofs, felling trees, re-laying drives and patios, sending children out to beg or sell stuff on the highway, scrap-metal collecting

Dislikes: Women, the age of consent, reading, New Age Travellers, being called a pikey, paying taxes, eating hedgehogs

Earnings: £90k

Offspring: Twelve children by eight different mothers (one of which turned out to be a niece)

Drives: New Japanese 4x4 crew cab pick up

Most likely to say: "I'll fix yer feckin roof lady!"; "I'll be back tomorrow to finish off…"

Tramp

A filthy solitary derelict, often found propped between park bench and cashpoint machine, smelling of dried urine. By night he sleeps in a cardboard box by the ring road; by day he drinks the hand gel from the hospital foyer if he can't beg enough spare change for a can of Special Brew.

In his favour, he harms no one but himself; you won't find him running amok in the town centre with a shotgun and a Glock, or axeing 100,000 public sector jobs or snorting cocaine whilst his building society goes belly up. He's simply a homeless alcoholic who's lost his marbles and in Scotland this means he drinks marginally less than the locals.

His daily routine is lonely and cold. He feels bad if he drinks and worse if he doesn't. At his time of life he should be in a Parker Knoll watching his grandchildren play but instead he finds himself muttering in an underpass or being moved on by the police. On the plus side, he's never had to change his underpants or pay tax.

Characteristics

Reading Material: Yesterday's news

Favourite TV Programmes and Films: Hasn't had a TV to watch since 1984, though occasionally looks in through the window of Curry's and expresses surprise that Angela Rippon's still alive

Most likely cause of death: Exposure

Favourite Music: The music died from his life at about the same time Angela Rippon should have. From time to time, however, he has a sing-song under the railway arches with the old fella with the harmonica

Political Views: Over the years he's been on the streets, he's kept a close eye on the price of domestic heating fuel, and reckons that on balance, he's probably not so badly off love!

Ego Issues: Loneliness and poor self-esteem issues are what drove him on to the streets, and loneliness and poor self-esteem are what keep him there

Fears: The cold, the dark, stag parties

Likes: Soup vans, a clean sleeping bag, a fresh tin of Brew

Dislikes: Begging

Earnings: On a good day, enough for a four pack and a bacon buttie

Offspring: Two, somewhere, though they wouldn't recognise him now if they stepped over him

Drives: He used to drive long ago, but these days traffic scares him

Most likely to say: "Gurraaaaafafukyerbaarssttddd"

Village Idiot

Fortunate enough to have an uncle who is also his father. Usually spotted pushing a broken bicycle and wearing wellingtons in a heat wave, this unfortunate type is likely to have only two biological grandparents. He's not dangerous, at least you don't think he is, but whenever you see him he's always several miles away from the last place you spotted him, still striding along with head down muttering to himself, especially in sheeting rain.

It's unclear why village idiots love walking so much. One possible reason is rural cutbacks, which means he now has to serve several villages in the local area. His behaviour indicates at best a level of self-neglect and social withdrawal that makes conversation strained and at worse that he can't remember where he hid his axe since the last time the voices came. Either way, you always make a judgement call that he wants to be left alone.

He sometimes sits stinking out the back rows of the local church making parishioners feel awkward and a bit nauseous, and now and then he does a bit of lacklustre begging. You've heard talk that he lives in a caravan in the hills so you assume he's self-sufficient but you wish he'd show a bit of common sense sometimes and at least buy an umbrella or catch the bus. Then you wouldn't feel so guilty for driving past without offering him a lift.

Characteristics

Reading Material: Road signs, discarded newspapers

Favourite TV Programmes and Films: Black and white TV broke down in 1979 then never got it fixed, The Good Life, Butterflies, Star Wars

Heroes and Role Models: Pictures of Lady Di plastered all over his wall

Most likely cause of death: Basic neglect

Favourite Music: Silver band and whatever's in his head

Political Views: He likes the postman

Ego Issues: None

Fears: Brain-eating parasites, crows, milk wagons

Likes: The postman, baby, doing jigsaws, walking, collecting his toenail clippings, staring directly at total eclipses

Dislikes: Falling off walls, running with scissors, only breathing through his nostrils on Bank Holidays

Earnings: £20 a week for doing 25 hours for the farmer who's a right bastard

Offspring: None

Would like to drive: A tractor

Most likely to say: "Will you marry me?"

Would-Be-Gangster

78

71

30

75

70

He has grown up watching his older brother wreck his prospects by acting like a dick, wearing thick chains and being the Big Man, so he started even younger. He's always on the lookout for anyone who might be disrespecting him because he has no self esteem and he thinks he can gain it by fighting, so long as he's got three mates to back him up.

He has no ambition, no academic qualifications and his only aspiration is to be respected and he will fight anyone who disrespects him although he doesn't deserve anyone's admiration because he hasn't achieved anything. He has the bouncy ghetto walk and a fake blaccent which makes him look and sound stupid and consequently unemployable. His pierced eyebrow consolidates a future on benefits but he blames "so-sigh-e-eee" for his lack of opportunities. If he hadn't been so obsessed with gaining respect he might have amounted to something.

His girlfriend is fat and spotty, works in a chip shop and always gives out five sachets of ketchup when one is required. She also thinks that wearing a belt where her waist should be makes her look thin. You think he can't look a bigger twat until he puts his cap on. His thigh jiggles when he's sitting down because he's a mindless hyperactive twitching little git.

Characteristics

Reading Material: Won't learn to read until he goes to prison.

Favourite TV Programmes and Films: Get Rich or Die Tryin', Things Fall Apart, Gun, Teen Cribs

Heroes and Role Models: So Solid Crew, Tempa T, Skepta

Most likely cause of death: Knife wound

Favourite Music: Grime

Political Views: They is takin' our jobs thou', innit

Ego Issues: He boasts about his non existent sex life more than Cherie Blair.

Fears: his gang leader, retribution, being shanked, disenfranchisement (but can't spell it), being outnumbered

Likes: Respect, twitching, bling, drugs, impressing other gang members, stare-downs, graffiti

Dislikes: Disrespect

Earnings: Benefits, small time drug distribution

Offspring: Girlfriend pregnant

Would like to drive: Can't afford to drive but once he has broken the law enough times to buy a car it certainly will have blacked out windows and big alloys

Most likely to say: "Is you disripektin' me thou'?"

Skinhead

82

97

34

3

28

Fifty-nine-year old male who doesn't know what he stands for any more. He still lives on fish and chips, still listens to ska music but can't get a fight, is divorced and has a couple of kids to two different women who won't let him see them. The women have red hair and mullet hair cuts with a jagged fringe and live in council houses with broken children's toys in the front garden and one boarded up window.

He fondly remembers buying an SS180 scooter when he was 17. In his youth he spent many hours sitting in the bath to shrink his jeans to get the extra-skinny-legged look; now he does it to relieve his piles. He kept the crop even when everyone else was becoming a suede head. He used to hang around in a huge crew but now there's only a few skins left. He remembers when the thickness and colour of braces and laces meant something, and when the size of check on his Ben Sherman shirt denoted his status within the crew. He still has an encyclopaedic knowledge of box weave shoes, ox-blood brogues, officer boots and Dr Martens. The skinhead movement has had so many revivals that he doesn't know whether he's sober or pissed, racist, mod, reggae or punk.

Characteristics

Reading Material: Daily Mirror

Favourite TV Programmes and Films: Radio 2, Made In Britain, This Is England

Heroes and Role Models: His mum, Alf Garnett

Most likely cause of death: German skinheads, scooter accident, old age

Favourite Music: Ska, rocksteady, and early reggae before the tempo slowed and songs focused on black nationalism and Rastafari

Political Views: Ranges from far left to far right but mainly apolitical

Ego Issues: Still proud to be working class, hates being thought of as gay

Fears: German skinheads, seagulls and gays

Likes: Ilford Palais, Brighton, seaside

Dislikes: Racists, Stormfront, National Alliance, Nick Griffin, chavs and students, how the skinhead movement was hijacked by racists and football hooligans

Earnings: Benefits, scaffolding for cash

Offspring: Two, estranged

Would like to drive but actually drives: His old SS180/1989 F Reg white XR3

Most likely to say: "We used to go down The Palais"

Boxer

65

68

50

75

25

As a kid, he was a gobby, skinny runt who never knew when to shut up but got away with it because everyone knew he'd knock your teeth out faster than you could say, "Shut your face, you skinny ginger twa—"

So when he took up boxing it was inevitable that he would excel at it. Weighing in at barely nine stone, he was as hard as nails and had a right hook as fast as an adder's tongue. His finest hour was at Madison Square Gardens, where he proved un-hittable, and emerged world champion. The bright lights of Vegas beckoned and life looked good.

But all that changed after a left hook put him under the surgeon's knife, fighting for his life, and closed the book on his boxing career. At the age of 28, he found himself back home in Leeds, living off his memories and his mother's scrapbook. Twenty years on, he has trouble remembering words, after the clot on his brain affected his speech. He's angrier than ever but can't do anything about it because it also affected his balance.

For her part, his mother's just glad to have him home. She polishes his championship belts every day while he's out feeding his ferrets or fetching the paper.

Characteristics

Reading Material: Autotrader, The Sun, Racing Post

Favourite TV Programmes and Films: Rocky films, Raging Bull, the tape of his Madison Square Gardens championship fight

Heroes and Role Models: 'Battling' Jackie Turpin, Muhammad Ali

Most likely cause of death: Blood clot to the brain, septicaemia from a ferret bite

Favourite Music: Judas Priest, AC/DC, Abba

Political Views: Would love the chance to go one round in the ring with Cameron

Ego Issues: Knows he coulda been someone. Resents the celebrity status of fighters like Eubank and hates that they were better looked after than he was

Fears: Flights of stairs, enclosed spaces, hospitals, gangs of youths, the dark, spiders, heights

Likes: His Mum, her cooking, his ferrets, backing the dogs

Dislikes: The success of his contemporaries

Earnings: Lives off the interest of his world championship winnings, which his mother makes sure he spends wisely

Offspring: None. He has never been in a relationship except with his ferrets

Drives: Not allowed

Most likely to say: "I was Champion of the World once, me"

Hunt Saboteur

He likes his beard, his dreads, his mung beans and his vegetable plot. He only washes with home-made organic soap, which doesn't work, and enjoys a vegan diet. He is evangelical about the need to protect the planet, about unfair farming practices and, most of all, about those who continue to flout British legislation prohibiting hunting. His back is lashed with scars from being horse-whipped back in the pre-ban days.

He organises the local hunt saboteurs of a weekend and is never short of camouflage gear, balaclavas, citronella spray, hunting horns or compasses. He keeps his digital camera fully charged at all times and is prepared to crouch behind a gorse bush for as long as it takes to catch the hunt in the act.

Until recently he earned his living putting his horticultural expertise to good use at the local garden centre. But his triumphant footage of a top celebrity chef hunting with dogs saw his name plastered all over the papers after the case went to court. Although the final ruling turned out to be a triumph for Animal Rights, the owners of the garden centre where he worked quietly gave him the sack.

Characteristics

Reading Material: The Sabotage Times, A Vegan Taste of India

Favourite TV Programmes and Films: He doesn't own a TV because he lives without electricity

Heroes and Role Models: Dalai Lama, Heather Mills

Most likely cause of death: Trampled by horses

Favourite Music: K.T. Tunstall

Political Views: Left wing, anti-hunt, anti-animal testing

Ego Issues: Is so eco he can't wipe his arse in your guest loo

Fears: Man's ultimate destruction of the planet, Clarissa Dickson-Wright

Likes: Mung beans, bamboo fabric boxer shorts, tantric sex

Dislikes: Electricity, the M25, David Cameron

Earnings: Currently looking for work

Offspring: None, but he's open to whatever the Universe wants to throw his way

Drives: Pushbike although will get into his mate's ancient Land Rover if they're off to sabotage a hunt together

Most likely to say: "Can I have some more mung beans with that?"

Fat, 34 (2 Kids)

This lovelorn porker was destined for doughiness since the day aged three her mother gave her first Happy Meal. She is in complete denial about her weight because she looks at her dainty but podgy feet as a sign that she "is not that big". After demolishing a whole cake she will pat her stomach and say that was her little naughty treat then she wonders why the only men she can attract have "commitment problems".

She talks constantly about her weight loss yet gains a stone annually. She thinks supermodels are gross skeletons, even the plus-size ones. Each year she lavishes more attention and money on her hair as it becomes the only thing that her friends can compliment her on without embarrassment. Rosy cheeks are a sign of high blood pressure. Friends tell her she looks young, but the skin is stretched to breaking point. She has lots of friends on Facebook but few who want to have coffee with her and listen to her yap on about how good she's been so far today while tucking into a huge chocolate muffin. In a few years she will seek refuge in spirituality of sorts and demand a gastric band on the NHS. At the moment she spends most of the time thinking about the love of her life who got her pregnant then buggered off with a slimmer woman.

Characteristics

Reading Material: Hello, TV Quick, Take away menus

Favourite TV Programmes and Films: How to Look Good Naked Even When You Don't, cookery programmes

Heroes and Role Models: Gok Wan, Jo Brand

Most likely cause of death: Busting her gastric band

Favourite Music: Compilation tape made by first boy friend in 1991

Political Views: Rights for single mothers

Ego Issues: She worries that people think she's fat

Fears: Yeast infections, body odour

Likes: Calling skinny people anorexic, her hair, her face, spending lots of money on hair and beauty products instead of just losing four stone

Dislikes: Taking responsibility for her size, eating healthily, her arse

Earnings: £12k

Offspring: Two; when they get fat she'll blame it on their genes rather than the crap she feeds them

Would like to drive: But has failed her test 9 times

Most likely to say: "I've tried all the diets and nothing seems to work"

Thai Bride

"I reary luv you long time." Most Thai Bride hookers with a heart of gold are pretty sure that they love their husbands prior to moving to the UK. They have a good two weeks to get to know them and in that time they have stopped sleeping with other men. (Well there was that one but he was a mistake).

She says that Thai men "don't look after women no good and that English gentlemen kind and faithful he take care of me". If you ask the man he'll say he's looking for someone half his age to take care of him, so someone is going to end up disappointed. The fatter and scummier the Brit the greater the attraction. A bald unemployed fifty-something wearing a football shirt and trainers is considered a prize catch.

Undressed she has the body of a poorly fed young boy and if you ask her what she really wants in life she will reply, "A Motorola flip phone". Once married she will make her husband's life hell, boss him around and complain that he doesn't earn enough money. They will argue all the time. Expensive clothes won't make her look any less like a prostitute, until she turns forty, when she'll get so fat she'll have to be removed from her bedroom by a team of paramedics with an industrial hoist.

Characteristics

Reading Material: Argos catalogue

Favourite TV Programmes and Films: Karaoke, Thai bride agency videos

Heroes and Role Models: Madonna, her friend who moved to England two years earlier

Most likely cause of death: Scooter accident, faulty industrial hoist

Favourite Music: Karaoke

Political Views: Respects Buddha despite shagging for a living, burning incense puts all that right

Ego Issues: Does not like being considered cheap or for sale

Fears: English food, Thai policemen, being sent home

Likes: Money, Madonna, and knows all the words to her songs, especially like "Rike A Virgin"; getting a British visa, discerning gentlemen, having sex with tourists, being treat nice like lady, teddies and stuffed animals

Dislikes: Thai men

Earnings: 10 baht for good time

Offspring: None despite successful sex change

Would like to drive but actually drives: Gets buses and taxis/would love a Mini

Most likely to say: "Ah, I, luv you long time!"

New Age Traveller

A young unwashed couple with at least three kids and another on the way, who have elected to step out of the 'capitalist conspiracy' of life in modern Britain and get 'back in touch with nature' in a ramshackle caravan which they park up on the side of the A39 in Somerset.

He spends his days rolling fags, waxing his mohawk and shouting at his scrawny dog, while she's busy soaking mung beans and dried fruit for tea and pondering where she should have her next piercing. Their kids are permanently in various stages of undress and hardly ever go to school, which is probably just as well because they smell like food waste and have stupid names like 'Crescent' and 'Aurora', a combination guaranteed to alienate them from normal children.

They subsist on state benefits but have plans to make enough to live off by selling her home-made falafel and dream catchers at summer rock festivals. In the evenings, they burn fence panels and sit around the embers with their other new-age mates singing songs about ley-lines to the beat of his bodhran, while the kids eat their mung beans and make collages out of tree moss and dead woodlice.

Characteristics

Reading Material: They don't read

Favourite TV Programmes and Films: They have no electricity and make their own music

Heroes and Role Models: They have no call for role models because they aspire to nothing beyond living with what nature provides. Though their mates who go door-to door selling their uninsured tree-surgery skills make a packet, which would come in handy.

Most likely cause of death: Magic mushroom overdose

Favourite Music: They enjoy a wide variety of their own folk songs

Political Views: The state is a capitalist conspiracy

Ego Issues: Think they are entitled to whatever they want, which they expect the state to provide for them

Fears: Hard work

Likes: Cider, an open fire, nature, skipping (helping themselves to discarded supermarket food), communal living, painting peace signs on their Doc Martins

Dislikes: The city, the Truancy Officers, bathing, Kylie Minogue

Earnings: State benefits and whatever she can make selling falafel

Offspring: Only three or four for the time being

Would like to drive but actually drives: Romany caravan/25 year-old Transit van

Most likely to say: "Do you want some lentil soup?"

Heavy Smokers

He has a hollow face as grey as granite and smoking is his whole life. He has not just turned smoking into an art form, he's a living nicotine sculpture; when he stands still he gets shat on by pigeons. He is still really angry about the smoking ban and hates Tony Blair and his "namby pamby liberal nanny state". He feels rejected from society and now only buys his cigarettes from abroad because he doesn't want his hard-earned Incapacity Benefit to line the pockets of the Exchequer. He reasons that he's been smoking all his life, so should be allowed to continue. That's the best argument he can come up with, especially if it's been a while since his last cigarette.

Like most smokers he thinks he's more interesting than a non-smoker. He claims he's a mental health sufferer whose only lifeline used to be sitting in the pub alone every lunchtime having a pint and a smoke. Since the ban he has no social life and no hobbies just like before. He sits at home smoking, or he would do if he hadn't recently sold up ready to emigrate to Majorca, only to find to his dismay that the law just changed there too. He thinks passive smoking is a myth and can't hear a trumpet playing without wanting to desecrate Roy Castle's grave.

Characteristics

Reading Material: Beer mats

Favourite TV Programmes and Films: Darts or any old crap, so long as he's smoking a cigarette

Heroes and Role Models: Hurricane Higgins

Most likely cause of death: Smoking

Favourite Music: The backing track to his life is the sound of traffic, rain and the hiss of outdoor patio heaters

Political Views: Has voted Labour all his life but never again, not since the summer of 2007

Ego Issues: Sensitive about people disapproving of his smoking

Fears: Running out of cigarettes, losing his lighter, getting fat if he quits

Likes: Smoking, drinking and watching darts on TV

Dislikes: Roy Castle, Tony Blair, searching for his lighter, how much it costs to smoke, hacking up a lungful every morning, smug ex-smokers

Earnings: Incapacity Benefit

Offspring: 2 non smokers

Would like to drive but actually drives: Roller/Nothing re-saleable

Most likely to say: "You've go to die of something, my Gran smoked 20 a day all her life and it didn't do her any harm"

Football Thug

 81

 76

 35

 75

 2

Cowardly brainless yob with tattoos and long-repressed memories of growing up in care, who loves drinking and cutting down alleyways to avoid the police and meet up with rival "crews" who "want it". He can't wait for the final whistle to blow so that he can run out in the street and start getting his head kicked in. There are only two types of football thug – obese baldies called Darren or malnourished chavs called Shane. When he isn't fighting he spends so much time scratching his balls that even his close friends suspect he has pubic lice.

An artisan in the noble sport of chinning, his favourite weapons are chair seats, bottles, paving slabs and his trusty Stanley knife, which he claims to use for his day job as a carpet fitter whenever he is stopped and searched. He has been charged several times for affray, violent disorder and GBH but has never been sent to prison.

On the terraces he spends most of the time with his arms spread wide above his head, making the Y shape of YMCA. He belongs to a firm of like-no-minded men who call themselves something immature like the Knives Business Crew, Mayne Line Service Crew, Frontline Faction – anything which makes them sound like they work for Railtrack or a hairdressers.

Characteristics

Reading Material: Text messages, The Sun

Favourite TV Programmes and Films: Radio 1. Favourite film, The Football Factory

Heroes and Role Models: Jackie and Bobby Charlton, Steven Segal

Most likely cause of death: Hitting his head on the pavement

Favourite Music: Oasis

Political Views: Shane and me jumped over the railings

Ego Issues: Growing up in the care system he quickly learned that all problems in life can be solved by throwing a chair at someone

Fears: Tear gas, water cannon, being outnumbered

Likes: McDonalds, kicking/spitting on people when they're unconscious, defending his "patch", playing Sunday morning football

Dislikes: Fines and court costs

Earnings: £25k

Offspring: Unknown, but the CSA is pursuing three cases against him

Would like to drive but actually drives: Old 3 series BMW with a cheap private plate. Would like to drive a chavvy Nissan Navara with all the bull bars roof rails, and alloy bits that they don't need

Most likely to say: "Yer gonna get it after the game"

Biker – (Hard)

77

91

15

4

40

Ex merchant-navy man in his late fifties, who now does stage crew work for bands and music festivals. He looks after his Harley better than he looks after himself. He's as hard as nails and wants to be harder than a proper Hells Angel. His gang is even more serious, and is called something like the Really Nasty Devils Claws, or Satan's Sphincter. He expresses his feelings on – and with – his knuckles but he has a good sense of humour once he's decided you're not full of shit.

He has had five bad bike crashes during his life and has broken his back in three of them. Those aren't rings he's wearing – they're clinch bolts holding his fingers on. He's as Old School as they get. He will always help a brother in need, but he'll knock you out with one punch if you touch his bike. He also has an encyclopaedic knowledge of the thousands of rides he's done and the highways he's hit.

Characteristics

Reading Material: Custom Bikes, The Mail

Favourite TV Programmes and Films: Easy Rider, Mad Max

Heroes and Role Models: Our boys and girls in Afghanistan and Iraq

Most likely cause of death: Volvo turning right

Favourite Music: Grateful Dead, Lynyrd Skynyrd, Guns 'n' Roses, Steppenwolf, Aerosmith, Motley Crue, Status Quo

Political Views: Motorcyclists against Government

Ego Issues: Is not as hard as his friends

Fears: Fighting, breakdowns and rain

Likes: Children gawping in awe as their parents nervously try to get them not to

Dislikes: Hates gays, and would kill one if he found there was one living nearby

Earnings: £25k cash in hand

Offspring: Unknown

Would like to ride but actually rides: Harley 883 Sportster/ Harley Custom Build

Most likely to say: "It's not leaking oil, it's marking its territory"

Fat Confident Young Girl

An increasingly common sight on the nation's streets, especially Cardiff and all northern towns, this misguided late teen wears boob tubes, short skirts and skinny heels despite her orange-peel legs, chubby face and ham-like forearms. She has hammer toes and borderline Type 2 diabetes and spends a fortune on blusher and minx nails, instead of just losing four stone.

The FCYG listens to what her body tells her it wants and it usually wants another box from KFC. However, being a fat minger isn't an issue – all the women in her peer group are even fuglier chubsters so she remains resolutely proud and loud, more so when drunk. Her philosophy is that it doesn't matter how many peach shots and bags of chips you have on the inside, it's what's on the outside that counts and she's sexy, just like her porcine celebrity role models – and if you don't agree that's your problem. At night she can be spotted tottering along arm-in-arm with an obese female friend sharing a banal joke and cackling like the siren sex-goddess she believes herself to be.

Characteristics

Reading Material: Seventeen magazine, Cosmo Girl, instructions on the packet of the morning after pill

Favourite TV Programmes and Films: Skins, Tricia, Glee, X-Factor, Britain's Got Talent, Take me out

Heroes and Role Models: Kerry Katona, Charlotte Church, Beyoncé

Most likely cause of death: Alcohol poisoning, fourth degree burns after trying to copy Katy Perry's Firework video

Favourite Music: Songs all fat girls listen to to feel better about themselves: You Are Beautiful (Christina Aguilera), Big Girl You Are Beautiful (Mika), Firework (Katy Perry), Just the Way You Are (Bruno Mars)

Political Views: Paedos should be castrated

Ego Issues: Having wished for larger breasts at 14, is now saving for a breast reduction

Fears: Being towed back out to sea while sunbathing

Likes: Her current Facebook profile pic which like all her others is a Fat Girl Angle Shot: high-contrast and snapped from above, showing face and cleavage but hiding a miasmic mass of chins and hoofing papaloopas.

Dislikes: Covering up, talking quietly

Earnings: £12k per year

Offspring: None - but lost count of the number of times she's been asked when it's due

Most likely to say: "Eeeh I'm starving, me"

Old Teddy Boy

He's a foreman at a frozen pea factory where he's worked since he was 14. He lives in a neat semi on a crowded seventies estate which his wife keeps spic and span in between her shifts at the local old folks' home. She gets up first every morning to cook him a proper breakfast and pack his favourite lunch for him, same as she has done every day for more than 40 years. He always pats her on the backside and refers to her as his girl.

Friday nights are a ritual: the entire family get spruced up and heads down the Working Men's Club for a night out. He takes longer to get ready than anyone else in the family. He touches up his roots with a spot of Grecian 2000, brylcreems his locks into as close to a DA as his receding hairline will allow, and gets out all the old gear which his wife has dry-cleaned for him every time there's a three for two offer on at Johnson's.

He looks a twat but no one says anything because they all know he's still capable of dishing out a good hiding after a few bevvies if the occasion calls for it. Besides, him and his old girl are as light on their feet as they ever were, and turn heads whenever they jive away to Eddie Cochrane.

Characteristics

Reading Material: The Sun, Caravan Club Magazine

Favourite TV Programmes and Films: Elvis movies, the football, the motor racing, the snooker, the darts

Heroes and Role Models: Buddy Holly, Elvis, Bruce Forsyth

Most likely cause of death: Lung cancer

Favourite Music: Elvis, Buddy Holly, Eddie Cochrane, Bill Haley & the Comets

Political Views: Does not vote but has not entirely lost the Teddy Boy rebel spirit that once defined him – he will still sneak a ciggie in a no-smoking zone and regularly walks the wrong way round IKEA.

Ego Issues: Protective about his age therefore has a go at anyone who spills his pint, eyes up his Mrs or looks at him wrong.

Fears: Male pattern balding

Likes: A bit of respect from the Mrs, the first cigarette of the day, reading the paper on the lav, cheese and pickle butties, dancing

Dislikes: Cliff Richard, Shakin' Stevens, Showaddywaddy

Earnings: £30k

Offspring: Two sons and a daughter, who love their Dad and wouldn't miss Friday night up the Working Man's Club for anything.

Would like to drive but actually drives: 50s American Classic/Has never passed his test

Most likely to say: "Only fools rush in"

Newspaper Vendor

 75

 89

 25

 7

 15

Old Billy has been selling newspapers for twenty years off and on. In his time he's been a soldier, a dosser, a pilgrim and there's a few years he won't talk about. His pitch has been in the family for the best part of a century. He used to be able to make a living but now his newspaper's in steady decline, thanks to the free papers, the Internet, podcasts and mobile phones. Both he and his product are dying breeds – there won't be any newspapers in ten years time, let alone newspaper sellers.

He stands near the bus stop for thirteen hours every day yelling "Get yer Standard" which sounds like "Gayerstanneer"

He used to enjoy a bit of banter with his punters, but nowadays they all seem much busier, too busy to stop and chat. He has a hardcore of loyal regulars but they too are dwindling and dying. His used to be a thriving paper rooted to the streets and the people, but not any more. He's asked for directions a hundred times a day – if they say please he helps them, if they don't he ignores them.

Characteristics

Reading Material: He has read a newspaper every day of his life since he was nine years old

Favourite TV Programmes and Films: Steptoe & Son, Carry On films, Bless This House, Morecambe and Wise, Tony Hancock, Grandstand, Match of the Day, the darts, It's a Knockout, always has Radio Five Live playing on his little transistor radio

Heroes and Role Models: His father and grandfather, Eddie Waring

Most likely cause of death: Traffic-pollution induced carbon monoxide poisoning

Favourite Music: Likes anything with a good beat: Chas and Dave, Abba, Spandau Ballet, Busted

Political Views: Believes every Cabinet since Thatcher's has been in the pay of Rupert Murdoch and doesn't trust any of them

Ego Issues: Sees how invisible he is to the City Suits who either stop to buy his paper or hurry past him every morning, but knows he is better informed about the state of the nation than any of them

Fears: His sons' disinterest in selling papers and the consequent death of his pitch

Likes: Selling papers, a nice bit of banter, a smiley face, a nice cuppa tea, the way so many Japanese tourists say please and thank you

Dislikes: Rupert Murdoch, rain, the way so many American toursists fail to say thank you

Earnings: Used to be enough to keep his kids in shoes and his wife in lipstick. These days, not so much, but he gets by

Offspring: Two well-balanced, hard-working kids with ambitions to get into IT, graphic design or something in media

Would like to drive: He uses the bus but his wife runs a little Clio which she keeps spotlessly clean and pine fresh

Most likely to say: "Gayerstanneer"

Miner (Retired)

Seventy-something called Arthur with lungs like empty crisp packets who left school at fourteen, did National Service with the Grenadier Guards and then put in a quarter of a century underground. He retired due to ill health in the mid-eighties and has spent the remaining years sitting in his armchair in his carpet slippers showing his grandchildren his Davy Lamp and vibration white finger and pretending to pull pound coins out of their ears.

He lives in a ground-floor flat in Barnsley with Beryl, his beloved wife of fifty years who is waiting for a hip replacement so has had to reduce her bingo sessions to four times a week. Every Thursday evening he walks to the Ex & Retired Miners Association Club with Walter his fifteen-year-old Jack Russell, where he drinks two double whiskies and a half of stout. They recently appeared in the Daily Mail after being robbed in their own home of their life savings of £814.50 by a twenty-two year old heroin addict who has never worked a day in his life.

Characteristics

Reading Material: Radio Times, Daily Mirror

Favourite TV Programmes and Films: Snooker, Emmerdale, ITV3

Heroes and Role Models: Arthur Scargill, Frank Sinatra

Most likely cause of death: Chronic Obstructive Pulmonary Disease (COPD)

Favourite Music: Nat King Cole, Tony Bennet, Vera Lynn, Hank Williams

Political Views: Has been a Socialist all his life and feels totally betrayed by New Labour and their chronic handling of miners' pensions and compensation scheme

Ego Issues: None

Fears: Dying before his wife because he knows she'll struggle on two thirds of his pension

Likes: Straight talking, no-nonsense

Dislikes: Women who swear

Earnings: £41.50 a week miners' pension, state pension

Offspring: Four children, including a bank manager, aeronautical engineer and two school teachers. Fourteen grandchildren

Drives: Doesn't own a car any more but used to drive an H reg Ford Orion Ghia

Most likely to say: "Since they shut the pit..."

Community Support Officer (Female)

She looks like Ronnie Barker in drag and wanted to be a dinner/lollipop lady but failed the BMI test. In her favour she is very approachable; in fact she is so large that you'd have to cross the street to avoid her.

She has recently learned to tell the time and her other duties include wearing hi-visibility clothing and sensible shoes, writing down the false names and addresses of truants, and watching abandoned vehicles burn until the fire brigade arrives.

She has no powers of arrest, and she can't investigate crime, falsify evidence, perform racial profiling or throw suspects down stairs like proper officers. She takes on all the routine and boring tasks so they can concentrate on the important business of posing inappropriately in photographs and playing hide and seek in their panda cars.

Characteristics

Reading Material: Swindon Gazette, Mills & Boon

Favourite TV Programmes and Films: CSI, Eastenders, All Star Family Fortunes, Who Wants To Be A Millionaire, The David Dickinson Show

Heroes and Role Models: Robocop, David Caruso

Most likely cause of death: Run over while directing traffic

Favourite Music: Elaine Paige, loves all West End Musicals

Political Views: Tory

Ego Issues: Hates not being considered as an officer

Fears: Blacks, Asians, gays, kids

Likes: US cop dramas, the way David Caruso takes off his sunglasses in CSI Miami, supporting the community

Dislikes: Blacks, Asians, gays, kids, cancellation of The Bill

Earnings: £9 an hour

Offspring: None

Would like to drive but actually drives: Anything with blue lights/Daewoo

Most likely to say: "Your disability badge is invalid"

Scaffolder

Whether aged 18 or 40 the scaffolder wears the same uniform of football shirt, shorts, tool belt and CAT boots, but takes his shirt off at the first sign of sunlight. Well-built, likeable and hard he pretends not to like people until he gets to know them. He hangs around with groups of similar-looking men, plays football and goes to the gym or mountain biking at the weekend. The older ones change their vocabulary to talk like the younger ones and the younger ones learn how to fight from the older ones.

He has a badly maintained flatbed, the cab of which is littered with half-consumed fizzy drinks, packets of cheap fags and food packaging purchased from petrol stations, but only ever one copy of The Sun, which lives in the window above the dashboard. Despite only being two years old his vehicle is so mistreated that it has no residual value whatsoever.

Listens to Radio 1 all day and shares an inexhaustible repertoire of obvious jokes and sayings that he repeats endlessly. Not content with the 50 hours of his week already spent with his work colleagues, Saturday night sees him in the same company. They love spending time together so much that they make jokes about being gay, but usually date Essex Girls.

Characteristics

Reading Material: The Sun, ScaffMag.com

Favourite TV Programmes and Films: Sky Sports, Harry Hill's TV Burp, Police, Camera, Action!, The Only Way is Essex

Heroes and Role Models: Ray Winstone, John Terry

Most likely cause of death: Falling through a board weakened by a mindless roofer, brickie or chippie cutting stuff directly on the platform

Favourite Music: Radio 1

Political Views: Tory voter

Ego Issues: Sensitive about old school friends calling him thick as he sees himself as a talented tradesman

Fears: Spiders, the dark

Likes: Essex women, blaming roofers, brickies or chippies when their scaffolding collapses, welding over weakened joints, eyeing up passing totty

Dislikes: Having to get up so early, HSE Inspectors, removal of ties and & unauthorised adaptions to the scaffolding, women who aren't orange, being pulled up on tiny gaps in the toeboards when putting scaffold up on the wrong house, bad weather, when his mate is late picking him up

Earnings: £9 – £27K, plus overtime, bonuses and accommodation costs

Offspring: 0

Would like to drive but actually drives: Porsche 911/Ford Cargo

Most likely to say: "Ay, Ay!"

Essex Girl (aged 40)

With two failed marriages and Caesarian scars under her belt, grown up Essex Girl is still the good time girl she always was but now she parties with supportive underwear and a whole lot more vodka.

A couple of decades of fags and booze have left her eyes puffy and her voice as raspy as Boy George's. After twenty summers on the Costa Brava her skin wouldn't look out of place in Sofa World. She had the boob and nose jobs and the lipo and now she really wants to find Mr Right, so he can pay to have her eye bags sorted.

She has a great relationship with her twenty-summink daughter Kayleigh, Tracey or Maisie, from who she borrows clothes, perfume, fags and the occasional boyfriend. She talks like a docker, and dances like a hooker and uses Lionel Ritchie lyrics as pick up lines.

She gets her money from alimony which she tops up by working at a spray tanning salon. She's still ambitious, though, and attends night classes to explore her artistic side and train to become a body art tattooist.

Characteristics

Reading Material: Trashy novels, Jilly Cooper if she wants something a bit more taxing

Favourite TV Programmes and Films: FM Brentford, Footballers' Wives, Vampire Diaries

Heroes and Role Models: Jenny Frost, Alex Curran, Toni Poole

Most likely cause of death: Smoking and drinking

Favourite Music: Lionel Ritchie, Barry Manilow, Michael Boublé, Wham!

Political Views: A bit beyond her to be honest but she always thought that Tony Blair a bit of a dish

Ego Issues: Doesn't understand women who get fat or don't tan but she'll hang around with them as it reflects well on her!

Fears: Getting old, losing her looks

Likes: Ordering cocktails with sexually suggestive names

Dislikes: Fillin' in forms 'n' shit, sorting Kayleigh's contraception, f'in' food shopping

Earnings: £14k pa salary, house, car, time-share in Alicante from her ex

Offspring: One daughter with great taste in men

Most likely to say: "Hello, is it me you're looking for?"

Confederate Enthusiast

These exclusively working class lorry drivers from Stockport hang around in groups and drive to cowboy shows in huge trucks that cost more than their houses. Here they park in circles and do their best to act American. Cultural activities include line dancing, talking about the World Series, and trying to outdo each other with stories of the time they "sure as hell could've gotten eaten by a gator". They are lovable though fairly stupid as evidenced by how much they like to buff up their ve-hickles and blow their bull horns at related events like Traction Engine Rallies and Steam Fairs.

They are into all things Americana, though mainly tools, license plates, weapons and flags. They have ten gallon hats and shiny American style number plates attached to the grilles of their vehicles just above the proper British ones in the hope that people won't notice the dusty yellow plate and think they are real Americans.

Psychiatrists have been unable to pinpoint why these oddballs should wish to be pigeon holed in this way, but the prevailing theory is that they watched Dukes of Hazard and/or BJ and the Bear at a crucial stage of their hormonal development. Sadly this has left them with the delusion that being American is impressive and cool.

Characteristics

Reading Material: Gun magazines, The Bible, TV Choice, books about the US civil war

Favourite TV Programmes and Films: Glory, Gettysburg, Gone With the Wind, North and South, Cold Mountain

Heroes and Role Models: Jefferson Davis, Robert E. Lee, Patrick Swayse

Most likely cause of death: High cholestorol

Favourite Music: Dixie, Country and Western

Political Views: Confederate

Ego Issues: His detailed knowledge of the mini series North and South gives him the confidence to hold his own in any company.

Fears: Communists, internet kill switch, terrorism

Likes: American cars, bikes, V8s, Dodges, Chevrolets, Plymouth, Pontiac, Ford, hot dogs

Dislikes: Obama, South Park, Seinfeld

Earnings: Hard to believe this fantasist could hold down a job.

Offspring: Two kids

Drives: Big American Vehicle, left hand drive, with Union Flags on long poles on both sides behind the cab

Most likely to say: "OK y'all, I'm gonna pull over in that there field and have us some beers"

Geordie

He is an inhabitant of Tyneside, but "Geordie" is an appropriate generic term for anyone from the north east of England. His speech patterns are a direct continuation of the 'language' spoken by Anglo-Saxon settlers in the Dark Ages who used to wear nothing but a T-shirt in the winter and smear themselves with orange clay before gannin doon the boozah.

Some Geordies protest: "Ahm not a Geordie Ahm frem Sunlun me" thus confirming with their unintelligible diction that they are to the rest of us Geordies. He supports his local football team with tremendous vigour as other than drinking and being nice, there is nothing else te dee. Newcastle is cold but friendly, the people are poor and those with money spend it on designer clothes and black or white Range Rover Sports which are essential for getting to Netto in the snow.

The Geordie is the salt of the earth and will dee owt fe ya as he continually reminds you, but you can always rely on him te dee summat daft in a crisis. If you were stuck in the pouring rain under a tree in Rothbury with only armed officers for company, you could bet a Geordie will appear with a dressing gown and a fishing rod.

Characteristics

Reading Material: The Sun, menu at fish and chip shop. Magpie programmes

Favourite TV Programmes and Films: Sky Sports

Heroes and Role Models: Gazza, Alan Shearer, Kevin Keegan

Most likely cause of death: Heat exhaustion after wearing a jumper

Favourite Music: Cheryl Cole, Sting, Bryan Ferry

Political Views: Labour but most of them get turned away from the polling station too late to cast their vote because of long queues at the kebab shop

Ego Issues: Ridiculously proud to be a Geordie, worried that people think he's from Sunderland.

Fears: Wearing a coat, Newcastle United losing, scousers, M1 Southbound

Likes: Going to watch the Magpies with Grandad and son

Dislikes: Kevin Keegan, Anthony Collins, Directski

Earnings: Not enough to go on a skiing holiday

Offspring: More than average

Would like to drive but actually drives: Campervan/Ford Fiesta

Most likely to say: "Away The Lads!"

(Horweir the Lards!)

Lollipop Lady

Large fluorescent post-menopausal woman of below average intelligence who is paid £5.77 an hour to stand at zebra and pelican crossings, wait for children to arrive with their parents, watch them press the button, wait for the green man, and then walk into the road to stand in front of traffic that has already stopped for the red light.

On other occasions she positions herself on busy T-junctions where no one should be crossing, least of all children, then suddenly leaps into the path of oncoming traffic without warning so motorists have to make an emergency stop. She complains about discourteous drivers who break the law by failing to stop, but if it wasn't for them she would be out of a job.

She claims her job is very difficult and demanding. She stands in all weathers stick in hand, which she uses to alert traffic to her presence, decapitate cyclists, scratch car paintwork, and accidentally hit children who are on the pavement waiting to cross. She knows the names of all the children and has been providing lollipopal guidance for seventeen years, even though originally it was a stop gap until she could find a full time job indoors.

Characteristics

Reading Material: Car number plates

Favourite TV Programmes and Films: The One Show, National Lottery Live, Deal or No Deal

Heroes and Role Models: She wanted to be a teacher but hasn't had time to train

Most likely cause of death: Run over by school run mum (see page 310)

Favourite Music: Chris de Burgh, Cliff Richard, Michael Ball

Political Views: Tory

Ego Issues: She is convinced that if it wasn't for her, hundreds of people a year would get run over. She thinks she's only a few steps down from a police woman

Fears: The animated germs in bleach adverts

Likes: Children, reducing child pedestrian casualties, the Churchill Insurance nodding dog, luminous coat, The Green Cross Code

Dislikes: Rain, aggressive drivers, council executives' remuneration packages, the 12 per cent salary increase just awarded to the town's chief executive

Earnings: £5.77 an hour

Offspring: Three cats

Would like to drive but actually drives: Mini/Can't afford to run a car.

Most likely to say: "I just like meeting people"

Lorry Driver

Thirty per cent of accidents on UK roads in which people are killed or injured involve HGVs. How can that be when lorries are only eight percent of vehicles? It's because ninety-eight percent of fat ageing teddy boys with no road sense answer adverts in Jobcentre Plus that say: "HGV License? Can you stay awake even when tired and bored? Able to steer a 40 ton truck with your knees while multi-tasking? Then look no further!"

He puts food on your table and the economy would grind to a halt if he didn't grind you into the central reservation to deliver his urgent consignment of bananas when you got in his blind spot. When is he going to get it into his thick skull that in order to overtake or be overtaken, at some point you are going to be in his blind spot? That's why it's called a blind spot, not an anti-matter vortex.

He justifies putting you in a wheelchair because his engine drowned out your horn, and his radio drowned out his engine, so the only way you can hope to get his attention is to remember this rule: "If he can't see your tits, he can't see you". But this doesn't mean all lorry drivers are the same – it's the minority of really incompetent ones who give the majority of merely complacent ones a bad name.

Characteristics

Reading Material: The Sun, porn mags, text messages while driving, 7 Steps to Success

Favourite TV Programmes and Films: None - just listens to Radio 1 or 2

Heroes and Role Models: Himself

Most likely cause of death: Texting whilst driving

Favourite Music: Radio 1 or 2

Political Views: Hates all Transport Secretaries

Ego Issues: He is marginally less opinionated and narrow minded than a taxi driver. He thinks he is a very good driver and considers himself a knight of the road

Fears: Fuel price increases, people braking up ahead because he doesn't observe the correct stopping distance

Likes: Killing cyclists, reading porn mags, full English breakfast, steering with his knees, overtaking another lorry slowly on a hill to block two lanes, texting while driving and Sally Traffic

Dislikes: Illegal immigrants hiding in his lorry, indicating, using his wing mirrors, braking, getting up at five o'clock in the morning, cyclists, foreign lorry drivers, working time regulations, M6 southbound, sleeping, Eddie Stobbart and Norbert Dentressangle

Earnings: £30k

Offspring: Two quiet kids of average intelligence who were pushed really hard to get into Uni

Would like to drive but actually drives: A bigger rig/The one he has got

Most likely to say: "If you think my job is easy, darling, climb into my truck and you'll see how hard it is. Har har har har"

Mod (46 this year)

In the early 80s he followed Paul Weller everywhere on tour, and still has the restraining order to prove it. He was part of the eighties Mod revival, but him and his mates bought the DMs and the fishtail parker, with a proud target emblazoned on the back, and covered their modified scooters with a thousand mirrors. They'd head down to Brighton for a run, where they'd sit on the sea front listening to an old Lambrettas album, or they'd head off en masse for a special screening of Quadrophenia.

These days they work Monday to Saturday in Halfords, B&Q or the local kitchen and bathroom fitters. They are fewer in number, style and hair, and don't go in for the gang warfare that they used to, but they still like to get together of a weekend for a run to Brighton. Their scooter almost always breaks down on the way, just like the good old days, only the AA sees to that now. They don't have the energy to park up in a lay-by and strip the engine down together like they used to.

Characteristics

Reading Material: Viz and Scooter magazines

Favourite TV Programmes and Films: Quadrophenia, Brighton Rock, Cash in Your Attic

Heroes and Role Models: Paul Weller, Pete Townshend

Most likely cause of death: Collision on his scooter with a B&Q truck

Favourite Music: The Who, Jam, Paul Weller, The Lambrettas

Political Views: Was secretly never hard enough to go the distance with 'Nazi rock', owned a pair of red socks but was never brave enough to wear them, though did shave his hair in 1983

Ego Issues: Thinks being a Mod makes him more interesting and subversive than his mates at work who like Sudoku and Top Gear

Fears: Old age, mobility scooters

Likes: Polishing his collection of vintage wing-mirrors

Dislikes: Driving his scooter in the rain

Earnings: £17 500 – £22k a year

Offspring: Two teenager daughters who think his Mod thing is "gay"

Would like to drive but actually drives: Vespa everyday/Forklift truck

Most likely to say: "You can't beat the smell of Castrol R"

Bouncer (Rough)

 71
 97
 26
 2
 25

As vain as a body builder but fatter and actually quite hard with it despite restricted mobility, the bouncer tries his best to be stony-faced because he has watched too many Westerns and martial arts movies and believes that inscrutability is power. He's charming and patronising to the ladies and sees every man as a potential loser/troublemaker. He drinks Red Bull to stay alert and has barbed wire and a pair of eyes tattooed into the back of his head.

He really wanted to be an international close protection bodyguard, but can't get the work because that gig goes to ex-SAS types who are intelligent, whereas even the Army turned him down as "psychologically unsuitable." The most he can expect to become is a driver for a rubbish celebrity.

The rougher the town the shorter, skinnier and more psychotic the bouncer. He sports a torn ear, a bitten nose and missing teeth, and fights for fun with other bouncers, except on Saturdays when he stands tall and proud on the doors of dingy nightclubs and bars taking the moral high ground and thinking he's making intelligent decisions as to who he lets in next. He thinks he's involved in social engineering but his job title is "door supervisor" not "people supervisor".

Characteristics

Reading Material: Sunday Sport, The Sun

Favourite TV Programmes and Films: Springwatch, Eastenders

Heroes and Role Models: Jean-Claude Van Damme, but he would never admit it.

Most likely cause of death: Heart attack

Favourite Music: Club music

Political Views: Pissed-up twats deserve to be ejected horizontally so they break their nose and kneecaps

Ego Issues: Anything penis or fertility related

Fears: Being friendly and personable, conflict mediation courses, the drudgery of a 9-5 job

Likes: Pat downs and purse searches, excessive use of force, chokeholds, letting four people in a group of six past the velvet rope then turning the other two away

Dislikes: Men who drink champagne, fake IDs, wearing his yellow visibility jacket, filling in incident logs, conflict resolution, plaid shirts

Earnings: 25k per year

Offspring: None - fears steroid-related infertility

Drives: He doesn't drive a car, he just stands in doorways with his arms folded

Most likely to say: " Sorry, lads"

Granny (Skinny/Grumpy)

The antithesis of cuddly granny (see page 234), skinny granny is always grumpy and always busy pegging out washing, with a fag stuck in the corner of her mouth. She moans that she can no longer send her grandchildren to buy her fags so she has to go herself. She likes the smell of the corner shop and she enjoys scowling at the women who won the Bingo.

It's always skinny granny who fights off robbers in the post office not because she's a hero but because they cut in front of her in the pension queue. She has long outlived her bald henpecked husband who popped his clogs decades ago to escape her relentless busyness. When skinny granny goes out she smears bright red lipstick on her gash of a mouth and buttons her coat up to the neck.

She never bakes like cuddly granny. She crosses the road without looking, steals from Lidl and you can't accurately age her – she could be seventy or ninety-five. She's always cold and there is a hundred percent chance that she will break her wrist during the next few months. While she is in hospital she will complain that you never visit.

Characteristics

Reading Material: Puzzler magazine, Daily Express, romance novels

Favourite TV Programmes and Films: Coronation Street, Jeremy Kyle, bad daytime TV

Heroes and Role Models: Margaret Thatcher

Most likely cause of death: Hypothermia

Favourite Music: Complains she can't hear anything so doesn't listen to music

Political Views: Hasn't followed politics much since Maggie invaded the Falklands, which she was right behind. Gets Labour activists to taxi her to the polling station then votes Tory.

Ego Issues: She is very manipulative and the ripples caused by her meddling spread out through the generations below her. Always feels like she should be treated with more respect.

Fears: Dying alone, dying in hospital, winter fuel bills, losing her independence as she gets older, Delroy Grant

Likes: Smoking, living frugally, buying lottery tickets, being cranky and judgmental, listing her ailments, moaning about the cost of a television license

Dislikes: Surprises, incontinence pads, children, being hugged, being called 'sweetie' or 'dear', people speaking needlessly slowly and loudly, immigrants, going to funerals

Earnings: Pension

Offspring: Four children, eight grandchildren

Drives: Just pushes a zimmer frame aggressively

Most likely to say: "I'll be dead soon and then you'll be sorry"

Homeless

He's everyone and he's no one, but his back story is a million miles from what you think. He never imagined that homelessness could happen to him. He's as likely to be a professor of obscure Middle Eastern studies who had an affair with a student, lost his job and everything else in the divorce, as a young offender with a background in care.

The only two things you can know with any certainty are that he doesn't want to sleep in a doorway and he feeds his dog before he feeds himself. If he didn't have mental health or alcohol problems before he came on the streets, there's a fifty per cent chance he'll have them now.

He'd like to find a job and get his life back together but he is slowly dying with no hope. He has no way out because he has no driving licence, no passport, no address, so he can't get work. But he has plenty to do – seeking food and shelter, keeping dry, clean and safe, avoiding the police, listening to Christians tell him about Jesus in exchange for some clothes or sandwiches, and – most important of all – finding somewhere to sleep.

Characteristics

Reading Material: Discarded newspapers

Favourite TV Programmes and Films: n/a

Heroes and Role Models: None

Most likely cause of death: Drugs, alcohol, circulatory diseases, suicide

Favourite Music: Sounds of the streets

Political Views: n/a

Fears: The cold, being attacked

Likes: Drink, drugs, warm weather

Dislikes: Being moved on by police, being ignored, shelters, Christian pigeons

Earnings: £35/week

Offspring: none

Drives: n/a

Most likely to say: "Spare some change"

Rugby League Lad

Happy and confident as a result of his school days where nobody hit him, the professional Rugby League player honed most of his professional skills fighting for fun in Castleford on a Saturday night. He is 6'4", 18 stone, and can sprint 100 metres in 10 seconds once every 2 minutes, and wrestle in between. He takes a punch in the face as a token of friendship and will not get cross so long as he can punch you back. He makes friends this way on and off the pitch.

Despite their professional status, Rugby League players get paid very little as they would play for free anyway. His career will last to his early thirties when he will become a car salesman, gym coach or something to do with sport in schools. As is often the case in the towns in which they are bred, they often marry young and have children by the time they are twenty. They make great dads and are usually bloody nice blokes but cannot help their children with their homework past the age of 9.

Characteristics

Reading Material: Back pages of tabloids, bedtime story to kids

Favourite TV Programmes and Films: This Sporting Life, Super League Show, A Question of Sport

Heroes and Role Models: Steve McNamara (GB Rugby League coach), Martin Offiah, Clive Churchill for playing with a broken arm

Most likely cause of death: Old age

Favourite Music: Power ballads, Tina Turner, Heart FM

Political Views: Tory

Ego Issues: Thinks he's so hard he's untouchable - probably not far off!

Fears: Recurring knee injury that takes him out of the game, – life after rugby league, his childrens' homework

Likes: Rugby League, a few beers with the lads, quiet night in with a few beers, celebrating end of game, the week, training session – with a few beers

Dislikes: Playing hungover

Earnings: £50 - £100k

Offspring: 2 young kids who watch every game Dad plays

Drives: Whatever the sponsors offer a discount on!

Most likely to say: "Fancy a pint?"

Essex Girl (Young)

Simple, fun, slightly shallow, aspiring glamour model who manages to combine surprising intelligence and dumbfounding ignorance in equal and oscillating measures.

She looks like a footballer's wife and considers herself to be socially mobile but has settled for an equally orange muscly guy who is either a bouncer, builder, scaffolder or in the army. Says "no, but seriously though" a lot but then never gets to the point. She holidays in Ibiza and is promiscuous and materialistic and wants to be famous. She is saving up for a facelift and to take her toddlers to Disneyland, in that order.

Enthusiatsically romantic, she likes to tell her girlfriends she has met 'The One' before then accidentally sleeping with one or more of his mates.

Characteristics

Reading Material: Comprehensive and wide-ranging i.e. both OK! and Heat

Favourite TV Programmes and Films: Watches The Only Way Is Essex and laughs at herself, but won't change; I'm a Celebrity; Jersey Shore

Heroes and Role Models: Cheryl Cole, Denise Van Outen, Katie Price, Jodie Marsh, Chantelle Houghton, Stacey Solomon, Victoria Beckham, Amy Childs

Most likely cause of death: Vodka shots, Jack Tweed, skin cancer

Favourite Music: Cheryl Cole, chart music and Ibiza classics

Political Views: She is fiercely pro choice – it should always be the woman's decision whether she spits or swallows

Ego Issues: Plays up to being an Essex girl. but hates being considered an Essex girl

Fears: Her boyfriend isn't attentive enough, which means that he doesn't tell her how gorgeous she is all the time on a loop

Likes: Nights out with the girls, cosmetic tattooing, tanning salons, nail bars and nightclubs

Dislikes: Crosswords, reading books

Earnings: £12–18k

Offspring: Two toddlers with names the same as current popstars have chosen; she dresses them in clothes like their dad wears with haircuts to match

Drives: Yellow Renault Megane convertible with a private number plate that sort of spells 'Denise'

Most likely to say: "I get really saucy after a few drinks. Sexy rude, not obnoxious rude"

BNP Supporter

Gaunt middle-aged latent homosexual called Terry who thinks he's intelligent and blames his lack of success and unemployment on immigrants and asylum seekers. He lives in a grey northern town which he claims as his own but actually he has done nothing for the town or the country.

He complains that he's treated like a second-class citizen in his own land and believes in putting indigenous British people first but if he'd ever read a history book he'd realize that he's descended from German, Viking and French invaders and that the only people who can truly claim to be 'British' are the Welsh who he also hates.

He draws most of his self-esteem from the grossly exaggerated stories of his grandfather Terry's heroism in the Second World War (he was in the Home Guard after faking an injury to avoid the front line). Terry believes that Grandad's heroism justifies the repatriation of all Pakistanis and gives him the right not to have to compete with any ethnic minority group for a job in Huddersfield. The truth is that the only reason his home town can still afford to turn its lights on is because the ethnic minorities which he hates so much generate all the income while he and his lazy friends claim social or go on the sick for a week with a broken flask.

Characteristics

Reading Material: Daily Mail, The Sun, Identity, Voice of Freedom, Britain Awake, Asian Babes

Favourite TV Programmes and Films: Sky Sports, WWII War Films, V and anything which features the classic extraterrestrial invasion plotline

Heroes and Role Models: Winston Churchill, Nick Griffin, Enoch Powell, Jimmy Hill, Bruce Forsyth, Anton Du Beke

Most likely cause of death: Excessive shouting

Favourite Music: National Anthem, Land of Hope and Glory, Wagner, Bad Manners

Political Views: Blames the immigrants and Europe

Ego issues: Has never got over being called needle dick at school

Fears: Mosques, Muslims (especially Pakistanis), Jews, The EU, getting a job, political correctness, homosexuality, being asked why he hasn't had children

Likes: St George's flag, inciting racial hatred, Holocaust denial, Islamaphobia, European elections, Cillit Bang

Dislikes: Foreigners, Equality and Human Rights Commission, foreign aid

Earnings: Income Support

Offspring: None

Would like to drive but actually drives: Tank/Nissan Cherry

Most likely to say: "There's no black in the Union Jack"

Emo

Emos are to some the tearful necrotic spawn of post-punk and emotional alternative rock; to others they are merely skinny young Goths seeking attention by acting depressed. Neither description is entirely accurate since Emo is a fake persona adopted to fetishize shyness and sexual confusion rather than conceal.

In Emoland every day is Last Halloween in Bridgend, reinforced by the writing of whiney poetry and mooning over websites of pink teddies. Lots of spoilt middle-class teens wear dark colours and sit crying in their bedrooms, so the acid test for an Emo is the belief that Weezer's album Pinkerton talks specifically about their life. Subsequently, despite the fact that every Emo band has rejected the label and then split up anyway as soon as they've got a record deal, hoards of angst-ridden acolytes continue to worship the pseudo-complexity and banal emotional palette of their lyrics, feelings shared by every skinny morose teen who can't keep a girlfriend.

To communicate his confused isolation and febrile sensitivity to an uncaring world the Emo wears thick black-rimmed glasses, slim-fit black jeans, tight black T-shirt, Converse shoes, studded belt and black rubber wristbands, all second hand. Dyed black hair is grown straight and lank so that it covers one or both eyes. Ironic shards of individuality may be expressed through blue, pink, red or bleached blond highlights and dark nail varnish. The girl Emo dresses the same only with less mascara.

Characteristics

Reading Material: Own poetry, Catcher in the Rye, suicide notes

Favourite TV Programmes and Films: American Beauty, Dead Poets Society, Ice Storm, Wonder Boys, The Virgin Suicides, Harold and Maude, You-Tube videos of Buddhist monks self-immolating

Heroes and Role Models: Toby McGuire, Edward Scissorhands, Gerard Way, Chris Crocker, anyone who cuts their fringe less often than their wrists

Most likely cause of death: They would have liked us to enter "suicide" but, of course, none of them have the courage

Favourite Music: Rites Of Spring, The Promise Ring, Weezer, My Chemical Romance, Green Day, any Emo band that sings seriously about mundane problems, with lyrics like: "My life is an abyss. because my girlfriend broke up with me [last year]. She says she already has a pussy and doesn't need another one . . . etc."

Political Views: Too self-obsessed to have an opinion worth considering

Ego Issues: Feel emotionally superior to everyone else because he/she cries a lot, but Emos never admit that they are Emo because they don't like to be labelled

Fears: Not being cool, people thinking he's gay just because he kissed a couple of guys

Likes: Merchandise from obscure Emo bands, tortured adolescent metaphors about unravelling knitwear, hanging out with other Emo boys and girls, messenger bags, self-harming, taking pictures of himself looking away from the camera, hair straighteners

Dislikes: Making eye contact, smiling, sunlight, being mistaken for a Goth, eating meat

Earnings: Without exception all Emos are funded by middle class parents

Offspring: No because, 'Hey, life, it would be so unfair to put someone else through this…'

Most likely to say: "Go away and stop trying to label me!"

Pub Landlord and Lady

HIM

80

106

20

75

HER

85

120

25

4

15

Fifty-something, overweight and over-optimistic, the Pub Landlord and Lady like nothing better than a nice bit of bling and a pub full of punters. She never forgets a punter's favourite tipple and he never forgets a vendetta. With a wardrobe modelled entirely on the stars of seventies British soap operas, and whatever's new this season at BHS, he fills the air with his Sid James laugh while she lights up the bar in her low-cut leopard print and her blonde 'do'.

After a failed venture to set up an English Pub in Fuerteventura, they have sunk every last penny they own into leasing a dingy and decrepit Railway Pub in a grim northern town where their only regulars are a few whippet-loving stout drinkers who eke out a half of Guinness for an hour or more and who rarely crack a smile.

Undeterred, they pour their energy into an endless series of poorly attended theme nights, brewery-sponsored promotions, and a weekly karaoke in which their rendition of Renee and Renato's Save Your Love, complete with plastic rose, brings a tear to the eye.

The reality is that 99 per cent of locals over the age of 9 years are smokers and since the smoking ban have taken to consuming their alcohol on street corners, park benches or at home on the sofa watching Harry Hill.

Characteristics

Reading Material: He reads the Sunday Sport and the local paper, she reads OK magazine and Jackie Collins novels

Favourite TV Programmes and Films: Cash in the Attic, A House in the Sun, Catherine Cookson mini-series

Heroes and Role Models: Den & Ang

Most likely cause of death: Full English breakfast

Favourite Music: Elvis, Barry Manilow, Tom Jones

Political Views: Help for Heroes, pro-smoking lobby, Tory

Ego Issues: Loved the ex-pat lifestyle and still can't quite get over the fact their dream had to end

Fears: Having to lose the pub

Likes: Big drinkers, outdoor patio heaters, Barbara Windsor

Dislikes: Teetotallers, the man from the brewery, the smoking ban

Earnings: Two months from bankruptcy

Offspring: One son in Fuerteventura 'living the dream'

Would like to drive but actually drives: Rolls Royce / 1989 XJS worth £1800 which costs £2000 a year to run

Most likely to say: "What can I getcha, love?"

BRADFORD HOTELS
FUNCTION ROOM 16
LICENSED FOR WEDDIN
CIVIL CEREMONIES
AND FUNERALS

Fat Bride

They say opposites attract but in this case all we can know with any certainty is opposites get married and that they probably met online. Her wedding gown is so large it makes her look like a coach load of skiers trapped in an avalanche. The groom is as thin as a whippet but with less of the innate grace and native intelligence. Maybe that's why he thinks he's marrying Megan Fox if he thinks at all. Regardless, the poor specimen is just supposed to keep quiet and sign his life away because she's the best he can get and it's her big day.

The photos are the giveaway – the bride always slightly angled to reduce her size, the bouquet held in front of her to hide her midsection, her head tilted so only two-thirds of her face is captured. Then she is made to lie down and twist the front half of her body upward to give her a waist, followed by a load of shots of her looking up at the camera to hide all the chins.

When two chubsters tie the knot it's easy to see how the mutual love of cakes has brought them together, but the fat bride/mentally subnormal skinny groom scenario also feels curiously inevitable, like watching a truck driver run over a motorcyclist. Will they be happy? Fat chance – or if you prefer, the odds are slim.

Characteristics

Reading Material: bridal magazines, slimming magazines, weighing scales three times a day

Favourite TV Programmes and Films: Big Brother, Hole in the Wall, Who Wants To Be A Millionaire? National Lottery Live

Heroes and Role Models: Kerry Katona, Queen Latifah, Charlotte Church, Beth Ditto

Most likely cause of death: Obesity

Favourite Music: Songs all fat girls listen to to feel better about themselves: You Are Beautiful (Christina Aguilera), Big Girl You Are Beautiful (Mika), Firework (Katy Perry), Just the Way You Are (Bruno Mars)

Political Views: Fat is a disease

Ego Issues: She's tried all the diets (except the eating less diet) and they haven't worked; she was born this way (no she wasn't) and she's proud to be big (no she isn't) .

Fears: Not fitting into the bridal Hummer, people will think she looks fat on her wedding day, eating less, hunger, wedding dress not fitting

Likes: Eating, her job at the cake shop, wearing tight clothes, her hair

Dislikes: Being fat, skinny girls saying they're fat

Earnings: £12k

Offspring: She wants to lose weight first

Most likely to say: "Where do you think you're going?"

Nurse (Ancillary)

Pallid, skeletal uniformed waif who shuffles around a ward clutching a stack of bedpans and soiled dressings. She has no clinical knowledge despite her eight years of experience. Her lack of expertise is largely due to her disinterest in all things medical combined with the attention span of goldfish.

She spends her breaks nibbling stale cheese and sauerkraut sandwiches and pickled onion crisps, as she fills a small notebook with plans for her forthcoming civil partnership ceremony with her life partner, Janine, who works as a part-time dinner lady while waiting to hear about a job with the Prison Service.

She was attracted to nursing because of the salary. Outside of work she avoids social interaction, preferring the company of reptiles which the couple keep in a large enclosure in the front room of their ninth floor flat.

The couple have decided to forgo the traditional exchange of rings in favour of a tattooed Celtic band around each of their ring fingers.

Characteristics

Reading Material: word-search magazines and the back of cereal boxes

Favourite TV Programmes and Films: Coronation Street, Prisoner Cell-Block H, ER

Heroes and Role Models: Sophie Webster and Sian Powers from Coronation Street

Most likely cause of death: MRSA

Favourite Music: Enya

Political Views: None, although she likes to watch the TV campaigns led by Jamie Oliver with a bag of chips and a Mars Bar in her lap.

Ego Issues: Has suffered from self-esteem issues since early childhood; she has felt warm and wanted since Janine tattooed her initials onto her inner thigh.

Fears: Germs

Likes: High-odour foods, working alone, pot noodles, cleaning procedures

Dislikes: Conversation, hospitals, people

Earnings: £11, 825

Offspring: None, although she has successfully bred from her extensive collection of reptiles

Drives: A motorbike, if she could pass her test

Most likely to say: Nothing

Rapper

He doesn't have an American accent so he has to fake one, but after criticism from other UK rappers he has settled on a ridiculous hybrid that is stuck half way across the Atlantic. He sings about booty, melanin and guns but he doesn't have a gun. The only thing he shoots are crappy homemade grime videos in some grubby underpass backed up by thirty of his hoodied wannabe rapper homies. But no amount of lunging towards the camera and pointing can make up for the desperate UK rap. Despite this he is responsible for making suburban youths everywhere talk fake gangsta-ese whether they is Indian, Polish or from Kettering.

His music lacks the edge, the aggression, the humour, the bitches and bling or even the samples (can't afford the license) of the American hip hop stars. UK rap is so rubbish by comparison that N-Dubz is considered one of the best things to come out of Camden and two of them are Greek. In fact it's so far behind, UK rappers are still saving up to buy monogrammed Louis Vuitton backpacks like Kanye used to wear.

Characteristics

Reading Material: The Anthology of Rap, Exchange & Mart

Favourite TV Programmes and Films: Radio 1Xtra, Radio 1, Capital FM, Grime Radio, pirate radio

Heroes and Role Models: Pretends it's Dizzee, N-Dubz or Tinchy but it's really Fiddy or Eminem

Most likely cause of death: Flat green bowling incident

Favourite Music: Fiddy, Dr Dre, Eminem, Jay-Z, even Lil' Scrappy, Vanilla Ice and Kanye West, just anything but UK rap

Political Views: Life's tough in the 'hood

Ego Issues: He knows he'll never be a dead legend like Biggie or Tupac because of his misfortune to be born in a country which fails to arm its most illiterate citizens

Fears: Flying, lifts, ferries

Likes: The US hip hop scene, Sir Tim Westwood, Dave Pearce, following Kanye West on Twitter

Dislikes: Pretends to dislike the bling and the bitches, saying that UK rap is healthier, less violent and materialistic

Earnings: Couldn't afford even one pair of Kanye's shutter shades

Offspring: None

Would like to drive but actually drives: Range Rover / but hasn't past his test after suffering a panic attack in the instructor's Renault Ciio

Most likely to say: "Is""innit" "yeh man!"

Cockney Street-Trader

 87

 130

 10

 28

 10

Once found in great numbers, cluttering up every high street and market square in the country, the street trader is now in decline, brought low by a combination of strict council licensing laws and eBay. A few hardy specimens remain in the shadier corners of the capital.

Recognisable by the fur-trimmed coat and indecipherable sales patter, the street trader most frequently specializes in fake perfumes and ripped-off 'designer' watches, both of which are liable to bring you out in a nasty rash. He's light on his feet, and possessed of an infinite cheeky-chappy charm that comes from years spent chatting up female punters and fast-talking his way out of fines for illegal street-trading from the neighbourhood bobbies.

His toothy grin sparkles with at least one gold cap and look closely and you'll probably see remnants of the pie and mash he ate for lunch. He has mistrusted every politician since Churchill, and has even less time for bank managers. In fact he boasts that he's never opened a bank account, and claims he earns his interest through an in-depth knowledge of the horses. He appears to be good at it too: he is certainly never short of a bob or two.

Characteristics

Reading Material: The Sun, street-trading bylaws, racing columns

Favourite TV Programmes and Films: Only Fools and Horses, Horse Racing, Ealing Comedies

Heroes and Role Models: Alexander McQueen, Derek Edward Trotter, Alan Sugar

Most likely cause of death: Septicaemia from a knock-off Rolex

Favourite Music: Frank Sinatra

Political Views: Far right, pro-hanging, anti-immigration

Ego Issues: Hates the idea of being perceived as dodgy, sees himself as having a lot in common with Alan Sugar

Fears: Poverty, bad debts, impotency

Likes: Barbara Windsor, pie and mash, jellied eels, the East End, a safe bet

Dislikes: Banks, bankers, politicians and the Chelsea Set

Earnings: Very, very little he's prepared to tell the tax man about

Offspring: Three or four that he will admit to; several he won't and a few he's not aware of

Would like to drive but actually drives: Roller/1985 Mercedes Estate

Most likely to say: "Cost you a pony up west, but for you, darling, a couple of knicker'"

Paint Sprayer

 78

 101

 28

 4

 26

This chirpy/manic young lad works in a crash repair centre where he prepares, sprays and finishes vehicles to the highest standard. He's got an up-to-date knowledge of solvent abuse, checking for moisture in the compressor and overcharging insurance companies.

He wears combat trousers underneath his overalls and for some reason he looks incredibly fit, like a soldier or plasterer. He covers his hair and clothes, but he is more cavalier about his nose and mouth. His occupational asthma, slight astigmatism and general air of barely contained hysteria discredit his bravado about not using an air fed mask when spraying 2-pack.

He is better paid than most of his mates who unlike him passed their exams at school, but look who's grinning now. He will probably marry a nail technician and live happily ever after raising a brood of manic children with cognitive abnormalities, but nice nails.

Characteristics

Reading Material: The Sun at lunch break

Favourite TV Programmes and Films: Sky Sports, Harry Hill's TV Burp, Police, Camera, Action!, The Only Way is Essex

Heroes and Role Models: Famous custom sprayers

Most likely cause of death: Chronic obstructive airways disease

Favourite Music: Distorted loud radio channels

Political Views: Blames feminism for lack of jobs for men

Ego Issues: Doesn't like to be teased about all the car doors that keep getting keyed

Fears: Work running out

Likes: Doing a perfect paint job, taking one day at a time

Dislikes: Doing written quotations

Earnings: £35k

Offspring: Not yet

Drives: Ford Focus

Most likely to say: "[coughs] Now then [coughs] Are you all right? [coughs]"

Protester

Dirty smelly pain-in-the-arse unemployed vegan eco-crusty anarchist, aged 18-35, who selfishly hijacks peaceful student protests about tuition fees and thinks smashing the windows of Millbank Tower and taking a crap in the foyer is an intelligent form of civil disobedience.

Sells Socialist Worker magazine, smokes rollies and wants to destroy capitalism but has nothing constructive to put in its place. He opposes all road building programmes but is happy to use existing roads, hospitals, public toilets, his mobile phone, and all the other benefits that law abiding tax payers provide in exchange for their labour. He looks to the rest of his community to pay for him so he can go round despising them for being unenlightened wage slaves whilst enjoying all the privileges of living in a modern capitalist democracy.

Characteristics

Reading Material: Big Issue, Socialist Worker, Stephen King, Michael Albert, Robin Hahnel, Thomas Pynchon, Noam Chomsky (owns a dog-eared copy of Manufacturing Consent: The Political Economy of the Mass Media, which he hasn't read and couldn't understand if he did)

Favourite TV Programmes and Films: Rambo, Lord of the Rings, 300, Japanese slasher movies

Heroes and Role Models: Che Guevara, Paul van Dyke, Ichi the Killer

Most likely cause of death: Police custody, infected cartilage piercing

Favourite Music: Berlin Techno and Anarcho-punk like Paul van Dyk, Crass, Flux of Pink Indians, Smelly Fish Flaps, Bus Shelter Piss Stains. (Basically any music that makes you want to rip the doors off a disused warehouse)

Political Views: This week he wants to ban tuna fishing and animal testing. Thinks more land should be given over for travellers. Believes property is theft and actual theft isn't. Supports participatory economics but the lazy bastard doesn't realise that he would be much worse off under a system that rewards sacrifice and effort.

Ego Issues: His sense of entitlement and abandonment issues began aged eight when his abusive father left home, he was promptly withdrawn from prep school and spent the rest of his childhood in relative poverty without a strong male role model to kick some respect for authority into him.

Fears: Anger management courses, return to work interviews

Likes: Cashing his giro, shoplifting vodka from German discount supermarket chains, taking drugs, causing major disruption, getting another eyebrow piercing

Dislikes: Eric Carle's consumerist manifesto The Very Hungry Caterpillar, the police, G20 summits, fish farms, inequalities of wealth, coercive hierarchy, wage labour, making a positive contribution to society, washing

Earnings: Jobseeker's Allowance, housing benefit

Offspring: Lives with his partner and their four underachieving children in a council house but dreams of moving to a yurt in a New Age commune somewhere in West Wales

Would like to drive but actually drives: 1960s Split screen camper/Ex- British Telecom grey Escort van (untaxed)

Most likely to say: "That's police harassment"

Ticket Collector

As a child, this was the kid who would never lend you his rubber, always kept his colouring pencils in their original packet and cried if he got his knees dirty. He showed neither aptitude nor enthusiasm for team sports, hated class trips and wore his uniform fully buttoned up and tucked in at all times. He would be the first to tell on any miscreant and consequently was always appointed 'Pupil In Charge' during any temporary teacher absence.

Fifteen years later, and he's still no more of a team player. His aptitude for rule books, timetables and keeping sundry pieces of equipment spic and span made him the ideal candidate for a railway ticket inspector, and he approaches his work with the same gusto with which he grassed his classmates up for every minor misdemeanour throughout his school days.

A rule is a rule, and he has no intention of ever making an exception. He likes his passengers in their correctly allotted seats and his boots nicely polished. He's such a pain in the arse that even his Mother's glad to see the back of him every morning.

Characteristics

Reading Material: The rail network's regulations, rules and bylaws manuals; a sudoku puzzle book, full UK rail timetable

Favourite TV Programmes and Films: Columbo, Inspector Morse, CSI Miami, Great Train Journeys

Heroes and Role Models: Isambard Kingdom Brunel, Sir Clive Sinclair

Most likely cause of death: Poorly maintained rail infrastructure

Favourite Music: Mike Oldfield

Political Views: Wants heftier fines for fare-dodgers; thinks ticket inspectors should have same authority as the transport police

Ego Issues: Wants to be a Transport Police officer

Fears: Unruliness, disorder, women, that his mother didn't screw the lid on his thermos tightly again.

Likes: Rules, trains, uniforms, Hornby

Dislikes: Questions, conversations

Earnings: £17,450

Offspring: As yet undecided and is currently weighing up the pros and cons

Drives: Makes full use of his staff rail pass

Most likely to say: "I'm sorry, Madam but you and your infant are going to have to alight at the next station"

Hairdresser

A woman with a robust conviction that cutting hair is an art form mastered only by an elite few. She regards her clientele as artistically derelict and therefore treats them with the condescension they deserve by talking to someone else while she cuts their hair, and not listening to their instructions.

She is appalled by clients who desecrate her creations with a hair brush. She name drops celebrity stylists although everyone knows she's only ever seen them being interviewed on TV on her day off.

Her salon boasts a number of impractically low-slung leather sofas and her monochrome minions scurry around the place, swaying timidly as they watch her work to strains of unsuitable music. She instructs them to learn by observation, not conversation, which is fortunate because her management style terrifies all but the most resilient into becoming temporary mutes.

She never eats during the working day, spends every spare minute of her breaks drawing hard on a menthol cigarette and allows herself an organic yoghurt with her flavoured vodka every evening to stave off osteoporosis and premature ageing.

Characteristics

Reading Material: Cosmopolitan, Grazia, and the gossip columns of the tabloids

Favourite TV Programmes and Films: Loose Women, Gok Wan, Eastenders

Heroes and Role Models: Nicky Clarke, Toni & Guy

Most likely cause of death: Something nasty after decades of working with carcinogenic hair dyes

Favourite Music: "I just love dancing, me"

Political Views: Whatever campaign is highlighted in Cosmo this month

Ego Issues: Tells people she works in fashion and considers herself a fashion consultant

Fears: Being behind-trend, old age, alopecia

Likes: Sexting, compliments, professional recognition, vodka

Dislikes: Only being able to afford shop rents in provincial Britain

Earnings: £25 – £35k

Offspring: 1 girl who has the same hairstyle as her mum despite being 3½

Would like to drive but actually drives: Black Golf GTI/Black VW Polo

Most likely to say: "Have you got any nice holidays planned?"

Roadies

The old roadie is an ageing rock 'n' roller who never grew up. He's on his third wife and is always on the look out for number four. He scrapes his thinning hair back into a ponytail and wears sleeveless vests all year round to display his extensive collection of tattoos. His mates call him Spunky, Sparky or Spanky but his real name's Brian.

These days he lives in Milton Keynes and earns his living long-distance lorry driving, but he's never short of stories about his days fooling around backstage with some rock legend.

He keeps a collection of back-stage passes glued to the walls inside his truck and refers to rock legends by the Christian names as if he's their best mate. He'll tell you lame stories about the time Mick [Jagger] treated all the roadies and crew to a slap-up dinner at the end of a tour and then turned up in his terry cloth dressing gown. Or the night in Birmingham when he sat up til 5am doing coke with a well known drummer and still did a five hour drive to get the set to Edinburgh. In fact, most of these stories happened to someone else – as did the countless encounters with women letting him cop a feel in exchange for a back-stage pass.

It is true, however, that he once plugged an amp in for Barry Gibb. In a shop in Cirencester

Characteristics

Reading Material: NME, The Sunday Sport, The Sun

Favourite TV Programmes and Films: Radio One, The Osbournes, I'm a Celebrity Get Me Out of Here

Heroes and Role Models: Ozzy Osbourne, Keith Richards

Most likely cause of death: obesity-related coronary heart disease

Favourite Music: Mick (Jagger) and the lads, Ozzy, Dave (Bowie)

Political Views: Like he was only saying to Bono the other week, he thinks the AIDS crisis in them third world places is shocking

Ego Issues: Hates it when clients forget his name

Fears: Sharon Osbourne, getting to the end of the bottle, progress of digital music hardware

Likes: To drink, having a bird on his arm, his collection of back-stage passes, egg and bacon butties

Dislikes: Setting up PAs for weddings

Earnings: Up to £30k, if he can be arsed to put the miles in. Which he generally can't

Offspring: Claims to have lost count, but then not good at counting '2, 1, 2, 1, 2,' etc

Would like to drive but actually drives: 1960 Corvette Stingray/Capri

Most likely to say: "When I was on the road with the Stones"

Goths

Somewhere in their revisionist pasts many Goths have suffered personal or societal trauma – broken homes, violent or abusive parents, late homework, or a sub-culture of victimisation. Many leave off their lame suicidal thoughts in exchange for a cultural phenomenon which protects them from the very worst society has to offer by cunningly donning the garb of the very worst society has to offer.

The Goth wardrobe lies in the murky No-Man's Land between Victorian mourning attire and sadomasochistic weekend-wear. The Goth stamps out its past pain by piercing, tattooing and stapling body-parts at will. The face-full of metal, weird skull implants and ripped fishnets, appear to gain them membership to a special family, enabling them to feel the part when group-reading Mary Shelley's one hit wonder.

The downside is that they are left with very few career options. Limited to specialist music stores and penny arcades in desolate British seaside towns, the average Goth exists within a narrow income bracket.

Nonetheless, the hard-core Gothic enthusiast has made an academic study of 18th and 19th century Gothic horror novels, frequents Architectural Reclamation Yards and is a connoisseur of eighties Death Rock. Twice a year, they head off in their thousands to the Yorkshire seaport of Whitby to celebrate everything Goth in the ruins of Dracula's Abbey. At those times, Whitby becomes a place not even the Count would be seen undead in.

Characteristics

Reading Material: Mary Shelley, Daphne du Maurier, Anne Rice, Poppy Z Brite, Mick Mercer's 'Hex Files'.

Favourite TV Programmes and Films: Early gothic horror movies, Bram Stocker's Dracula, The Hunger, The Addams Family

Heroes and Role Models: John Galliano, ('haute goth'), Mary Shelley, Robert Smith

Most likely cause of death: Suicide pact

Favourite Music: Bauhaus, The Cure, the Damned, Dead Can Dance

Political Views: Apathetic

Ego Issues: Feel invincible as long as you don't meet them in their PJs

Fears: Speaking out in class, conventional dating, airport security check points

Likes: Wired underwear, Whitby, black stuff

Dislikes: Christmas, hot weather

Earnings: £5.77 an hour

Offspring: They have little Goth babies who they get pierced before they turn six weeks old.

Would like to drive but actually drives: A old cheap Peugeot or Renault with 3 other goths in the back; would like a hearse, but can't afford to run one

Most likely to say: "Yeah? You're the one who's weird"

Graffiti Artist

There are two types of graffiti artist – the intelligent talented ones and the thick twonks who think that tagging a bus shelter is a radical statement of urban youth, even though it's done as indiscriminately as dropping litter or hocking chewing gum onto the pavement. Sadly there are hundreds of the latter and only a handful of the former. (By the way, a test for graffiti is this: if it's depressing it's crap; if it makes you laugh, say "wow", or even think, it's art).

To some he is a genius, to others a vandal; he provokes outrage and admiration in equal measure and believes he is an urban warrior creating guerrilla art, but he still wants to turn his hobby into a career. He's probably unemployed but he does get the occasional commission to paint a legal wall, or the toilet in some crappy nightclub or restaurant. He's spurred on by Banksy and his millions, but he's unlikely to achieve that level of success because he is a talented tearaway from an inner city estate while Bansky is rather predictably a former public schoolboy from the Bristol Cathedral School.

Nowadays he feels under pressure to create provocative statements and gone is the time when he could get satisfaction from spraying his tag twenty times in an underpass. If he's truly talented he'll quit the streets and get a job at Apple or Sega, but most likely he'll keep signing on whilst sneaking out to spray his territory.

Characteristics

Reading Material: Walls, The Guardian, GRAFF; the Art & Technique of Graffiti

Favourite TV Programmes and Films: Skins, daytime TV, Southpark

Heroes and Role Models: Banksy, Luke Egan, Tom Bingle

Most likely cause of death: A train related accident, solvent blow-back

Favourite Music: Hip hop

Political Views: Anarcho-punk

Ego Issues: Conflicted. He wants to be famous on the streets and respected by his graff peers but he also needs to remain anonymous. He's painted himself into a corner.

Fears: Getting caught, the police, graffiti-resistant paint, that he's wasting his life

Likes: Spray cans, Sharpies, culture jamming, being subversive, ghetto fame, getting rich

Dislikes: Capitalism, being poor

Earnings: n/a

Offspring: 0

Would like to drive but actually drives: Mountain bike/Volvo P1800

Most likely to say: "Nice one!"

Most likely to spray: "NikNak96" or some similar ego-stroking nonsense

Fisherman

A trawlerman doesn't just catch fish. He has to be a sailor, tracker, butcher and mechanic and his life and safety depend upon taking calculated risks and staying alert during gruelling shifts in miserable conditions. His toughness comes not only from his strength and temperament, but from suppressing the possibility that each voyage could be his last. He is also hardened to the uncertainties and disappointments of returning home with nothing to show for days at sea.

His livelihood and those who depend on his catch are suffocating under a complex system of quotas imposed by a bunch of suits in Brussels but he is too busy trying to land a catch to dwell on how it has corroded his soul. There is nothing he can do to stop the EU parasites so he has no choice but to tolerate them like a whale with barnacles. His wage is declining but he prefers being out at sea to staying on land. Besides, his wife can't stand the smell anymore.

Characteristics

Reading Material: Tide tables, EU directives, radar

Favourite TV Programmes and Films: Shipping Forecast, Trawlermen, Perfect Storm

Heroes and Role Models: Guy Barnett, Jimmy Buchan

Most likely cause of death: Drowning

Favourite Music: Knows what he likes, but can't name any

Political Views: Hates the Spanish fleet

Ego Issues: Doesn't like people to see rust on his boat

Fears: Mermaids, kelpies, being swept overboard, outcome of quota talks, tearing the nets on the propeller, The Fog

Likes: Fishermen's Friends, Rick Stein, calm weather

Dislikes: Fishing quotas, Common Fisheries Policy, discarding 50 percent of his dead catch to comply with EU law, bad weather, gruelling shifts, mermaids, the French, Prince Charles and green campaigners

Earnings: £25k despite a capital investment of £800k

Offspring: Three, all of whom have left the town to find work

Most likely to say: "Nothing"

Gossip (The Local)

81

106

30

4

15

The old stereotype of Nettie at Number Nine scoping the neighbourhood and delighting in petty scandals is still alive and twitching but it takes considerable effort to imagine the damaged child who cowers beneath the floral print polyester.

She grew up in post-Edwardian austerity with a control freak father whose rages could only be pre-empted by paying careful attention to his moods and movements. She quickly learned that gleaning privileged information about others was the best way to deflect attention from herself while getting her siblings into trouble and clawing her back some of the self-worth stolen by a domineering parent.

Widowed twenty-five years ago she has become so adept at informational warfare that it has never occurred to her that if she moved from her village to a city she would lose her identity and have a nervous breakdown. She has little awareness of neither the harm she causes nor her own unpopularity. Being a supposed repository of local knowledge gives her the illusion of power, so she has dedicated her life to finding out as much as she can about everybody else to gain the influence she craves. .

Characteristics

Reading Material: The Daily Mail, Woman's Weekly, OK Magazine

Favourite TV Programmes and Films: Eastenders, Coronation Street, Deal or No Deal

Heroes and Role Models: Cilla Black, Dale Winton

Most likely cause of death: Stroke, information overload, eaten by her owns cats

Favourite Music: Bob Monkhouse, Russell Watson, George Formby

Political Views: She's very vocal on the politics of her immediate environs, but has no stance on wider issues

Ego Issues: She finds herself beyond reproach in a morally derelict world

Fears: Blindness, deafness, busting her knicker-elastic in public

Likes: Port and lemon, aprons, Google Streetview, pressure bandages on her legs

Dislikes: Being the last one to know

Earnings: State pension, supplemented by the occasional win on the bingo

Offspring: Daughter who contacts her once a week and has learned to be highly selective with her news

Drives: Doesn't run a car, but makes full use of her Free Bus Pass

Most likely to say: "Just between you, me and the gatepost . . ."

Seaside B+B Owner

Plump, impersonal and passive-aggressive, the seaside landlady runs her guest house by a strict and complex code which she thrusts into guests' hands upon check-in on a laminated sheet headed 'House Rules'. She never makes eye contact and addresses everyone with a disdainful regional accent, checked by a self-conscious over-pronunciation of almost every consonant.

Top of her list of 'Don'ts' is a pathologically enforced smoking ban. Dare to stick your head out of the bathroom window for a cheeky late night gasper and you'll face her wrath at breakfast, when she'll withhold the Full English until the illicit smoker owns up. As she likes to remind every guest under the age of 45 at check-in, nothing gets past her.

Mealtimes are a bleak, institutional affair: the tension is as heavy as her speciality fish pie and stays with you almost as long. Check-in and check-out times are enforced with military precision and the house is riddled with mysterious 'restricted' areas from which she is quick to evict stray guests.

She has perfected the art of misleading sales blurb: her brochure describes "spacious sitting rooms" (a chair and coffee table squeezed at the end of the bed) and "well-tended grounds" (the back garden of her Victorian end-of-terrace). Despite condemning her brow-beaten husband to a biannual refurb of all communal areas, she clings resolutely to a tired, 1980s show-home look guaranteed to make every guest feel suicidally down-at-heel. However suicide is also expressly 'not permitted' in the guest bedrooms.

Characteristics

Reading Material: Catherine Cookson, Jackie Collins, Women's Weekly, Reader's Digest

Favourite TV Programmes and Films: How Clean Is Your House, Coronation Street, National Lottery Live, Countdown, Deal or No Deal

Heroes and Role Models: Kim Woodburn and Aggie MacKenzie

Most likely cause of death: High cholesterol

Favourite Music: Jim Reeves, Engelbert Humperdink, Daniel O'Donnell, Susan Boyle

Political Views: A lifelong Tory; thinks Labour-voters are common; vehement about the abuses of local councillors

Ego Issues: This woman doesn't have an ego, she has a Narcissistic Personality Disorder. Every stranger is the focus of her contempt and she has yet to check-in a guest she believes worthy of residing at her establishment

Fears: Rule-breakers, yobs, smokers, hooligans and anyone from the Midlands

Likes: Quiet people, steam puddings, Domestos

Dislikes: Guests, Trip Advisor

Earnings: Turnover £11k in an average year; maximum capacity turnover

Offspring: One - see Gay Mental Health Worker, p.112

Would like to drive but actually drives: Mercedes/Lada estate

Most likely to say: "Breakfast is any time between 8 and 8.15"

Gay Mental Health Worker

 86
 115
 29
 8
 28

Bizarre camp male with short spiky hair and long pointy sideburns. He minces around being very helpful and seems to enjoy mopping up blood and being physically assaulted. He is a proactive member of the community doing really good work but it is hard to respect him because you suspect that after a hard day on the wards dealing with gimps and psychos, he spends the evenings at home doing something rather unsavoury.

In common with most mental health workers he has suffered his own mental health problems in the past and this has led him into a caring career. Quite how his own acute problems qualify him to talk un-medicated schizophrenics down from the roof is open to question.

Since the NHS cuts, his role has expanded to include anxiety management and cognitive behavioural therapy; this consists of making cups of tea and telling 'clients' to put some clothes on and pull themselves together. He hates being hampered by bureaucracy, but is unhappy with how the Tories have addressed this: a recent green paper stalled Labour's policy of developing communication infrastructures about communication infrastructures, by giving all the tables, chairs and biscuits to GPs.

Characteristics

Reading Material: Psychology Theory for Dummies, Independent, Working with Serious Mental Illness (Without Telling Your Boss), Oxford Handbook of Headcases

Favourite TV Programmes and Films: Shutter Island, Silence of the Lambs, American Psycho, Seven, Seven Pounds, One Flew Over the Cuckoo's Nest, Coronation Street

Heroes and Role Models: Nick Clegg

Most likely cause of death: Murder or suicide

Favourite Music: Dead Can Dance, Pet Shop Boys, Dimmu Borgir, Cradle of Filth, Marilyn Manson, Amon Amarth

Political Views: Liberal Democrat

Ego Issues: Defensive about his own cleanliness

Fears: His mother, intimacy

Likes: Nothing

Dislikes: Everything

Earnings: £14,750

Offspring: n/a

Drives: Hates cars

Most likely to say: "It's not their fault"

WARD 6

Sec
L

Streetwise Asian

This good looking young lad with way too much hair gel and way too much attitude is the scourge of the Asian community. He and his friends model their behaviour on short-arsed British-Yemeni boxer Naseem Hamed and think they can fight as well as him, so they strut around like they own the streets.

Nobody knows where they get their money from but it can't be legal. They spend more on accessories than the car itself, their blinged up Nissans are just the first step towards a 70k Black Range Rover with tinted windows and alloy wheels that are so inconceivably large that they make the car look like a badly drawn cartoon of the original. Like their hero, most of them will end up doing time for dangerous driving.

They is owning the streets innit. In their own minds they are big city boys like their counterparts in LA or NY; the truth is the streets they own will be home to Aldi and Netto, A Womens Institute and fishing tackle shop.

Characteristics

Reading Material: REVS and EVO magazine

Favourite TV Programmes and Films: Teen Cribs, Pimp My Ride, Xena Warrior Princess

Heroes and Role Models: Naseem Hamed

Most likely cause of death: Poor driving

Favourite Music: Bollywood, rap, fusion, garage, white noise – who knows?

Political Views: There should be no tax and that innit coz I is a free spirit man you know what I is saying YEH?

Ego Issues: Too long to list

Fears: His dad

Likes: Big alloy wheels

Dislikes: Working

Earnings: Undisclosed, no one has ever been able to find out, especially the government

Offspring: Not yet

Would like to drive but actually drives: Range Rover/Blinged up Jap stuff with blacked out windows and shiny wheels

Most likely to say: "Wickid man innit."

Motto: "Bling it, pimp it, steal it, leg it" (as opposed to 'legit')

Footballer (Lower League)

84

105

28

30

Lower League Player, is making the most of his brief bottom division career before becoming a PT instructor. When he is forced to quit with a knee injury he will spend the rest of his life lamenting what might have been, just like thousands of others who scraped a few games in the youth team.

He complains that football was his only way out of the gutter but he doesn't appreciate that in middle class areas children are deprived of the chance of becoming footballers by all the other opportunities that are thrust in front of them, including good schooling, secure home life and material comforts. He was given the perfect conditions to become a top footballer – zero brains, rubbish schooling and no other prospects.

He has played some great shots and scored some fantastic goals, as good as any of Rooney's, and he's better looking, but because there was no one important watching they will lead nowhere and he won't even get himself a sexy wife. He has little incentive to train and improve when he's only being paid £500 a week. He knows only too well that the premiership players were only a little bit better than their peers when they got head hunted aged twelve and then nurtured during their teens; that knowledge and the fact that they are all hailed as naturals and geniuses with the ball, will eat him up for the rest of his life.

Characteristics

Reading Material: The Sun, Being Jordan: My Autobiography, TV Quick

Favourite TV Programmes and Films: Sky Sports

Heroes and Role Models: Zinedine Zidane, Diego Maradona

Most likely cause of death: Alcoholism

Favourite Music: Whatever the missus plays, dance music, R&B

Political Views: Tory

Ego Issues: Bitter and angry about missed opportunities; he will spend the rest of his life feeling hard done by

Fears: His sons won't respect him because he's not a proper footballer, that he's settled for a plainer wife than he should have got

Likes: Football, dreaming about playing in the Premiership, practising his goal celebrations, paying for sex, diving in the penalty area, fighting outside night clubs, badge kissing

Dislikes: Ronaldo, Ashley Cole, Gary Lineker, strong winds

Earnings: £25k

Offspring: Not yet

Would like to drive but actually drives: Wants a black Bentley Arnage. Drives a first generation BMW X5

Most likely to say: "Are you f*****g blind, ref?"

Kebab Shop Owner

Benign, swarthy and hirsute gentleman of indeterminate racial and national origin, the kebab shop owner is a mystery figure about whom little concrete is known. When you first frequent his steel-clad emporium this uncertainty doesn't bother you but over time as your waistline increases and he comes to recognize you as one of his regulars, you feel compelled to ask him where he's from in a clumsily inappropriate gesture of welcome. This is because you are by now genuinely interested in his origins but you hesitate because you don't want to offend. He may have been born here, although his accent suggests otherwise, and maybe it's racist of you not to know whether he's from Mexico, Greece, Pakistan, Spain, or Eastern Europe. Plus you won't really want to pursue the conversation once your curiosity has been satisfied. And what if he should proudly declare he's from Ukraine? "Ah, right" you'd reply, eyebrows raised feigning polite interest, followed by an awkward silence because you'd know nothing about his homeland, except that it used to be or maybe still is somewhere in Russia.

Characteristics

Reading Material: Kyiv Post, Ukrainian Journal, Emergency Prohibition Notices

Favourite TV Programmes and Films: Radio Ukraine International-Kyiv, Gala Radio-Kyiv, Molode Radio from Kyiv, Little Britain, EastEnders

Heroes and Role Models: Vitali Klitschko and Wladimir Klitschko

Most likely cause of death: High cholestoral, salmonella

Favourite Music: Kobza, Mariana Sadovska, Rihanna

Political Views: Mistrust of wealth since the fall of the Soviet Union saw thousands of bureaucrats getting rich through corruption

Ego Issues: Works twelve hour days for the sake of his children, who come first

Fears: E.coli, listeria, shaking hands through a doorway, whistling indoors

Likes: Vodka, chess, stuffed cabbage rolls, chicken Kiev, poppy seed cake

Dislikes: Cockroaches, health inspectors, kebabs

Earnings: £35k

Offspring: Three children brought up to do well in school, keep out of trouble and not stick out

Would like to drive but actually drives: Toyota Corolla/Toyota Landcruiser

Most likely to say: "Chilli sauce?", "Why you askin' where I am from?"

Rasta (Community Leader)

Now that Notting Hill has been invaded by so many yuppies and ethnic minority groups this chap is considered a "proper Londoner" even by those who initially gave his grandparents a hard time.

He is a bloody nice bloke and a local political activist who is well respected by the local council. For most of his life he's been on a collision course with the local police who have always equated black community relations with criminality. He hasn't had it as tough as his father's generation, but he's old enough to have had drugs planted on him and he remembers the bravery of the Mangrove Nine.

He is active in organising the carnival, which often comes under criticism for its policing cost to the London taxpayer, although – as he is quick to point out – this is dwarfed by the £100 million it brings into the local economy annually, unlike the Olympics which will cost a £1 billion bail-out, enough to police the carnival for the next 170 years without the legacy of a terrorist bomb threat before the flame has even gone out.

Characteristics

Reading Material: Bible, Kebra Nagast, The Promise Key, My Life and Ethiopia's Progress, Royal Parchment Scroll of Black Supremacy

Favourite TV Programmes and Films: Newsnight, PM on Radio 4, Jules Holland when good music on

Heroes and Role Models: Bob Marley, Haile Selassie, Marcus Garvey, Frank Critchlow

Most likely cause of death: Old age

Favourite Music: Reggae

Political Views: Afrocentrism, decriminalisation of cannabis, does not vote out of principal

Ego Issues: Mildly paranoid but only about paranoia

Fears: More and more as time goes on

Likes: Jah, Afrocentrism, Ital, Livity, Zion, spiritual use of cannabis, natural living, Jesus was black, locks, patience, Notting Hill Carnival, Macpherson Report

Dislikes: Meat, Babylon, World Bank, isms and schisms, the word "Rastafarianism", alcohol

Earnings: £30k

Offspring: Two grown up professionals

Drives: Datsun Cherry

Most likely to say: "I don't think long-term cannabis use causes paranoia, what made you ask?"

Dog Track Bookie

81

121

30

30

Young "Artful Dodger" type with sharp eyes, a good looking young lad, if not a little thin and sickly. In fact he looks like a greyhound cross – bright eyes, sleek hair, alert, nervous, damp nose, possibly constipated. Despite his appearance he is a bold odds-maker who intimidates adults with his confidence because he only looks about eleven but he's bright, personable and reliable; if he wasn't he would go out of business. He only gets twitchy when mug punters ask him for multiple each way prices.

His jailbird dad took him to his first greyhound race when he was a small boy and taught him to calculate the return on a bet. Since then all he wanted to be was a bookie and he's been setting up his pitch trackside since before his voice broke. He is brilliant with numbers and could bamboozle a senior partner at KPMG with his complex odds, even though he left school with few qualifications and his attention span lasts between 30 to 45 seconds, the length of a dog race. After an afternoon by the rails he drives home like a maniac so he can blow his meagre takings playing online poker. One day soon, as he keeps telling his mates in the pub, he will expand and develop a better chain than Ladbrokes.

Characteristics

Reading Material: Betfair odds, race cards, Greyhound Star magazine, Racing Post

Favourite TV Programmes and Films: Sky Sports, Ross Kemp: Extreme World, Jackass

Heroes and Role Models: Jack Tweed, Gary Lineker

Most likely cause of death: Poor diet and no exercise

Favourite Music: Sugababes, JLS, Chris Brown, boy bands with "Crew" or "Squad" in their name

Political Views: There should be no tax on betting

Ego Issues: Regrets going for the gunmetal finish on his alloys instead of the 5 spoke gloss black

Fears: Getting done over on the way home

Likes: Clubbing, gambling, McDonalds, pimping his car, alloys from Halfords

Dislikes: Girls who don't wear make-up, lesbians, gays

Earnings: £18k

Offspring: Soon to be a dad

Drives: C Class Mercedes

Most likely to say: "You can't say fairer than that, sir"

Insurance Salemen

83

91

30

40

5

The insurance salesman is young, loud and reeks of stale cigarette smoke, Aftershave, and the Ginsters pie he ate in the car on the way. He'll arrive at your door clutching a faux-leather briefcase, call you "Dear", "Love", "Darlin" or "Mate", regardless of age and sex, and shake your hand with an unpleasantly sweaty palm.

He'll ask for three sugars in his cuppa and eat as many custard creams as you put on the plate. He pitches his product at you fast and loud, talks over any interruption and manages to fill a half-hour appointment spouting nothing that anyone can trust. In any case, you're too intimidated by the amount of product in his hair to concentrate on his patter.

He will bombard you with his limitless supply of anecdotal horror stories, is blinded by ambition and devoid of conscience. He'll counter your queries with nonsensical statistical reassurance and has no compunction about using exaggeration, omission or shameless deceit to seal a deal.

He spends his Friday nights getting drunk on Strongbow and luminous shots while pursuing the perfect companion from among the armies of women in stilettos and hair extensions out on the town. He hasn't found her yet.

Characteristics

Reading Material: The Sun and nothing else but company sales guff since leaving school at 15

Favourite TV Programmes and Films: Glengarry Glen Ross, Match of the Day, The Only Way Is Essex, Take Me Out, Austin Powers

Heroes and Role Models: Al Pacino, Jonathan Ross, Sid Owen, Ben Clarke from The Apprentice

Most likely cause of death: Liver disease

Favourite Music: Cheryl Cole, Lady GaGa, JLS, Miley Cyrus, Joe McElderry (until he came out)

Political Views: Votes Tory because he thinks it will lower his tax bill

Ego Issues: Believes he is as shit-hot a salesman as Al Pacino in Glengarry Glen Ross. He's a goal-oriented idiot who thinks that life is one big deal that needs to be closed

Fears: Not hitting target

Likes: Making a sale, binge drinking, the conviction he gets every Friday night that he'll pull

Dislikes: Losing a sale, binge drinking, waking up every Saturday morning alone

Earnings: He'll tell you his commission takes him up to somewhere around £35k a year. His Top Man wardrobe tells you differently

Offspring: Possibly, if he doesn't fry his fertility in tight underwear, cheap man-made fibres and too many cigarettes

Would like to drive but actually drives: BMW 3 series/Vauxhall Astra

Most likely to say: "You see the thing with me, right, coz I tell the truth, yeah, a lot of people will tell you anything"

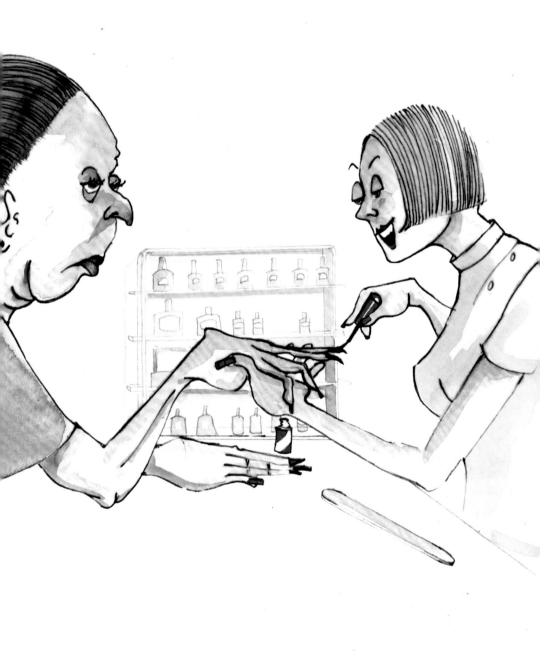

Nail Shop Girl

86

99

26

4

28

Pretty and upbeat young woman called Donna who loves her job because it's creative, fashionable and allows her to talk a lot. The only drawback is that she has to keep her own nails short. She left school with a handful of GCSE passes and then did a Level 2 NVQ in Nail Services. Her course cost about £600 which she paid for herself because she is methodical and focused. She says "if you see what I mean" a lot and goes up at the end of her sentences.

She is popular with her friends because she practises her techniques on them, so they get free manicures. She feels like a professional and within her peer group she commands the respect of a Beverly Hills plastic surgeon. The chemicals she works with every day are neural toxins so her IQ will actually diminish as she becomes more experienced. She wakes every morning with a nose encrusted with bogeys formed from the nail dust of rich women but she doesn't envy her pampered customers because she has her own life and ambitions. In five years she wants to be running her own mobile salon, marry a handsome shop fitter and live happily ever after. Both the name of her salon and the names of her eventual kids will mentally include one or more 's's replaced by a 'z'.

Characteristics

Reading Material: Trade catalogues, Daily Mirror, Hello, Grazia

Favourite TV Programmes and Films: I'm a Celebrity; Jersey Shore, romcoms, Michael McIntyre, Eastenders

Heroes and Role Models: Serena Williams, Rihanna, Christy Turlington, Anita Roddick

Most likely cause of death: Chemical poisoning

Favourite Music: Rihanna, Katy Perry, Shontelle

Political Views: Doesn't agree with hospital parking charges

Ego Issues: She's very down to earth and friendly despite her lofty career heights.

Fears: Archaeologists, Phil Harding, nail fungus, broken skin

Likes: The hottest nail shapes, colours, or lengths

Dislikes: Clients dipping their fingers into their handbags to answer their mobiles before the acrylic has dried; clients telling a long anecdote about how they broke their nail

Earnings: £14.5k

Offspring: Not yet

Would like to drive but actually drives: Fiat Panda/Fiat500

Most likely to say: "You've got lovely nails"

Bouncer/West End Doorman

82

110

10

3

40

He's born and bred in the East End and lives and breathes London. He knows the West End as well as any cabbie after thirty years or more as a doorman. He works outside some of London's most exclusive venues, and is known as 'Sid' or 'Bert' by the glitterati, with whom he is excruciatingly obsequious and always sure to over-emphasize his Hs.

He has never gone a day without shaving and can tie a perfect bow tie in fifteen seconds. He keeps his shoes polished to a military sheen, is always careful never to eat raw onion and combs hair oil into his eyebrows before every shift.

He'll bore his wife to tears over his eggs and bacon telling her what a smasher that Kate Moss is or how Russell Brand's a diamond in the rough. His greatest life moment was being asked to make a cameo appearance in a Bond movie as a doorman. The scene was cut during editing but he still pauses the credits to show everyone who comes to his house his name, telling them to "make an orderly queue for autographs, ladies and gentlemen" and cackling with laughter every time.

Characteristics

Reading Material: The Daily Mirror, war novels, Dick Francis

Favourite TV Programmes and Films: The Bond movies, the motor racing, the horses

Heroes and Role Models: Michael Caine, Roger Moore, Terence Stamp

Most likely cause of death: Lung or throat cancer, emphysema

Favourite Music: Partial to a bit of Elvis

Political Views: Fiercely pro-monarchy, thought Thatcher was the only one with any balls

Ego Issues: Years of holding doors open for the rich and famous have given him ideas above his station

Fears: Retirement

Likes: His job, his suit, Kate Moss

Dislikes: Paparazzi, tourists, Vinny Jones, Grant Mitchell

Earnings: £24k

Offspring: Two sons, one is a bouncer, the other an electrician

Drives: Would like to be driven

Most likely to say: "Good evening Ladies, and may I say how lovely you're looking this evening?"

Game Keeper

The Game Keeper lurks in a corner of every rural pub in the land, where his seat is sacrosanct and an unspoken local lore makes sure it remains so. He lives alone, works alone and drinks alone, and has long since lost the art of conversation. His paper-thin, blue-grey complexion belies the fact that he has spent the better part of his life outdoors on some godforsaken moor shooting things, though stand within ten paces and the overwhelming aroma of high tar cigarettes might help explain his pastiness.

His only companions are his two dogs, most commonly spaniels trained to fetch the kill. On the back of his 4x4 at any given time you are likely to find a broad cross-section of British wildlife: badger, rabbit, deer or pheasant. All of it dead of course.

When he's not out on the moor or downing pints of beer at the pub, he's at home failing to relax in his comfortless, barely fit-for-purpose lodgings. He has no need for television, telephone or central heating and distracts himself by stripping down his rifles, re-setting his badger traps and plucking pheasant and skinning rabbit until the pub opens.

Characteristics

Reading Material: Lady Chatterley's Lover, Horse and Hound, Sir Arthur Conan Doyle, the racing columns

Favourite TV Programmes and Films: Doesn't own a TV, the wireless radio hasn't worked since Dame Judi Dench made a cameo as the silent Pru Forest in 1989 and thinks the cinema is for courting teenagers

Heroes and Role Models: His father, and his father's father before him

Most likely cause of death: Unknown, no one's ever seen a dead one

Favourite Music: Hasn't listened to music since his brief foray into courting in the early fifties

Political Views: He's never trusted any of them London folk but the hunting ban was the final straw

Ego Issues: Gets very cross if a new member of bar staff does not know what he drinks

Fears: The city, the death of his dogs and the closure of the village local

Likes: Solitude

Dislikes: Skittles night, pub quizzes, and anything else which makes for a full pub

Earnings: Enough to keep himself in gunshot, ale and tobacco

Offspring: None

Would like to drive but actually drives: Landrover 90/but recession has driven him to a Suzuki Jimny

Most likely to say: "Humph." (if he is addressed in the pub

Druid

 83

 129

 30

 6

 27

 75

To paraphrase – 'A society that has lost its beliefs will believe in anything" and as the established church gradually falls into decline a spiritual vacuum is created.

As long as you have a list of rules (punishments to suit for transgressors) and a highly stylised set of rituals with fancy dress to match, you too are free to create your own religion. It's not so much about prostrating yourself at the feet of a deity with the sole intention of getting a fast car and a cushy afterlife but satisfying the ego of self appointed chief priest.

A definite perk for a poptastic potentate is that he gets the pick of the women and is sure to assist their spiritual well being by a laying on of hands at any and every opportunity.

It is therefore of no coincidence whatsoever that the modern day Druid is a twentieth century phenomenon seeking to reconnect man with nature. Had this been attempted at any other time in our history (save the pre-Christian era) then the participants would have been summarily rounded up and tortured, stabbed and burnt in front of a packed house on a busy bank holiday weekend.

The Druid may well angrily defy the doubters and the nay sayers because he doesn't frankly have the first idea himself what it's really about and can conveniently make it all up as he goes along. Still, don't knock it, it makes no more or less sense than most other belief systems and if it gives you comfort then go for it and "LO, YOU TOO WILL SOON BELIEVE!"

Characteristics

Reading Material: J. R. R. Tolkien, Harry Potter

Favourite TV Programmes and Films: Time Team, Desperate Housewives, Lord of the Rings, Harry Potter

Heroes and Role Models: Gandalf, Getafix, Obi-Wan Kenobi, Albus Dumbledore

Most likely cause of death: Mistletoe poisoning, judge records an open verdict

Favourite Music: Ambient new age CDs for sale in motorway service stations and garden centres with names like "Healing Vibes"

Political Views: Claims to be a Green but votes Tory

Ego Issues: Despite professing a belief in reincarnation, his sole aim is to sleep with as many gullible flakey women as possible before he dies

Fears: Uncertain future of Stonehenge visitor centre; planned wind turbines at Callanish Stones

Likes: Megaliths, solstices, equinoxes, oak trees; there are no archaeological finds or written records about druids so he can make up any old crap

Dislikes: Romans; stubborn stains

Earnings: Mining/jewel crafting; grants from the Welsh Assembly

Offspring: Lost count

Drives: Your girlfriend

Most likely to say: "I'm a druid"

Jockey

75

109

20

4

30

Horseracing is the only sport where being a chippy little runt is a distinct advantage. He left school at thirteen to become a stable hand and then spent years eating less than a catwalk model, shovelling horse manure, grooming and being groomed. The racehorses are all inbred monsters with brittle bones and the jockeys with fragile egos. It's a seedy business where only money matters and novices struggle to get noticed, so unless he was born into the equine set he will have lost most of his wages to bunging the right people to advance his career.

He has no academic qualifications, just a killer instinct, a sore arse and a determination to win. He buys all his clothes from Adams and reeks of horse sweat and Lynx. He can't talk properly; even the ones who aren't Irish or Italian and still have most of their teeth are unintelligible. His head is too big for his body so he looks like a gonk with a Noel Edmonds haircut.

Horses and jockeys are expendable and he knows it. Racing is scary but he's not allowed to show fear, least of all to the horses, so he stores up some serious mental health issues which usually surface in arrogance and a sleazy attitude towards women.

Characteristics

Reading Material: Racing Post

Favourite TV Programmes and Films: Horse racing, Seabiscuit, eighties movies about selfish go-getters of small stature, usually played by Tom Cruise

Heroes and Role Models: Frankie Dettori, Genghis Khan, Bernie Ecclestone

Most likely cause of death: Horse/alcohol

Favourite Music: Only listens to the sports channel

Political Views: He's a typical aspirational Tory who thinks that because he works hard and looks out for himself that the rest of society should operate like that too

Ego Issues: If he wasn't a jockey he would be an unremarkable short arse; this is his one shot at making something of himself or join the circus

Fears: Not being able to carry on racing

Likes: Women, horses and winning

Dislikes: People generally except the wives of rich owners and trainers who like him very much and bring the best out of him. PETA, walking horses, shovelling shit, Inland Revenue, saddle soreness

Earnings: £80 per ride, 10% prize money

Offspring: None

Drives: Anything with a cushion on the front seat . . . probably a Mercedes

Most likely to say: Generally aggressive and snappy, but his voice is so high pitched and squeaky that fortunately it's above the aural range of most humans

Amateur Body builder

86

101

20

25

Unlike professional body builders, a few of whom are intelligent and manage to earn a bit of money or political influence from their narcissism, the Amateur Body Builder has the same obsessive personality, vanity and tiny penis only without the discipline. Consequently he never attains the ripped look that he longs for because he's too fat and doesn't train correctly. He lifts too much weight which he can't control, and has a thick-necked friend to spot for him, and motivate him with moronic phrases like "Cum on Steve" and "one more" whenever women walk into the gym. This makes him grunt loudly like the brainless meathead he is. His vocabulary largely consists of adjectives like ripped, shredded, crazy and freaky, all of which he aspires to be. When it's cold his black North Face Nuptse jacket makes him look even fatter.

When he isn't over-training or posing in the mirror this grotesque obsessive is researching synthol and protein shakes on the internet or prodding his chest to see how firm it is. He thinks women find him attractive but he can't seem to get one. Once a month he stays home and bleaches his hair. He's desperate to get huge because then women will find him irresistible but his biggest muscle gains are in his jaw and forehead from all the straining and gurning he does.

Characteristics

Reading Material: The Mirror or Sun, Flex, Muscle and Fitness, Steroid Times, porn

Favourite TV Programmes and Films: Ross Kemp on Gangs, YouTube clips on bodybuilding and synthol fails (which won't happen to him), Patrick Swayze movies, especially Road House

Heroes and Role Models: One word: "Arnold". Also Dorian Yates, Ronnie Coleman, Nasser El Sonbaty

Most likely cause of death: Multiple abscess infections and cardioembolic stroke from injecting too much synthol

Favourite Music: Listens to crap American deathcore bands while he pumps, like Impending Doom, Carnifex, Winds of Plague, Born Of Osiris

Political Views: Votes Tory because he believes that life is about the survival of the fittest

Ego Issues: He thinks his calves are disproportionally small, which makes him feel deeply insecure, so he compensates by making his biceps even more disproportionately large

Fears: Cardio, that someone in the gym will lift more than him, not growing lean muscle mass

Likes: Oiling up, looking in the mirror, Ephedrine, HGH, protein, horse steroids, amino acids

Dislikes: Being challenged on his objectives

Earnings: Likes being big as it makes up for low esteem brought about by low earnings

Offspring: Infertile

Drives: As flash a brand as he can afford even if it's older. Audi, BMW or Golf

Most likely to say: "How much can you bench?"

Motto: "We are what we repeatedly do"

Designer (Weird Trendy Type)

86

140

10

5

28

Open any Sunday supplement or a trendy design magazine and you'll find a high-contrast black-and-white shot of one of these pretentious pillocks staring blankly out at you, with one finger touching their chin, or posing against a wall with an expression so serious you'd think design was actually important.

The male version has an ugly face and even uglier thick glasses and cheekbone definition that indicates that he matters more than you. If he was pudgy, he just wouldn't fit, so does that mean there's a heap of talented pudgy designers being overlooked, or do they starve themselves as a career choice?

The female version is almost pretty but again self-absorption, chiselled facial features and ugly slitty red rectangle glasses give her a hardness and make you suspect she's just angry.

Both name drop obscure designers/artists/authors to appear ahead of the curve. Both think design will save the world. They are desperately unoriginal in their choice of clothes and demeanour and style. They are certainly never friends with sales and marketing people without whom they wouldn't exist.

Characteristics

Reading Material: Design Week, Creative Review

Favourite TV Programmes and Films: Art house films like Memento or Eternal Sunshine of the Spotless Mind are too mainstream. Prefers installation video art like Gillian Wearing before she won the Turner Prize

Heroes and Role Models: People you have never heard of, (as soon as you might have, he will change his mind)

Most likely cause of death: Pretention overdose

Favourite Music: Minimalist tripe like Steve Reich and John Adams. Used to like Philip Glass before he became mainstream

Political Views: Keeps politics secret – prefers to defy labels, but actually because he's too trendy to admit to being a reactionary Tory

Ego Issues: Spends his life serving a new aesthetic where ugly ducklings like him don't have to become swans

Fears: Being like everybody else; doesn't realize his design consultancy is just like every other design consultancy

Likes: Sneering at clichés; sitting in comfortable chairs designing stuff that places style over comfort; loves Postmodernism because undermining frames of reference allows him to talk down to people who like what they like while passing off his ugly subjective bullshit as art so long as he can stroke his chin and talk it up; Helvetica

Dislikes: Aestheticism, beauty, having to provide corporate branding solutions

Earnings: £90k

Offspring: Two serious looking kids; married a French woman so they'd be naturally skinny

Drives: Karman Ghia or Volvo P1800

Most likely to say: Four or five syllable words that end in 'ation' like aspiration, inspiration, motivation, innovation, formulation, implementation, application

Salesmen (Old, Carpet)

 78

 108

 28

 40

 10

You can judge a country by its carpet salesmen. In the US he is a fast-talking professional making good money; in hotter climes he is a haggling supremo; in the UK he's a grey little grebo from a bygone era who spends the day slowly pacing the aisles of an empty warehouse unit waiting for customers to amble in. He's no shark, just an even-tempered Vauxhall Astra driver called Roger or Derrick who is basically honest but still manages to cause mild customer discomfort with his Brylcreem comb over, cheap shoes and gigolo walk.

Carpet selling in the UK means helping boring couples choose the cheapest option and payment protection with the credit. He has spent twenty years in the same shop without losing his sanity, which shows that he doesn't ask much out of life. Sometimes he wears a pink shirt to work.

On a good day he projects confidence, knowledge and trustworthiness; on a bad day it's disinterest and mild impatience. He's happy with his lot, his diabetic wife with her chimp-like stature and his two unremarkable kids. He comes into his own when it's time to patiently explain all the hidden costs, like grippers, threshold bars and why you have to buy 1200 square feet of carpet when your floor is only 900.

Characteristics

Reading Material: Various vehicle magazines

Favourite TV Programmes and Films: Strictly Come Dancing, anything featuring Ray Mears, Peter Purves or John Craven

Heroes and Role Models: Peter Purves

Most likely cause of death: Old age, but still at work

Favourite Music: Dave Matthews Band, Jimmy Ray

Political Views: Thatcher had it right.

Ego Issues: Likes to be thought of as honest and wishes UK salesmen were respected like they are in the USA

Fears: Downturn in the retail sector

Likes: Carpet samples, carpet selling best practice, airport luggage carousels, playing board games, sitting down meekly by the changing room while his chimp-like wife tries on new bras, watching his tortoise eat a piece of lettuce

Dislikes: Inspiral Carpets, hardwood floors

Earnings: £28k

Offspring: Two unremarkable kids

Would like to drive but actually drives: Jaguar XKR/Ford Focus

Most likely to say: "Are you being looked after?"

Trainspotter

93

143

10

24

Indistinct through the mist at the end of the railway platform the trainspotter stands stork-like, camera hanging expectantly round his neck, notebook and pen poised in either hand waiting with barely suppressed ecstasy for the 9.05 from Reading to Birmingham New Street. If he is "bashing" he may well board the train with the intention of discovering a branch line which he can describe in microscopic detail on his return home.

If he has neither the time or the funds for such a giddy experience (you can only take so much excitment in one week) he may just note the registration numbers of the rolling stock, checking movements and cross-referencing with fellow enthusiasts as to the whereabouts of individual coaches over any given expanse of time.

It is the numbers that fascinate him. You see numbers are reliable, they are a constant and don't cheat on you and walk out.

Far from being autistic , the trainspotter is simply misunderstood. He is used to the sniggers from the cattle (his term for ordinary train users) and the dismissive way he is often treated by railway officialdom. He is a maverick and despite being the last person to be aware of this does nobody any harm. Ask him a simple question and he will happily keep you occupied for three hours while he answers it.

Characteristics

Reading Material: train timetables, data book, Electric Locomotives of the West Coast Main Line, British Railway Steam Locomotives 1948-1968 and hundreds of similar titles; Railway World; Rail Enthusiast; Asperger's Gazette

Favourite TV Programmes and Films: The Railway Children, IEC Test Card, Cricket, Red Dwarf, Dr Who, Star Trek

Heroes and Role Models: Sir James Dewar (inventor of the thermos flask); all train drivers, Kryten

Most likely cause of death: Pushed under train

Favourite Music: Ladyhawke, Aphex Twin, underground electronica, Korn

Political Views: He lacks empathy and interpersonal skills so it is inevitable that he votes Tory or BNP

Ego Issues: He has significant difficulties in social interaction and repetitive patterns of behaviour

Fears: Terrorist attack, being arrested as a suspected terrorist

Likes: Trains, serial numbers of trains, thermos flasks, playing Lego Batman on the Wii, Clapham Junction, York station and nearby National Railway Museum, jam sandwiches

Dislikes: Beeching, old gricers – trainspotters with tape recorders

Earnings: £28k

Offspring: Two surprisingly normal kids

Would like to drive but actually drives: The Orient Express/Daewoo

Most likely to say: 'Actually it's not a train it's a locomotive'

Hill Farmer

He's a man of few words who spends his days frowning inscrutably at women, children and tourists and who always sits on the same seat in the village pub. He likes his wellies neatly turned over and no one has ever seen him without his dog or his crooked walking stick, even though he apparently hates the former and only uses the latter to threaten children with, silently.

He's one of a dying breed of hill farmers who hasn't a penny to his name, can't afford to run the generator and hasn't married. He stubbornly refuses to open his farm to middle-class urban professionals who want to park up their camper van in a field of dairy cattle and get back to nature once a year.

Instead he continues to swear at his dog and tramp up and down the Welsh hillsides herding sheep and selling their lambs for a pittance to a large supermarket. The only extra money he's been able to earn was from a high street opticians after a film crew spotted him inadvertently sheering his dog.

Characteristics

Reading Material: Barely literate

Favourite TV Programmes and Films: Doesn't own a TV; his radio only picks up Welsh speaking channels

Heroes and Role Models: Six generations of his family were hill farmers: who needs a role model?

Most likely cause of death: Trapped in unserviced machinery, exposure, foot and mouth

Favourite Music: Has been known to temporarily stop growling when within earshot of a male voice choir

Political Views: Sons of Glyndwr

Ego Issues: Too consumed with disapproval to have time to consider his view of himself

Fears: Eye contact, TB, lesbians

Likes: Talking through his nose ("noss") and growling at children

Dislikes: Road signs in English – keep the buggers out, don't help them find their way!

Earnings: Enough to keep him in wellies and whisky

Offspring: None, though he's delivered a lot of lambs in his time

Drives: Thirty-two year old Land Rover

Most likely to say: "Bloody rambler"

Nurse (Lovely Female)

88

120

 10

 9

25

A patient, empathetic angel, who's easy on the eye and reaffirms your faith in humanity. She quietly manages any number of incompetent and sleep-deprived medical personnel and at the end of every shift goes home to a clutch of well-fed, well-mannered children and an adoring husband.

Years spent in inner city A&Es have left her deceptively tough. She's dealt with every kind of drunk, can have you in an armlock in seconds and operates within a top-secret encoded system with which she ruthlessly categorises and condemns every other patient.

At the weekends, she unwinds with tequila and regales her non-medical mates with horror stories of what caustic soda can do to your foreskin or what a dachshund can do to an unconscious 83 year old if left alone long enough.

During her single years she would frequently get off shift, head to Amsterdam and party for 24 hours straight before flying home and turning up for another shift without a wink's sleep. After a quick purge in the staff loos and a thick cup of machine coffee she would be back suturing a ripped testicle with a rock steady hand, a reassuring smile and no one any the wiser.

Characteristics

Reading Material: Biographies of South American dictators, The Rough Guide to just about anywhere, foreign-exchange nursing programme manuals

Favourite TV Programmes and Films: Medicine Man, Evita, The Mission, any reality TV shows about emigrating, Motorcycle Diaries

Heroes and Role Models: Shirley Valentine, Mother Teresa

Most likely cause of death: MRSA

Favourite Music: Anything new from the world music section of HMV

Political Views: Prone to angry rants about the under-funding of the NHS and about western betrayal of the developing world. Fond of late-night tequila-induced debates about the Cuban Revolution

Ego Issues: Generally ego-free with the exception of inferiority compex around female GPs

Fears: Living out her old age in rural England doing Sudoku, working on the garden and ticking off the days until the next visit from the grandchildren

Likes: Glastonbury Festival, working weekends, the knowledge that she has the ability to be financially self-sufficient should the need arise

Dislikes: Women who don't work, waiting in line, time-keeping, rural England

Earnings: £26K

Offspring: Three well-adjusted teenagers

Would like to drive but actually drives: Renault Scenic/Beetle convertible

Most likely to say: "I am sorry to keep you waiting"

CALVERT'S GUIDE TO THE BRITISH

DHLPTX

Keep
at a

Nursery Manager

This affable, fun-loving woman and mother of two is devoted to the children in her care. She's larger than life and loves the unabashed affection of a well-cared for toddler. She sees being entrusted to look after other people's children as one of the greatest privileges there is and never misses an opportunity to make her views on child-rearing clear. Privately, she cannot understand how any woman could put career over her own child but is professional enough not to let her nursery mums know that.

She is fastidious about health and safety and imposes rigorous hygiene spot-checks on her staff at a moment's notice. Her open, affectionate nature and her sunny personality make her the ideal wife and lover, if only she could persuade a man to stick around long enough to find that out. She consoles herself after-hours with copious packets of jaffa cakes and macaroni cheese and pledges that tomorrow she will start her new health and fitness regime. And one day, God willing, she will take her children, leave Wimbledon behind and open an orphanage somewhere where the sun always shines.

Characteristics

Reading Material: She scours parenting magazines and manuals for the very latest educational techniques for raising confident and intelligent children.

Favourite TV Programmes and Films: Panorama, Newsnight, Question Time

Heroes and Role Models: Maria Montessori, Floella Benjamin

Most likely cause of death: High cholestorol

Favourite Music: Motown, anything with heart and soul

Political Views: Believes the government hasn't invested enough in early years education; wants a Scandinavian system of state-funded parental leave; votes Labour

Ego Issues: Suffers from poor self esteem when it comes to relationships, feels good about herself when she's with the children; comfort eats

Fears: Being alone

Likes: Story time, messy time, food

Dislikes: Middle class professional mothers that are more interested in Little Raphael learning French at the age of 2 than they are about his emotional health

Earnings: £18k – £25k

Offspring: Two, her raison d'être

Would like to drive but actually drives: An ambulance in Africa/A hatchback in traffic

Most likely to say: "Who wants to read the Hungry Caterpillar?"

Soldier (Squaddie)

 82

 106

 25

 2

 50

Young enthusiastic recruit who after one or two false starts in life opted to shelter under the umbrella of the military for salary. His hobbies include drinking, fighting and criticising civvies. He claims not to care what civvies think but he still craves their approval and demands their respect.

He uses lots of squaddie speak which combines swearing, jargon and acronyms, and affects a Ross Kemp accent, which is ironic since Kemp affects a squaddie accent. Who's copying who? He adds "ey" or "o" to the end of everyone's name, so Blake becomes "Blakey" and Rob becomes "Robbo". He's never happier than when he's alongside his pals and charged up with adrenalin, whether that be at work or on a night out.

Locals try to beat him up for a laugh and when he loses a fight this is doubly bruising because it means he is not very good at his job. He jokes about using a "kebab compass" to find his way back to base after a night "on the lash" and regularly gets refused entry to nightclubs. However, he does deserve our admiration because he puts his life on the line for both dubious and worthy causes around the globe. So the next time you are put off your reading material by their loutish behaviour on a train journey, spare a thought for the ones that won't be coming home, for their families and for their loved ones and toast their youthful arrogance and the fact that you would have run away. Still, don't let that put you off playing Call of Duty 3.

Characteristics

Reading Material: The Sun, Viz, Loaded

Favourite TV Programmes and Films: Top Gear, Match of the Day

Heroes and Role Models: Anyone in the SAS

Most likely cause of death: Unsatisfactory equipment

Favourite Music: Radio 1

Political Views: While he spreads democracy abroad his postal vote never reaches UK in time to be counted

Ego Issues: Demands respect, not as mentally tough as he knows he should be

Fears: IEDs, army cut-backs and being dropped from the football team, homosexuals

Likes: Fighting, swearing, playing practical jokes, getting drunk, challenging other squaddies to pull-ups competitions

Dislikes: Cold chips, flat lager, officers

Earnings: Twenty percent less than a traffic warden

Offspring: A baby daughter and toddler son with a grade 2 haircut like Dad's

Would like to drive but actually drives: Lamborghini/Bedford truck

Most likely to say: "Can't wait to go home!"

Basketball Player

His defensive rebound is second to none, his bank shots are faultless and he is the slam-dunk king of the circuit. He got ignored as a child and grew tall to get noticed; that's why so many basketball players come from poor backgrounds. Now he walks with a swagger, has more attitude than Dennis Rodman and his pick of the girls. His future looks bright all thanks to a late growth spurt caused by neglect.

Everything about this guy says Harlem or the Bronx except he was born and raised in a three-bed semi in Walthamstow and left school a couple of years ago with six GCSEs, an A Level in Art and a gene-given talent on the basketball court.

A scholarship to play college basketball in at the San Diego University will give him a glimpse of riches to come, but it will be nearly impossible for him to make it big in the NBA, not for lack of talent and commitment but because his name isn't nearly stupid enough.

Characteristics

Reading Material: Fade Away, Slam or basketball magazines

Favourite TV Programmes and Films: Doesn't have time for TV or film – too busy training and impressing women

Heroes and Role Models: Michael Jordan, Magic Johnson, Chauncey Billups

Most likely cause of death: Old age and obscurity

Favourite Music: Eminem, Black Eye'd Peas, Kayne West, Dr Dre, Jay-Z

Political Views: Thinks the British government should do more to stamp out gang violence and inner city knife crimes and promote urban regeneration schemes

Ego Issues: Is torn between the confidence gained by girls' attention and the crushing blow of once being told he was too tall to be sexy

Fears: A career-breaking injury, becoming a mobile phone salesmen

Likes: Nike, basketball, the States, being tall, beating the buzzer

Dislikes: Growing pains, gays, being ignored

Earnings: Nothing yet, but he hopes his college basketball career will help him turn pro

Offspring: No way

Would like to drive: Hummer

Most likely to say: "you know . . . you know . . . you know . . . laik . . . you know"

Morris Dancer

He's called Phil and like most of his friends he's never been without some errant version of facial hair during his adult life. He has also enjoyed an incisor-spiked smile long before David Bowie and Avril Lavigne made them fashionable. He is quite manly in that his back is hairier than the norm, but not so creepy that children would jump out of a swimming pool to escape.

He enjoys grubby hobbies like renovating boats and building model steam locomotives, but he's not macho. He would never start a fight in a pub, for example, even if someone knocked over his pint of real ale or if their eye lingered too long over his girlfriend's ample tie-dyed bosom; he would be more likely to shake their hand and make such a big deal about there being no hard feelings that the offender could end up mildly threatened by his overt friendliness.

He will suffer fools – he frequently laughs too loudly at crass jokes, in a manner reminiscent of a TV archaeologist from Wiltshire – but he gravitates naturally towards those who show respect for century's old traditions, such as skipping around pub car parks and shopping centres seemingly without embarrassment, waving handkerchiefs, festooned with bells and ribbons and decked with fresh flowers.

Characteristics

Reading Material: Real Ale Enthusiast, Christianity Magazine, Sandals!

Favourite TV Programmes and Films: Radios 2 & 4, Top Gear, Ice Road Truckers

Heroes and Role Models: Cecil Sharp, William "Merry" Kimber; he can tell you the names of men who danced on his village green a century ago, if you're foolish enough to ask.

Most likely cause of death: Run over by electric milk float (ironically not wearing any bells)

Favourite Music: Fairport Convention, Steeleye Span, The Albion Band, Mike Oldfield

Political Views: Christian democrat or Conservative

Ego Issues: Leaps around in public dressed like an idiot to compensate for chronic shyness

Fears: Morris dancing dying out: for some reason they can't attract youngsters

Likes: Leapfrogging over up-ended brooms, clashing sticks, growing facial hair

Dislikes: All other Morris Dancing teams, who do it wrong, shaving, women

Earnings: n/a

Offspring: Four children from his first marriage and six grandchildren; none of them Morris dance

Drives: Supports a boring British tradition while driving a boring French car like a Peugeot 307

Most likely to say: "Three pints of Black Sheep, please"

Postman on a Bike

82

112

25

4

20

Friendly chap who likes people and doesn't seem to mind that his bike is ancient and heavy. He is chubbier than you'd expect considering the amount of exercise he does every day, but that's because at least half his job involves sorting his own mail and eating family sized packets of crisps.

He would love to get in early and finish early like in the old days, but now he's not allowed to start delivering until 10:15 so he has to skip breaks instead. All he wants is to be left alone to do his job quickly and efficiently and he feels like he gets crapped on by everyone. He can't even drop red elastic bands on the floor any more.

Before long the post office will have died the death, ruined by a combination of bosses who don't consult and prioritise modernization above morale, and the Union types who, in common with many of the other industries, have crippled the business. People are off sick with mental anguish because one of their managers questioned why they work at less than half the speed of their slowest comrades. Apart from Postman Pat and the old pillar boxes, this entry may be the only proof that postmen in uniforms every existed.

His bike is being phased out and sent to Africa because apparently the roads are too dangerous, so without consultation the bosses are looking at various options from crappy mobility scooters to yet more vans. They will be sure to choose whichever the postie likes the least.

Characteristics

Reading Material: The indecipherable hand-written addresses of old ladies, demotivating memos from senior management, the job ads

Favourite TV Programmes and Films: A House in the Country, A House in the Sun, Cash in Youth Attic, Miss Marple, Countdown

Heroes and Role Models: Phil Spencer, Alan Titchmarsh

Most likely cause of death: Septicaemia from an infected dog bite, cycling accident

Favourite Music: Billy Joel, Bon Jovi, Paul McCartney, U2 or anything with 80-100 beats per minute

Political Views: Opposed the cessation of the Royal Mail's monopoly in 2006, thinks anti-cycling Health & Safety regulations are a joke, voted in favour of Industrial Action in 2007 and in 2009

Ego Issues: Makes far too much of the fact that his work keeps him outdoors and active, when in fact he has a cholesterol level of 238

Fears: Dogs; no matter how clichéd, some of those beasts are deadly

Likes: An eye-level letter box, a tidy garden path, prawn cocktail flavour crisps

Dislikes: People who let their "friendly" but noisy dogs out of the house to greet them without warning; ground-level letter boxes, tower blocks, having to wear shorts for work in the summer

Earnings: £21, 700

Offspring: 2.4 kids and a tidy wife

Drives: He'd be quite happy to stick with his bike, but nobody asked him

Most likely to say: "My package appears to be too large for your slot, Mrs Brown"

Young Estate Agent (Oily)

The Oily Young Estate Agent is instantly recognisable from the fog of cheap aftershave he leaves in his wake, not to mention his shimmering hair (doused in an oily 'product'), and his shiny manmade fibre shirts and armpits.

His face has the reddened remnants of late adolescent acne and his Southern-fried-chicken-fed neck bulges over the enormous knot of his garish oversized tie. Still young enough to smile with hopeless optimism through the recession fuelled property-slump, if it wasn't for his vast collection of iPhone apps, he would have nothing to do during the empty office hours after he's cold-called everyone in the area to try to talk them into moving house.

Those precious few house-hunters who are misfortunate enough to walk through his door are treated to his many glib assurances before he systematically tries to push them into making viewings to see absolutely everything in the window which falls neatly above their price bracket.

He will answer technical and important questions without hesitation and with absolute disregard as to the consequences for the viewers.

He has all the grace and charisma of a call centre operator, hardly surprising because that's what he was until a couple of months ago. He spends his weekends drinking at local branches of Wetherspoons and attempting to pull by laughing too loudly and singing George Michael songs with his arm around his mate's neck.

Characteristics

Reading Material: The Daily Mail, Martina Coles, GQ Magazine, Chris Ryan

Favourite TV Programmes and Films: The Chris Moyles' Show, Top Gear, The Gadget Show, Bond Movies, The Football, Location Location, Location, Million Pound Drop Live

Heroes and Role Models: Sir Alan Sugar, Phil Spencer, Deborah Meaden

Most likely cause of death: Heart disease

Favourite Music: Katie Perry, Ollie Murs, Robbie Williams

Political Views: He'll get stuck into any issue you care to debate, but he has no idea what he's talking about. Votes Tory because his perception is it makes him middle class

Ego Issues: Overcompensates for his lack of education and poor body image by telling everyone he's "in property"

Fears: The country going into a double dip recession; being asked what a double dip recession means

Likes: Lager, making a sale, Billericay

Dislikes: Working for a woman, paperwork

Earnings: £25 - £50k OTE – which he will not hit

Offspring: None

Would like to drive but actually drives: BMW/company mini with nasty decals

Most likely to say: "Seriously though, no but, err, I would seriously buy this if I wos you!."

Cyclist (Fat)

He's something senior in marketing or distribution and lives in the Home Counties with an attractive wife and two or three kids, who he's always far too busy to help with homework or take to swimming club. He's on the wrong side of 40 and he's preoccupied with his spreading paunch and the fact that he can't easily see over it to pee any more. Still, he's always been goal-oriented and he doesn't see any reason to think that getting fit should be any different.

Step one: he gets geared up, heading into a specialist cycling shop to invest in an aero-dynamic cycling jersey and lycra shorts, and a Felt AR3 road bike, constructed from an advanced carbon-fibre, which, he is reliably informed, "slices through the wind like nothing else". After picking up a six pack of high-energy rehydration drinks, he heads home as unfit as ever, but more than four grand poorer.

Step two: he downloads a training software package which he fills in over a few beers, a Kung Po Chicken and egg fried rice.

All that remains is to get out on the open road, feel the wind in what remains of his hair and get the blood pumping. Which he will do. Any day now. Just as soon as it stops raining. And once he's put the pedals, front wheel and saddle on the bike.

Characteristics

Reading Material: Cycling Weekly, The Independent, John Grisham, David Nicholls, Stieg Larsson

Favourite TV Programmes and Films: Top Gear, Mad Men, The Sopranos, Shane Meadows movies

Heroes and Role Models: George Clooney, Alan Sugar, David Walliams

Most likely cause of death: Pulmonary embolism

Favourite Music: Pulp, Oasis, Elbow, Snow Patrol, Radiohead

Political Views: Lib Dem/Labour tactical voter

Ego Issues: Doesn't feel or act like a fat guy, believes he has something of value to offer in every conversation

Fears: Hair loss, ear hair

Likes: Talking, networking, holidaying in Tuscany, take out food

Dislikes: Simon Cowell, exercise

Earnings: £40 – £60k

Offspring: Two or three lithe and athletic kids, who take after their mother

Drives: Company car and a 4 x 4

Most likely to say: "I'm thinking of training for the London to Brighton"

Part Time Firefighter

He lives in rural England where the local fire crew is made up of a long list of 'reserves' – men who work nine-to-five as a chippie, a farm hand or a sparky but who could at any moment be called upon to sort out a burning bus stop, hay rick or school bike shed. In reality this only happens once a month, but he wears his regulation 'firecrew' shirt, with the word 'firecrew' embroidered on the breast pocket, at all times just so that everyone knows he's a Fire Fighter.

When talking to attractive shop assistants, nurses, school teachers, housewives, girls in bars, bank clerks, and the woman in the post office he makes sure to casually mention "I'm a Firefighter" as soon as possible in the conversation just in case his shirt doesn't alert them to macho bravery, albeit on a very part time basis.

He lives in a village of 1,500 people; they all know he left school with two GCSEs in Food Technology and Horticulture followed by an NVQ and working for his dad. Half of them even know he had a recurring problem with threadworm through his primary years. But he's sure that the shirt compensates for all that: everyone knows women love a Fire Fighter.

Characteristics

Reading Material: The Sunday Sport, The Sun, Penthouse

Favourite TV Programmes and Films: Secret Diary of a Call Girl, Take Me Out, Sex Tips for Boys, Sex Tips for Girls, Backdraft, Towering Inferno

Heroes and Role Models: Clint Eastwood, Prince Harry, Fireman Sam

Most likely cause of death: Old age

Favourite Music: Blur, Oasis, Robbie Williams

Political Views: Votes Tory because his Dad always has done

Ego Issues: Likes his uniform

Fears: Backdraft (but that only happens in big fires)

Likes: Going into the pub in his uniform after practise, his uniform, his chest, Lynx

Dislikes: The last week before payday, being called Fireman Sam by the local cynics

Earnings: £5.77 – £10.06 per hour

Offspring: Two

Drives: His dad's Ford Focus

Most likely to say: "Yeah, no, I am a fire fighter, yeah"

Folk Singer (Female)

Raised in a northern mining town and just old enough to remember what a working miner looks like, she is most often found in a remote pub in some semi-derelict northern fishing community. She's the only woman in the place, clutching a pint of syrupy brown ale and mid-way through preparing her next roll-up as her three-legged dog lies at her feet.

She's never been any good with women and has surrounded herself with barrel-chested, full-bearded, professional drinkers. In company she boasts that she's never needed a man, but she regularly cries herself to sleep over the great love of her life: the executed death row serial killer she pen-friended twenty years ago.

By night, she resurrects dreary hundred-year old songs that everyone hated the first time round. The folk singers of the distant future will probably do the same thing with James Blunt. She trills her way through every vowel sound in words such as, 'farthing', 'hunger', 'Sunderland' and 'shipyard'. She sings earnestly, while some bloke and his Northumbrian bagpipes drone on in the background. Despite the finger she places reverently in her ear, her tuning is always terrible and her voice clears the bar of anyone but alcoholic shepherds and clinically depressed Fisherman (see page no 107).

Characteristics

Reading Material: True-crime, anthologies of Nineteenth Century Northumbrian Street-Ballads, anything by Dave Pelzer, Nabokov's 'Invitation to a Beheading'

Favourite TV Programmes and Films: CSI, Dead Man Walking, Last Dance, The Green Mile, Monster, late-night Radio Four broadcasts such as, 'Healing in the Open Air'.

Heroes and Role Models: Norma Waterson, Ewan MacColl, Peggy Seeger

Most likely cause of death: Low immune system from years of lentil soup

Favourite Music: Anything written before 1945, obscure, northern, depressive and bull

Political Views: Uninformed left-wing; anti-death penalty

Ego Issues: Misguided conviction that she has exceptional vocal skills, in spite of the fact that her career has never extended beyond a half dozen pubs within a four mile radius. She believes she has an innate ability to heal broken spirits; she's a 'fixer'

Fears: Attractive women in large numbers, dying alone

Likes: Getting to the end of a set without the room emptying, true-life stories about commuted sentences

Dislikes: Confident, goal-oriented women, last orders

Earnings: £30 a gig and whatever she can make selling her CD at car boot sales

Offspring: A three-legged dog

Would like to drive but actually drives: She dreams of one day owning an orange VW campavan; meantime, she makes do with a rusty scooter.

Most likely to say: "This next song has special memories for me… Thank you – that was 'The Pitman's Fiery End'"

Folk Singer (Male)

This guy's easy to spot: he's the one holding court in the public bar, strumming a battered guitar and belting out folk songs he's written himself. His lyrics are inevitably filled with rhyming sexual puns, and naturally, he lingers with great emphasis on words such as 'yore', 'rock' and 'hunt', just to make absolutely sure the audience knows what's coming. They always do.

He pauses in between songs to fire out a few tortuous one-liners at anyone stupid enough not to have left already. He's sporting a home-knitted pullover that he's selected from his extensive collection of Professor Mick Aston rip-offs, and gobbets of the local real ale dance in his beard, alongside bits of pork scratching and shreds of pipe tobacco.

He's married to Miriam, an almost mute woman who could carry a tea-tray on her backside and stays in nights watching old episodes of Time Team for the knitting patterns. Despite spending every summer convincing the tourists in his little Cornish fishing village that he's a fourth-generation yocal, he was in fact born and raised in Stourbridge where he spent his working life in the local tax office.

Characteristics

Reading Material: The Daily Mail, The Oxford Anthology of Rhyming Profanities

Favourite TV Programmes and Films: Carry On boxed sets, Countdown, the horse racing

Heroes and Role Models: Jethro, Bill Oddie, John McCririck, Sid James, Richie Havens, Martin Carthy, Pete Seeger

Most likely cause of death: Burnt in a wicker man by angry mob

Favourite Music: His own

Political Views: Mistrusts Europe, feminism and vegetarianism, and left-wing politics

Ego Issues: Believes his talent, sense of humour, physique, after shave and beard make him irresistible to women, despite a life-time of sexual frustration to prove otherwise

Fears: Closing time, laryngitis, emotional intimacy, closing of the pit, folk music dying out

Likes: A good breakfast, the horses, being the loudest man in the pub

Dislikes: Pasta, the French, men who don't drink

Earnings: A comfortable pension from the tax office

Offspring: Unhappily married daughter in Dudley

Would like to drive: Split screen camper

Most likely to say: "Alcohol killed my first wife. I got home drunk one night and shot her." (Or any other Jethro one-liner)

Indian Restaurateur

Pleasant 49-year-old Bangladeshi who runs the business with his wife and two daughters; the youngest is due to start university and his oldest has recently graduated. Food is a family tradition – his father, grandfather, uncles and brothers are all involved in the restaurant business. He is a great father and has high ambitions for his children.

He is fed up of correcting people who assume he is Indian, so now he doesn't bother. He is passionate about every aspect of his restaurant from the wallpaper to the hot towels and mints. He's brilliant at remembering people's names – even if they have been only once – and he is loved by his regulars.

He is individualistic, has a natural warmth and charisma and is effortlessly brilliant at customer service. He provides jobs for twelve staff and he recently received a good citizenship award from the Mayor but he still has to suffer abuse and occasional vandalism of his premises from groups of unemployed white chav scum (see pages 12 and 13) teens jealous of his natural intelligence and self-determination.

Characteristics

Reading Material: Jamjamat, The Times, Tandoori Magazine, Kazi Nazrul Islam, Souptik Chakraborty, Salah Choudhury, weeklyblitz.net

Favourite TV Programmes and Films: The Kumars at No. 42, MasterChef, Midsomer Murders, Jamie Oliver's Food Revolution

Heroes and Role Models: Salah Choudhury, Madhur Jaffrey, George Best

Most likely cause of death: Old age

Favourite Music: Bangla

Political Views: Proactive anti-jihadist and cricket fan

Ego Issues: Doesn't like being asked where he's from

Fears: Chavs, Bangladesh Awami League

Likes: Good food, intercultural understanding, Roshgulla, Keski Mas Bhuna, scrumpy

Dislikes: Long hours, ignorant customers, greedy bastards who come in for the lunchtime buffet menu, Cobra beer

Earnings: £50k

Offspring: Two daughters

Would like to drive but actually drives: Bentley/ E Class Mercedes

Most likely to say: "Somebody will be out to take your order"

Paramedic

81

115

29

6

5

Perennially cheerful, everybody's best mate and in careful control of almost every aspect of his life, the Paramedic can handle drug-addled teens, disorientated grannies and fat businessmen in cardiac arrest without ever losing his natural high. Gun-shot victims, frightened women in labour and the psyched-out and unwashed feel safe and reassured in his hands. And at the end of his shift, everyone wants to take him out for a pint.

He's a glass-half-full guy; in fact, optimism is the only thing he does to excess. His trademark whistle and his preference for Abba songs and show-tunes, mean that staff at the local A&E can always tell he's coming. His shoes are always brightly polished and he owns an endless supply of brightly-patterned novelty socks reserved for work days, in case he finds the need for an upbeat talking point.

He is the perfect father and when he's not coaching the under-11s football team and running the local scout troop, he spends his downtime taking yoga classes and studying aromatherapy in a bid to soothe his neurotic wife. Too many hours spent alone and awake, wondering if her husband's been stabbed, shot or injected, have left her a broken woman. Still, he doesn't let her half-hourly panic calls get him down when he's on duty; she's still his Little Sunshine.

Characteristics

Reading Material: The Daily Mirror

Favourite TV Programmes and Films: X-Factor, Gavin and Stacey, I'm a Celebrity Get Me Out of Here, Harry Hill's TV Burp, Morecombe & Wise re-runs

Heroes and Role Models: His dad

Most likely cause of death: Heart failure (paramedics couldn't get there on time)

Favourite Music: Abba, show tunes, Phil Collins

Political Views: Floating voter: they're all much the same to him

Ego Issues: He has none

Fears: Causing his wife unnecessary distress

Likes: His life, helping people, having a laugh

Dislikes: People dying on his watch, Anne Robinson

Earnings: £20 to £25k

Offspring: Two or three, usually boys, generally well-loved and well-fed with a love of team sports

Would like to drive but actually drives: Harbours a secret desire to drive a First Responder's Honda ST 11000

Most likely to say: "You have been in the wars, haven't you, love?"

Back to Work Mum

Nice but dull run-of-the mill mum who has lost her figure and bladder control after her third child and is now returning to work 16 hours a week as an administrator somewhere in Swindon. Here her main office concerns will be keeping her biscuit drawer well stocked, updating her Facebook and leaving work early to collect whichever of her kids is puking in the nurse's office today.

Four years ago she oozed sex appeal and now she feels guilty about returning to work too early and not feeling sexy enough to make love with her husband for the last 2 years and nine months. She forced him to have kids too early and now she has realised too late that there's more to life than breeding (something he knew all along which was why he was so resistant). When they are grown up she will probably leave him for someone she met in a chat room, lose two stone and travel the world to find herself. In the meantime she comfort eats to keep post natal anxiety at bay and plays Angry Birds on her iPhone when she should be working, or at least pretending to work by filling in her timesheet.

Characteristics

Reading Material: Slimming World Magazine, Jamie Oliver cookbooks

Favourite TV Programmes and Films: The Mentalist, Desperate Housewives, Relocation, Relocation, Loose Women

Heroes and Role Models: Lorraine Kelly, Ann Diamond

Most likely cause of death: Heart attack

Favourite Music: Ricky Martin, Enrique Iglesias, Take That

Political Views: Would like to send her children to public school but can't afford it

Ego Issues: Suffers ambivalence about being away from home

Fears: She worries that her husband doesn't fancy her any more since she gained all the weight (he doesn't)

Likes: Scarves, drinking Kopparberg cider when the kids are in bed, Russell Brand

Dislikes: Her bum

Earnings: £5,200

Offspring: Three children, ages twelve, ten and eight.

Would like to drive but actually drives: Old Renault Espace or Toyota Previa

Most likely to say: "Guess how many calories there are in this biscuit"

Golfing Amateur

78

98

20

2

20

75

A retired bank manager who talks a pretty good game and considers himself to be an intellectual and even a contrarian social critic. Take a character like Christopher Hitchens, remove his brain and fill his skull with bunker sand and you have a rough approximation of the conversational poise of the amateur golfer, always your second choice of company for an evening in the clubhouse.

You don't see soccer players kicking imaginary balls or snooker players sliding an air cue through their fingers, because that would be moronic, but the golfer, not content with playing three times a week can't hold a conversation without taking imaginary golf swings.

He wears a Lyle & Scott polo shirt and worships the club pro. He's always complaining about his sore back but never connects it with his bad golf technique. From June to August he falls asleep watching the golf on TV and sitting on the remote control so no one can turn over. Golf pervades his whole life from his car (must be able to fit the clubs in the boot) to the way he drones on about how amazing Rory Mcilroy is because he can drive 400 yards. He still believes that a couple of minor tweaks to his grip and stance will see him 'get down to single figures'.

Characteristics

Reading Material: Daily Telegraph, books on golf

Favourite TV Programmes and Films: Golf, snooker, Mastermind

Heroes and Role Models: Colin Montgomerie, Rory McIlroy

Most likely cause of death: Heart attack on the 18th

Favourite Music: Eddie Cochran, Elgar

Political Views: Acts like a Tory, votes BNP or UKIP

Ego Issues: He derives most of his self-esteem from his golf handicap and the rest from getting chummy with the club pro

Fears: His putting going off form, ethnic minorities

Likes: Shirts with collars, graphite shafts, new boxes of balls

Dislikes: Getting out of breath, lower back pain, sensible trousers, people being admitted to the clubhouse without a collared shirt, women players, players in front taking too long, pitch-and-putt, jeans, asylum seekers

Earnings: £36k pension

Offspring: Two grown up children

Would like to drive but actually drives: 3 series BMW or C Class Merc

Most likely to say: "Fore!… Ooof, my back!"

London Cabbie

A national institution as treasured as the Crown Jewels, the London Cabbie is a breed apart. With his Fred Perry polo shirt and his large thick lensed glasses, he'll give you a cheeky grin as he has a quick butcher's at your whistle and flute and ask, 'Nice threads, mate. What you done this time?' And before you've had a chance to clunk click, he'll launch into his specialist chosen subject for the day, which is generally something to do with the Congestion Charge, Boris Johnson, or how many of our "overseas friends" are doing a dodgy line in unlicensed private hire cars.

He'll have a packet of Benson & Hedges on the dash and his mother's rosary dangling from the rear-view mirror, God rest her soul. On the rare occasion that the conversation runs dry, he'll fill the silence by breaking out into a Perry Como number which he celebrates with a hearty, husky chuckle.

He's a cheeky, cheerful chappy who loves life, won't drive south of the river and stops the same time, same place every day for a bacon sarnie and mug of tea. The only time you're ever likely to see his dark side is when you ask him to take you to Colindale half an hour before he goes off shift.

Characteristics

Reading Material: The Sun, The Sport, The Evening Standard

Favourite TV Programmes and Films: Capital FM, Only Fools and Horses, The Sean Connery James Bond Boxed-set, Mastermind, The Italian Job, Mona Lisa

Heroes and Role Models: Michael Caine, David Jason, Fred Housego, Bob Hoskins

Most likely cause of death: Coronary heart disease, self-inflicted decapitation

Favourite Music: Whatever has a jaunty tune and works well with the substituted lyric, "na, na, na, na, na"

Political Views: He has a view on everything, just don't get him started

Ego Issues: Doesn't understand anyone who doesn't want to live in London

Fears: Very heavily pregnant passengers in rush hour traffic

Likes: Open questions, good tippers, a good laugh

Dislikes: Germans, Mancunians, Brummies, the Welsh, the congestion charge, cyclists, Boris Johnson, Ann Robinson, the cost of personalised number plates, anyone who works in a pinstripe, toffs, the smell of kebabs, foreign food, private minicabs, hen parties, Colindale, New Labour

Earnings: About £30k

Offspring: Probably, and he's not afraid to give them a good belt across the ear when it's called for, neither

Drives: New shape Black cab which they never shut up whining about

Most likely to say: "I had that Alan Yentob in the back of my cab once!"

Massage Therapist

She became a massage therapist because she strongly believes in the healing benefits of deep tissue work and because she realised that she could earn £45 an hour for the same amount of physical work she was getting paid £6.50 and hour for at the local bacon factory.

Although it only took her 2 weeks and a trip to the clearance bookshop to become 'fully qualified' she enjoys the marketing benefits of working from a rented room at the local surgery who are equally as focused on increasing their income at two hundred times the rate of inflation.

Many of her clients ask her if it will hurt to which she replies "No dear, I never put anyone in traction on purpose". She claims the reasons many of her clients cry during treatment is due to the release of pent up emotion although any clients brave enough to say so just say it hurt a lot.

She worries about not having enough return clients to put her son through medical school. She is very spiritual and is considering adding a number of other treatments to her repertoire including, Hopi Indian ear candling, crystal healing and Reiki.

Characteristics

Reading Material: The Suma catalogue, Healing Today, Yoga for beginners

Favourite TV Programmes and Films: Lonely Planet, Gardeners World, The Green Mile

Heroes and Role Models: Barefoot Doctor, Dr Bach, Anita Roddick

Most likely cause of death: High cholesterol

Favourite Music: Earth, Wind & Fire, Gladys Knight and the Pips, 50 Cent

Political Views: Publically Liberal, privately Tory

Ego Issues: Sees herself as on a par with doctors

Fears: God and the Devil, Health and Safety Act

Likes: Communicating through touch: applying oil, increasing blood flow, rolling and kneading, slapping, punching, elbowing.

Dislikes: Visible signs of arousal, third party liability insurance premiums , sceptics

Earnings: £16 – £20k

Offspring: Two children

Most likely to say: "Sorry, does that hurt?"

Plastics (School Girl Type)

Manipulative little queen bees aged thirteen and upwards who consider themselves to be teen royalty amongst the various classroom factions at school. They attach themselves to the pretty alpha females in the year and then try to push away anyone who threaten this closeness, because they can't share friends. They trawl for gossip and suffer the indignity of appearing approachable and friendly if it furthers their need for material to destroy the lives of the innocent targets of their hatred.

Their image is clean cut with long straight hair, pelmet skirts (as worn by celebrities) and enough make-up to make them appear ten years older. They hang around in groups of three or four and are indistinguishable from one another. They are academically unremarkable but have been known to read an entire copy of Bliss magazine in one sitting. They are generally middle class and bear a massive grudge because their brothers have been sent to minor public schools but the money didn't quite stretch to them.

Their default setting is monosyllabic but when communication is forced upon them a spokesperson is pushed to the front of the group. Culturally dead, their main interest (apart from always trying to lose three pounds) is music, but only if it appears in the Top 40.

Characteristics

Reading Material: Vogue , Grazia , Cosmopolitan (they like to pretend they understand the more adult publications)

Favourite TV Programmes and Films: The only Way is Essex which is spelt out in the acronym TOWIE , Mean Girls , Skins and Made In Chelsea

Heroes and Role Models: Elexa Chung , Kiera Knightley and Kate Moss

Most likely cause of death: complications during plastic surgery

Favourite Music: Top 40

Political Views: As soon as she is old enough to vote she won't bother voting.

Ego Issues: Compensates for being dull and characterless by trying to be the prettiest of all her identical-looking friends

Fears: Being FRAPED - having your Facepage hacked into and obscenities left there without your knowledge

Likes: Dieting, talking about how fat she is, looking in the mirror, posting hundreds of photos of herself pouting on Facebook

Dislikes: Grammatical correction

Earnings: n/a

Offspring: n/a

Drives: obviously too young and stupid to drive but if they did they'd drive a Mini (new version obviously)

Most likely to say: "Oh my GOD Shu 'urp ! I was like totes amaze!"

Air Hostess

She grew up with big dreams of independent womanhood and becoming Miss England, but soon downgraded her aspiration to opening bags of peanuts and fetching stuff for people in the air. Political correctness and EU legislation mean she doesn't have to be pretty or polite any more, but she still can't be overweight, a dwarf or a heterosexual male.

As a flying skivvy her skills include wearing a tight uniform and too much blue eye shadow, responding to call lights, checking Ralph Fiennes isn't cavorting with one of her co-workers in the toilet, and keeping passengers alive long enough so they hand over all their spare cash in exchange for scratch cards and tiny packets of Pringles.

Dead behind the eyes from years of patient friendliness and lonely hotel layovers, she projects an image of bored professionalism (a transferable skill when she' transfers to a job in hospitality). The minimum height requirement of 5ft 4" is so she can reach the overhead lockers and meet and satisfy the requirements of the marketing team.

Characteristics

Reading Material: Hello, OK and in-flight magazine, Sophie Kinsella, Marian Keyes

Favourite TV Programmes and Films: Sex and the City, Strictly Come Dancing, Who Katie Married Next, Red Dragon, The English Patient, Schindler's List

Heroes and Role Models: Cheryl Cole, Evangeline Lilly, Brian Dowling

Most likely cause of death: Deep vein thrombosis, blood poisoning after botox

Favourite Music: "Ooh I like anything me." Loves to dance, more confidently after five Sabai Spritzers, that song about air hostesses by Busted

Political Views: Thinks fox hunting should be banned; doesn't realise it already is, considers herself a feminist but likes admiring glances from male passengers

Ego Issues: Reminds everybody that she has an HND from a polytechnic which she really wishes had been called a university when she was there

Fears: Lifts, Middle-Eastern men with beards, losing her looks, not meeting her sales targets for peddling perfume, cheap headphones and overpriced pillows

Likes: Pilots, Ralph Fiennes, feeling feminine

Dislikes: Being portrayed as a sex object; the ground staff who see her as a sex object; Japanese businessmen

Earnings: £30k plus whatever she makes in commission

Offspring: None

Would like to drive but actually drives: New shape VW Beetle/New shape Audi TT

Most "Could you put your seat in the upright position, please, sir"

Barmy Army

He's pushing fifty, is the life and soul of every party, a great dad and always remembers to appreciate his wife's cooking or kick a ball around in the back garden with the boys (while his daughter watches feeling unloved). He's worked hard to build up a successful but boring business across the South East and lives a comfortable life in an artless seventies-built Georgian style house in Upminster.

He holidays with the family twice a year in his time share in Alicante and sinks a great deal of his income into private education for his kids. But his passion is football. He's never missed an England home game and thinks nothing of splashing five grand on a foreign fixture. He even had to move his wedding day because it clashed with a friendly against Croatia.

He will talk for hours about the Euro-divas taking a dive or our nation's urgent need to address its youth system. He and the lads show their mindless allegiance by painting red crosses on their faces and dressing up as medieval religious extremists; they could teach the England players a thing or two about commitment.

Characteristics

Reading Material: Daily Mail

Favourite TV Programmes and Films: Match of the Day, Five Live, Harry Hill's You've Been Framed, Wipeout, Take Me Out

Heroes and Role Models: Bobby Moore, David Beckham

Most likely cause of death: Heart attack on the terraces, flying seat

Favourite Music: Marc Bolan, David Bowie, Roxy Music, Lou Reed

Political Views: The current England manager should be fired, and football has lost touch with the working man

Ego Issues: Huge ego – he supports Spurs

Fears: England's almost total lack of technically gifted footballers

Likes: Weekends away with the lads, drinking, his wife's steak and onion pie and mash, sending death threats to Ashley Cole

Dislikes: Ashley Cole, Emile Heskey, John Terry, Fabio Cappello, Steve McClaren, high wage lifestyles of England players

Earnings: £80K

Offspring: Three teenagers, brats, spoiled and indulged

Drives: BMW X5

Most likely to say: "At the end of the day . . .the boss played him out of position, again"

Welsh Singer/Rugby Player

Most Welsh rugby players have played to an international standard from the age of 6. Perhaps they are mad about rugby because it gives a small nation the chance to beat up its more highly populated neighbours on a fair and level playing field. Even when they are defeated their loyal fans continue to sing bravely and in tune.

International players come in two basic types – they either look like Tom Shanklin, Gareth Thomas, Gethin Jenkins, Neil Jenkins, John Yapp, Martyn Williams, (close cropped gingery hair, pointy or broken nose, hard as nails) or Steve Jones, Gavin Henson, James Hook (longer black hair and better looking and hard as nails). The dark haired version is rarer today but if you consider the legends who wore the red shirt in the past they were more common but also crazier and a bit uglier than the modern crop probably because of the sideburns. Prime examples of these classic Ted Hughes/Tom Jones hybrids from the golden age of bardic rugby include Mervyn Davies, John Dawes and Phil Bennet.

Characteristics

Reading Material: The Mabinogion, Daily Post, Dylan Thomas, tea towels

Favourite TV Programmes and Films: Even with a twenty-foot booster aerial, television reception in Wales is rubbish. The only channel that broadcasts perfectly is S4C

Heroes and Role Models: Tom Jones

Most likely cause of death: Slate or coal

Favourite Music: Tom Jones

Political Views: They complain about English people moving into Wales and pushing up the house prices, but how else are they going to learn to speak English properly so that they can beg from the tourists that bring money into Wales?

Ego Issues: They always speak Welsh in the presence of non-Welsh speakers, like anyone cares what they are talking about anyway – probably how great coal mining used to be or the price of slate

Fears: Dentistry

Likes: Their national symbol of a deformed onion, slate, playing the harp, that thick ugly Welsh pottery

Dislikes: Anne Robinson, A A Gill

Earnings: £50k + PAs

Offspring: He hasn't landed one between the posts yet

Drives: What ever the sponsors are heavily discounting

Most likely to say: "As long as England lose"

Traffic Copper

75

99

25

2

Crass unreconstructed male with a banal sense of humour since subtlety usually passes him by. He's tall, well-built and a bit of a moron who sees issues in black and white, especially when a black man drives past in a new BMW. His day consists of hours of boredom interspersed with moments of abject terror. He's either complaining it's too quiet or that he's too busy.

He has the dangerous trait of being below average intelligence while thinking he is smarter than most people. He thinks he's an expert in human pyschology and he's got lots of anecdotes about incidents he's attended, usually involving druggies or car crash decapitations. He tolerates and humours those who are clearly brighter and better educated than him but he writes them off as gay liberals who wouldn't last a day doing his job.

In the same way that the Daily Mail tries to classify everything in the world into things that cure and things that give you cancer, the traffic cop sees a world in terms of coppers and potential suspects.

He has great respect for the brave men and women of the British Armed Forces and wishes he had been a Marine but he holds little sympathy for poor single mothers and the disadvantaged because the only ones that come to his attention are the law breakers, so he lumps them all in together. He's seen a lot of weird stuff in his career; there are only so many times you can wrestle a naked drunk to the ground before it starts to colour your vision of humankind.

Characteristics

Reading Material: The Daily Mail

Favourite TV Programmes and Films: Terminator, Predator, Universal Soldier, Life on Mars (thinks it's a documentary)

Heroes and Role Models: Jean-Claude Van Damme, Philip Glenister

Most likely cause of death: Boring police-related anecdote

Favourite Music: Top Gear compilation driving music

Political Views: He votes Tory because he has seen first hand the scrounger scum created by namby pamby liberal politics

Ego Issues: Thinks he's smarter than he is, what's more, he thinks he's fooling everyone that he's smarter than he is

Fears: Armed assailants, high speed chases in built-up areas, fast-tracked Oxbridge graduates

Likes: His uniform, taking a mildly intimidating length of time to approach a female driver that he's just pulled over

Dislikes: A shift full of careful drivers, being followed by a TV camera crew, single mothers and crack whores

Earnings: £19 - £30k

Offspring: Probably

Would like to drive: The Met's Lamborghini patrol cars

Most likely to say: "Who do we think we are then... Jensen Button?"

Highland Caber Tosser

With his ginger hair, lily white skin, big calves, white vest and kilt, this great lug looks like he just stepped off a box of Quaker oats. He's cheerful and friendly – men who can blow up hot water bottles and pull trucks with their teeth always are – but he can't be understood because his Scottish accent is too strong. He asks questions like "Hawee skaloo moo hiya areee?" to which you can only smile and nod.

He wears his pubes outside his clothes and loves showing off his pudgy knees when he wears a kilt. His diet consists of nipples and titties, Scotch eggs, deep fried confectionery and lurid orange fizzy drinks. He always gets pissed before using public transport, and on Burns night he'll get a tear in his eye paying tribute to a lecherous and incompetent farmer who wrote pages of gibberish about sheep's intestines and tam 'o shanters that not even the Scottish can understand.

He despises everyone who lives further south than him. He is crap at all sports except throwing telephone poles to see how they land. He has never forgiven the English for the highland clearances, when his ancestors shouldn't have been living in places fit only for sheep in the first place. All his mates are freemasons or unemployed welders.

Characteristics

Reading Material: Robert Burns, Compton Mackenzie, William Dunbar, The Herald, Martin Lewis

Favourite TV Programmes and Films: Braveheart, Coronation Street, The World's Strongest Man

Heroes and Role Models: Rob Roy, Mariusz Pudzianowski, Martin Lewis

Most likely cause of death: Heart disease (invented by the Scottish)

Favourite Music: The Proclaimers, anything bagpipes, James Last and his Orchestra

Political Views: SNP

Ego Issues: Feels very pleased with himself because he can throw a telegraph pole straighter than most people

Fears: Scotland leaving the UK

Likes: Bagpipes, sheep's intestines, whisky, meths, his pudgy knees, deep fried confectionery

Dislikes: Being called Scotch, underpants, highland clearances, Geoff Capes

Earnings: n/a

Offspring: Two little hernias

Drives: White 1980s Transit van

Most likely to say: He specialises in gibberish bollocks expressions like 'Many a mickle makes a muckle'

Farmer's Wife

A plump jolly breeder who unlike most married women has a husband who loves both his job and her. She is shy and kind, has a simple outlook on life and makes the best of everything, despite the long hours, crippling debts, juggling raising a young family with doing the books, learning to operate the computer, running the farm shop and doing numerous odd jobs from feeding hens to ordering fencing. She grew up on her parents' farm, the seventh generation of her family who has worked the land and just twenty miles from her husband. They met at age nineteen and married three years later. With both pregnancies she was mucking out pigs when her waters broke. She hasn't had a holiday for four years.

She plucks turkeys at Christmas, which she hates because of the cold, but even though it makes her hands bleed she does it cheerfully because they need the extra money. She also breeds puppies in her kitchen and tries not to worry about her son's dyslexia because he's going to be a farmer when he grows up. She has a heart of gold, is completely without pretention and would do anything for anyone so much so that she periodically suffers quietly with depression because her own needs always come last.

Characteristics

Reading Material: Farmers Weekly, John Deere catalogue, W.I. magazines

Favourite TV Programmes and Films: Countryfile, The Archers, South Riding

Heroes and Role Models: Prince Charles, William Hague, her grandmother

Most likely cause of death: Old age, varicose veins

Favourite Music: Radio 2

Political Views: Conservative

Ego Issues: Worries she has not done enough for her children

Fears: Blind mice, phasing-out of the milk quota system, being priced out of the locality by shortage of affordable homes, paperwork and red tape, diseased livestock

Likes: Bisto gravy, EU subsidies, pig roasts

Dislikes: Change, Tony Blair

Earnings: Annual losses are offset by selling off land

Offspring: Three children; the boys will become farmers and the girls will marry farmers

Drives: Muddy RAV4

Most likely to say: "And please get that cat off my sideboard!"

Old Lady Racist

She's on every High Street in the country, shuffling along with her net-bag, her comfy shoes and heavy woollen coat with a beatific smile and her kindly words to everyone who gives up their seat on the bus for her. She'll strike up conversation with almost anyone queuing at the Post Office and can talk forever about the weather, her coach trip to Bognor and how she's looking forward to putting her feet up in front of Countdown with a nice cuppa and a slice of Battenburg.

But watch her walk twenty minutes out of her way to avoid shopping at the local corner store. Ask her who does her window cleaning and she'll tell you, "A black boy . . . he's nice though". Listen as she books her next set and perm and you'll hear her say, "I don't mind who does it for me, my love, as long as it's not that new coloured girl you got in: I couldn't understand a word she said, last time". Her rampant racist remarks are delivered without hint of malice. The smile never fades from her face. Confront her about her offensive terminology and she'll be dismissive, telling you, "That's just what we called it in my day".

Characteristics

Reading Material: The Sun, Radio Times, Puzzle Books

Favourite TV Programmes and Films: The Dick Emery Show, It Ain't Half Hot Mum, Are You Being Served?

Heroes and Role Models: The Queen Mum

Most likely cause of death: Senile dementia while being cared for lovingly by a nurse from Trinidad

Favourite Music: Ray Charles, The Ink Spots, Nat King Cole, Johnny Mathis, Shirley Bassey

Political Views: Anti-immigration, anti-EU

Ego Issues: Insists that she's "not one of them racialists" but can't shake the feeling that the bread and milk sold in the local corner shop is grubby

Fears: Suicide bomber on Matlock High Street, Delroy Grant

Likes: Dale Winton, faggots and peas, Terry Wogan, the snooker

Dislikes: That Graham Norton, women in trousers, foreign food

Earnings: State pension, a little her late-husband set aside for a rainy day

Offspring: Two grown children and a clutch of teenaged grandchildren

Would like to drive but actually drives: Rides the bus for free with her bus pass but covets a mobility scooter so she can stop worrying about every Muslim student who gets on carrying a rucksack

Most likely to say: "I'm not a racialist but—"

Thai Bride Suitor

77

96

20

3

Dave from Birmingham goes out to Thailand twice a year, loves that you can have a threesome for ten baht and accepts trips to the STD clinic as par for the course. He enjoys unprotected sex with the girls because he sees it as a sign that they fancy him because they let him 'go bareback'. Now he's decided it's time to settle down and get looked after by a woman half his age.

If he's stupid he will stay in her home village in Thailand, buy a house in her name (foreigners aren't allowed to own property) and get murdered by her Thai boyfriend two years later. If he's slightly less stupid he'll bring her back to the UK where he can strut around Asda proudly with his catch, hugging her tightly around the neck using that amorous elbow restraint technique so favoured by possessive men. He will regularly boast to his friends how young she is and how good she looks naked.

They will be at each other's throats within a year when she realises that she'd rather be back home growing rice than living with this loser and he discovers she's not so full of Eastern promise as he expected.

Characteristics

Reading Material: Generally he doesn't read, he just looks at the pictures

Favourite TV Programmes and Films: The football, the snooker, the cricket, the darts, the motor racing, the boxing, the late night adult only channels

Heroes and Role Models: His mate One-Eye'd Pete who's bagged himself a proper cracker, and first put him on to the idea of shopping for a bride in Thailand

Most likely cause of death: Heart attack

Favourite Music: Karaoke

Political Views: Apathetic, though he does resent the unspoken disapproval he gets from the immigration officials he meets to get her paperwork sorted

Ego Issues: Believes that she believes he's sex on legs

Fears: Impotency, abandonment, being fleeced

Likes: Being cooked for, sex on demand, having his laundry done, free green curry

Dislikes: Not knowing what she's saying when she's calling home

Earnings: £18 - £30k

Offspring: Doubtful

Drives: Vauxhall Astra

Most likely to say: "You should see my missus in a bikini"

Pit Girls

It is the Pit Girl's resposibility to stand in a crop top with her hot pants wedged between her cheeks and maximize brand awareness and quantitative influence by creating positive associations between the sponsors and her large breasts. She does this by holding a placard or branded umbrella near her large breasts. Adding pizzazz to the pit stops requires the same core skills as the Golf Sale Man, but thanks to gender inequality, the pay is much better.

She sashays around the pit at Silverstone in 7-inch platform heels getting ignored by all the drivers and mechanics. Her spandex two piece leaves little to the imagination because the pit guys have none – they are too busy tweaking the engines, poring over computer readouts and examining tyres. For the first time in her life she experiences what it's like to be ignored by men; consequently she will feign disinterest whenever the camera is pointed at her.

Characteristics

Reading Material: Cosmo, Elle, Red

Favourite TV Programmes and Films: Grand Prix

Heroes and Role Models: Jordan, page 3 girls

Most likely cause of death: Knocked down in the pit lane

Favourite Music: The ringing in her ears

Political Views: Feels the ban on tobacco advertising is a step too far

Ego Issues: She wants to meet and marry a racing driver; if she is lucky she will end up dating Peter Andre. Brolly girls are ranked lower than models and beauty queens.

Fears: Old age, flying, being ignored, getting knocked down

Likes: Her perky smile, her boobs, mixing it with top celebrities, being taller than Bernie Ecclestone

Dislikes: Condescending remarks when she describes what she does for a living

Earnings: About thirty seconds worth of fuel

Offspring: "Not until I'm 31"

Drives: Beetle convertible or Golf

Most likely to say: "I can't . . . I can't hear you. I'm wearing ear plugs"

Village Type

He's the man who knows everything and yet is party to nothing. He's on the local parish council, chairs the Village Hall Committee, is a Rotarian and plays for the village cricket, skittles and bowls teams, even though he is reliably rubbish at all of them. He tuts at every piece of litter and stares menacingly at anyone between the ages of 7 and 19 who appears to be having a good time.

His favourite pastime is to take a stroll around the village making a note of every tree which encroaches upon public highways, which he then details in a letter to the parish council. He takes pub quiz nights very seriously indeed, and likes to give words of advice to the quiz master in the pub car park afterwards, as to the relevance and validity of the questions set. He is famed locally for organizing the bi-annual Village Ball, which is a damp affair in a large marquee, where villagers are invited to spend £60 a throw for a ham salad, a crap comedian and a soulless band who play seventies Easy Listening numbers.

Characteristics

Reading Material: Parish council newsletters, the local paper, the Times

Favourite TV Programmes and Films: University Challenge, the Bowls, the Cricket, Eggheads, Mastermind

Heroes and Role Models: The local Tory Councillor, Des Lynam, Richard Whiteley

Most likely cause of death: A routine operation will turn into something of a sticky wicket, which will leave him hit for six. Still, he'll have had a good innings

Favourite Music: The Pasadena Roof Orchestra, Mantovani, Tommy Steele

Political Views: Campaigned against the move to introduce speed signs to the village on the grounds that it would bring down house prices, similarly vociferous against the campaign to erect street lights, for the same reasons, votes Tory

Ego Issues: Officious and anti-social with a vast general knowledge which he feels the need to impart in all circumstances in order to assert his intellectual superiority

Fears: Life without committees

Likes: A nice bit of ham and piccalilli, a well-tended lawn, his hugely successful 'please do not let your dog fowl here' signpost campaign of 1998

Dislikes: Children, teenagers, 'in-comers', the WI's Elvis Impersonator nights

Earnings: Lives off a comfortable civil service pension

Offspring: Two, miraculously, both currently live in New Zealand, which is hardly surprising

Drives: A Rover

Most likely to say: "If I could be permitted for a moment to draw your attention to sub-section . . ."

Bullying Sporting Dad

Ever since he watched a docu-drama on the childhood of the Williams sisters, this deadbeat nobody dreamed of raising a sporting prodigy. He can't play tennis so he drags his uncoordinated six-year-old son onto the golf course three times a week and tries to impart to him the benefit of his 24 handicap. Sadly, for every Tiger, Venus and Serena, there must be a thousand of these flunkee dads with their cheerless offspring.

He's spent their savings on individual lessons from the club pro, a bespoke set of clubs and a pair of state-of-the-art-golf shoes which he's already had to replace twice because Junior had a growth spurt. He records every professional tournament and makes his son sit and analyse each shot, pausing the footage to draw diagrams and illustrate what made it work with an animated power point presentation.

His son has inherited all his father's skill so he's rubbish. Adding to the problem is that the boy also hates the game and envies his friends' ability to collect football stickers and watch Tracy Beaker. Frustrated by the unsatisfactory progress of his master plan, his single-minded father attempts to push his son on further and faster by bellowing at him on the eighth hole. And the ninth. And the tenth.

Characteristics

Reading Material: A Father's Story: Cristie Kerr, A Great American Golfer, Tiger: The Real Story, Golf Today Magazine, Raising Tennis Aces

Favourite TV Programmes and Films: Golf, Golf!

Heroes and Role Models: Earl Woods, Richard Williams, Anthony Hamilton

Most likely cause of death: Embolism

Favourite Music: Music has no part to play in his life

Political Views: Tory

Ego Issues: Believes his parenting will result in a new British sporting legend, therefore by definition, all other forms of parenting are inferior to his

Fears: Mediocrity

Likes: Being right

Dislikes: Slackers, rain, the disapproving glances of the club pro

Earnings: £28 – £32k

Offspring: One six-year-old who is already showing signs of significant self-esteem issues

Drives: Peugot

Most likely to say: "Come on!, You're BETTER than that"

Labour Politician

81

104

15

8

He's a late entry to politics and only snuck in on a protest vote at the last election because of a late swing against the long-serving Tory MP after his six-figure expense claim fraud for lawn feed, hedge trimming and sundry damages to his property caused by mice, squirrels and drunken constituents.

A former comprehensive school teacher he has a wide range of personal quirks and a disarming habit of sneaking up on someone without them knowing he's there. It came as no surprise to his former students and colleagues that his acceptance speech on Election Night went on for 45 minutes and included a full account of the professionalism of his local NHS trust for enabling him and his wife to finally conceive by IVF. His staff remember it well: he commemorated 'Conception Day' every year by bringing a vanilla cream bun for every member of staff.

He will recoil in horror from anyone sucking on an extra strong-mint as he claims he's allergic to the odour of spearmint. At the Commons, he specialises in voting with the majority on every issue, largely because he is as ill-informed as a politician as he was as a science teacher. Decades of close shaves with parents accusing him of poor teaching and unprofessional forms of classroom discipline have developed his skill for talking in well-considered spin.

Characteristics

Reading Material: He skims through the Guardian every morning and lingers over Roald Dahl novels with his daughter every night

Favourite TV Programmes and Films: He used to be a devotee of Countdown but that's a thing of the past now that he can't get home for four o'clock; he watches Question Time to see if he gets a mention

Heroes and Role Models: Aneurin Bevan, Neil Kinnock, Peter Snow

Most likely cause of death: Anaphylaxis after exposure to spearmint

Favourite Music: Vanessa May, Brotherhood of Man, New Seekers

Political Views: He believes in the principle that the state should intervene on behalf of those who cannot help themselves; he secretly believes that the rich should be punished for their wealth.

Ego Issues: Believes he has a natural affinity with women and children, despite years of evidence to the contrary

Fears: Extra strong mints, press conferences

Likes: The leather-topped desk he's acquired for his Constituency office; his parliamentary secretary, hush puppies, satchels

Dislikes: Posh people, because he feels inferior

Earnings: £38-45k expenses, even under the new system

Offspring: A daughter called Miriam, the apple of his eye

Would like to drive but actually drives: Mercedes Estate but feels it may look bad for his constituents so drives a Renault Espace

Most likely to say: "If you will just let me finish . . ."

Loud Female Found At Every Major Race Meeting

She's called Vera, Stella or Barbara and works as a barmaid at her local golf or rugby club, somewhere in the Midlands. She gets drunk on gin and orange every Friday night without fail, and holidays in Lanzarotte or Tenerife, which she pronounces Ten-er-ee-fee no matter how many times the waiters try to correct her.

Every year, her and 'the girls' head off into town for a day of coarse jokes and posh-frock shopping. She returns with an inappropriately tight dress, shoes she can barely walk in and a ridiculous hat. All she needs is to get her upper lip waxed and she's ready for her Big Day At The Races.

The day starts with bucks fizz and ends in shameless binge drinking and a drunken rendition of Rolf Harris' 'Two Little Boys', which will reduce her to loud tears. She roars her horse on in every race and never fails to tell everyone around her which horse was hers, where it came and how close she came to winning that time. She repeats the phrase, "Never win a thing, me!" and "Oh well, it's only money" after every race, as if her run of bad luck or her philosophy on gambling is something that anyone cares about.

Characteristics

Reading Material: Jackie Collins romances, cocktail list

Favourite TV Programmes and Films: Gavin and Stacey, Eastenders, Casualty, Lark Rise to Candleford, Jersey Shore

Heroes and Role Models: Charlotte Church, Barbara Windsor

Most likely cause of death: Anything cholesterol-alcohol-or weight-related

Favourite Music: Shirley Bassey, Abba, Tom Jones, Robbie Williams

Political Views: Tory

Ego Issues: Struggles with her fading looks but thanks god for fake tan

Fears: Her husband's having an affair

Likes: Having an excuse to dress up, aqua aerobics because it's 'a scream'

Dislikes: Posh birds, people who take themselves too seriously

Earnings: £10k, but it's a handy bit of pocket money

Offspring: A daughter who's in hair and beauty and a son who's "something in computers"

Drives: An electric blue Micra with a humorous bumper sticker

Most likely to say: "It's only money, isn't it?"

WAG

Raised in a 70s semi somewhere in the South-East, this girl got all the education she needed at the local clubs. In the few years since she left school with two GCSEs and a ruthless wanna-be ambition, she set out to fulfil her goal to get hitched with a Premier League footballer with impressive drive, forward planning and dedication.

First, she equipped herself with all necessary qualifications: the designer heels, plastic cleavage and big hair. Then she studied, The Knowledge, learning by rote every club, hotel and airport lounge frequented by the largest number of desirable players.

From there it was a messy business of ingratiating herself, getting her face known, if not always her name, and working her way to the top. Single-minded in the pursuit of her goal, she was never afraid to shed friends, family and reputation along the way.

Now she lives in a multi-million pound pad somewhere in Cheshire with top-notch security system, monochromatic décor, a state of the art sound system and far too much gold. Her bikini wardrobe is housed in its own bedroom and she has a sports car for every day of the week.

She passes the long lonely season working on the vodka habit that will get her into Rehab as well as the front cover of Grazia magazine, and checking the gardener hasn't cropped the trees outside the walled garden that would enable the paparazzi to get a good look.

Characteristics

Reading Material: stories about her in the tabloids and gossip columns

Favourite TV Programmes and Films: Footballers' Wives, anything by Richard Curtis

Heroes and Role Models: Queen Victoria (Beckham)

Most likely cause of death: Botox-induced botulism of the lung

Favourite Music: The Spice Girls, Destiny's Child, Girls Aloud, The Saturdays

Political Views: Tory because she thinks that makes her middle class

Ego Issues: Thinks that hard work and dedication is all it takes to reach your goals; if you haven't, it's because you've not tried hard enough

Fears: Ageing, being seen without her hair extensions, carbs

Likes: Being in the glossies, vodka, Harvey Nichols

Dislikes: Sweating, eating, having to visit her family

Earnings: Somewhere in excess of £30 million

Offspring: Not yet, but she's in talks with Max Clifford about it

Drives: Depends what day of the week it is

Most likely to say: "Don' ask me!"

Chef (Anonymous, Provincial)

Unlike the Celebrity Chef (see page 287), the Anonymous Provincial Chef is super friendly especially if he's of Italian descent. He subscribes to the Ainsley Harriott school of cheesy grins and he wears novelty boxer shorts because he likes to give all the ladies something to read, except he can't seem to entice any back to his grubby bedsit above the restaurant.

He insists on coming out of the kitchen all the time to seek your approval and make you try complimentary dishes. In fact he is so overbearing and customer-focused that you can't quite believe his bonhomie or flamboyant Latin gestures are genuine and you suspect that he's probably second generation ethnic Croatian. He compliments all the female customers, even the ugly ones, and he makes such a fuss of you that you wish you'd gone to Pizza Hut where at least you'd be allowed to get through a plate of food without interruption.

His self confidence and ego are are overbearing, but not as tiresome as his need for approval. He considers himself to be remarkably talented and feels that it is only a matter of time before he gets a book and TV deal. All his dishes are derivative, he relies on three of his favourite TV chefs for ideas but he will change two minor ingredients and call them his own. He presents himself as a great architect of creative dishes, in reality he is just an enthusiastic bricklayer

Characteristics

Reading Material: Celebrity chef cookery books, celebrity chef memoirs, The Daily Mirror

Favourite TV Programmes and Films: The Hairy Bikers, Jamie's School Dinners, Nigel Slater's Simple Suppers, Masterchef

Heroes and Role Models: Heston Blumenthal, Massimo Bottura, Pierre Gagnaire, Hugh Fearnley-Whittingstall

Most likely cause of death: Alcohol

Favourite Music: Red Hot Chili Peppers, Fatboy Slim, Dave Matthews Band, My Chemical Romance

Political Views: If the country was run like a kitchen no one would be allowed to run or wear open toed shoes

Ego Issues: He is naturally obsequious and thrives in a strict hierarchy in which everyone knows their place; he gains satisfaction and self worth from giving service

Fears: Food poisoning in the restaurant, staff not showing up for work, forgetting to order something , bacteria

Likes: Stainless steel pots, being addressed as "Chef!"

Dislikes: Guests ordering off menu or a rare steak and then sending it back because it's too raw, Jamie Oliver, Gordon Ramsay, Marco Pierre White's hair and personality

Earnings: £44k

Offspring: No time

Drives: Mini Cooper Works

Most likely to say: "I let my ingredients do the talking" (then he talks to you for twenty minutes)

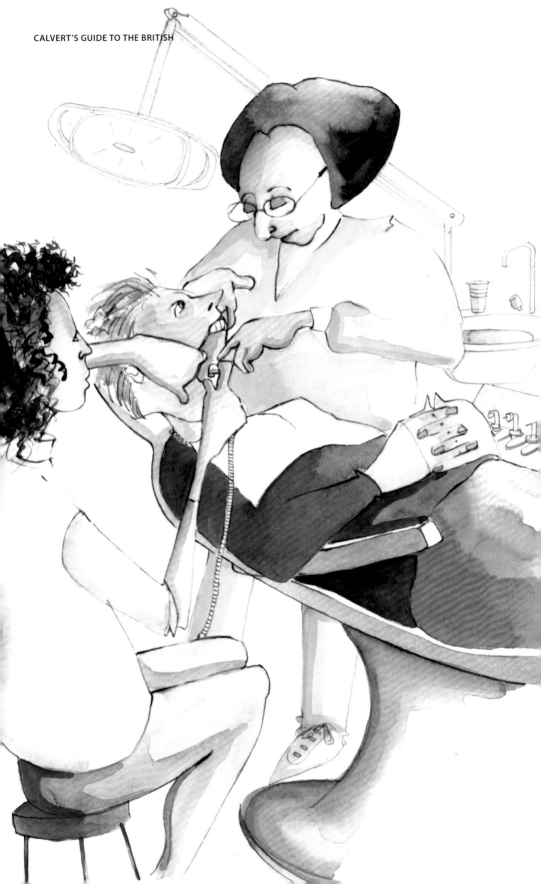

Dentist (Female)

A fastidious bright spark with a smart inner-city practice and a burgeoning waiting list. Her emphasis on holistic dental practices is heralded in the waiting room, where patients are soothed by an indoor waterfall and whale song. On the ceiling above the dentist chair is a faded collage of naff celebrities to distract the younger patients, compiled years ago by one of her children.

She owes her own academic success and financial security to her devoted parents who demonstrated the importance of a good education by subjecting her to four hours a night of extra tuition from the age of three. The extent of their pride in her is evidenced by the display of photocopies of her degree certificates in their downstairs loo.

Married with a grown family, her own parenting comprises a strictly supervised dental regime balanced by a fully democratic household. Consequently her offspring have been insufferably obnoxious since the age of four, but all have Oxbridge educations and perfect teeth.

Socially she's about as vivacious as novocaine and years of getting up close and personal with perfect strangers have left her with significant personal space issues as well as an unchecked hypersensitivity to nasal hair.

Characteristics

Reading Material: Whatever's on her Reading Group list for the month

Favourite TV Programmes and Films: BBC period drama, the Antiques Roadshow, Merchant-Ivory movies, anything with Kenneth Brannagh in it

Heroes and Role Models: Moira Stewart, Angela Rippon, Joan Bakewell

Most likely cause of death: Old age

Favourite Music: Vaughan-Williams, Elgar, Val Doonican

Political Views: Thatcherism

Ego Issues: Believes that to associate with anyone with imperfect dentition would be bad PR

Fears: Cavities

Likes: Teeth, pastel interior décor, the Soroptimists

Dislikes: Alcohol, Bollywood, the Milliband brothers, garlic

Earnings: £110k pa

Offspring: Three adult, Oxbridge educated overachievers, called Rupert, Henry and Verity

Drives: Toyota RAV4

Most likely to say: "Have you been shown how to floss?"

Born Again Biker

Most likely born between 1962 and 1969 this born again biker was brought up on a diet of Motorcycle News, The Isle of Man TT, Barry Sheene and Mike Hailwood

He had numerous self-maintained motorcycles between the ages of 17 and 29, loved taking girls on the back, and always dreamt of being a superstar road racer. He knows he had the talent and the looks but has forgotten quite how it never all came together. He has spent the last 20 years sitting at a desk in a boring business that has drawn the life out of him.

Despite a soulless career choice, he enjoyed 2 housing booms and has just received a letter from the dirty robbing insurance firm who sold him a 25 year endowment which is just about to pay him out 3% more than he put in. He has headed straight down to WHSmith to buy the latest Performance Bikes Magazine where he has carefully read a road test of the latest 200mph race-bred sports bikes.....and bought one.

Shocked and disappointed that he couldn't get his old leathers past his knees ,he has gone out and spent another £2000 on the latest racing suit, helmet, gloves and boots, not to mention black visor, back protector, toe sliders, knee sliders, visor tear offs and a small number plate.

He now hangs around his favourite biking cafes and market squares on a Wednesday night or Sunday afternoon sharing grossly exaggerated riding based anecdotes with likeminded storytellers who on the outside subscribe to the "NO FEAR" image but privately worry that their bike is too fast and that they might get killed.

Characteristics

Reading Material: Motorcycle News, Performance Bike, The Sunday Times

Favourite TV Programmes and Films: Sky Sports, Long Way Round, QI, Have I Got News for You, The Great Escape

Heroes and Role Models: Barry Sheene, Mike Hailwood, Bob Heath and James Hunt

Most likely cause of death: Rider error leading to a fatal collision with a stationary object.

Favourite Music: The Stones, Status Quo, Tom Petty, Van Morrison

Political Views: Lib Dem

Ego Issues: He craves female admiration and is more concerned with how impressed people are by his girlfriend, than how impressed she is with him

Fears: Rain, other men who ride quickly, ageing

Likes: Younger women, blondes, impressing pedestrians

Dislikes: Being teased about riding slowly, signs of ageing

Earnings: £38,750

Offspring: Two

Drives: Something too fast for him

Most likely to say: "Clipping the apex, winding it on, nailing it!"

Butcher

From quirky French black comedies set in post-apocalyptic apartments to Sweeney Todd (a barber by profession but a hobbyist butcher in his spare time), there's a good reason why the butchers that crop up in popular culture are psychos – it's because they are in real life. This solidly-built meat lover lives to chop up dead animals, dress their flesh and sell what he can't eat himself, which judging by his appearance, isn't very much.

His father was a butcher, and his father before him; in fact his family has been hacking carcasses since 1885, of which he is inordinately proud, skills passed down the generations. He's very polite to women, although he loves banter and sexist jokes when they're out of earshot, but he disapproves of women using blue language.

Traditional butchers are a dying breed; they are closing down all over the country (25 a month) as supermarkets put them out of business. If an average of three butchers work in each shop that means there's 900 tooled-up psychos with low self-esteem being added to the dole queue every year.

Characteristics

Reading Material: Farmers Weekly, The Mirror

Favourite TV Programmes and Films: Radio 1 & 2, Silent Witness. Cold Case, Casualty, Saw

Heroes and Role Models: Geoff Boycott, Henry Cooper

Most likely cause of death: E coli

Favourite Music: The Jazz Butcher Conspiracy, Meat Loaf, Leonard Cohen:The Butcher (butchers lack imagination)

Political Views: Tory

Ego Issues: He is very proud to be a butcher

Fears: E coli

Likes: Meat and meat preparation, tiles and stainless steel, his Advanced Certificate in Meat and Poultry (NVQ Level 3), framed on the wall

Dislikes: Flies, backache from standing all day

Earnings: £30k+

Offspring: Two meater eaters

Would like to drive but actually drives: Any high-spec Japanese made pickup like Nissan Navara or Toyota HiLux /a white Van with his name on

Most likely to say: "I've got something special in just for you, Mrs Naylor"

Social Worker

This patient, people oriented, thick-skinned, compassionate woman became a social worker because she wanted to help chavs, young offenders, the mentally ill, the socially disadvantaged, drug dealers and the disabled. She does this by taking middle class children away from their parents when they fall off a swing, while working class kids die in agony despite more than sixty visits from social services. How can this be?

The social worker would have us believe she is hampered by legislation and procedural issues and spends so many hours completing forms and ticking boxes that she doesn't have time to count the bruises and cigarette burns on the toddlers from the sink estate. In reality, it's because she's a woolly liberal who tolerates an unacceptable degree of rough and tumble from the plebs.

What she should do instead is apply some common sense: one sheet of paper, five questions.

1. Do the parents smoke in the house?
2. Do the parents turn the TV off when you come in?
3. Do they own more than one smelly aggressive dog?
4. Does the house smell bad?
5. Is everyone on benefits?

Five Yes answers and the kid should be taken into care. Simples.

Characteristics

Reading Material: Endless paperwork relating to new Local Authority policy; the tabloid coverage of the latest social services scandal, Alice Walker, Dave Pelzer

Favourite TV Programmes and Films: Eastenders, Coronation Street, Hollyoaks, Shameless

Heroes and Role Models: Pat Butcher, Barbara Windsor, Duchess of Kent

Most likely cause of death: Stabbed in the lift in an inner-city high-rise, crucifixion by the mass media

Favourite Music: UB40, Billy Bragg

Political Views: Labour

Ego Issues: Only ever wanted to help people, which makes her incapable of prioritising or making tough decisions

Fears: Lifts in inner-city high-rises

Likes: Dairy Milk and chardonnay in front of the telly after work, her cats

Dislikes: The media portrayal of social workers

Earnings: £23, 500 - £57, 500 depending on seniority

Offspring: She lives alone with her cats after two failed and abusive relationships

Drives: Dihatsu

Most likely to say: "I understand your predicament, Mrs Baxter, but you have to appreciate my hands are tied"

RIP

Art Student

73

89

5

10

20

Moody and inarticulate individualist who dresses in whatever retro style is currently in vogue, has bright red lipstick and back-combs her hair in a pompadour or ducktail. She yearns to do something different with her life but doesn't know what. She lacks the grades or linguistic skill to do anything so resorts to expressing her most intimate personal thoughts via the medium of suspending objects from a folding chair.

Art students are often portrayed as lazy potheads but the truth is most of them lack the intellectual rigour to tie their own shoelaces so to graduate they have to work longer hours than a five-year-old Sudanese camel jockey. She attributes her self-obsessed creativity to growing up in a seaside town with a single mother who pleasured sailors.

She financially supports her unemployed boyfriend, a confessional poet and fervent disciple of Amateurism – the expedient notion that being lazy and talentless for no money while sponging off your girlfriend is preferable to developing your skills and creativity through formal training.

After finally realising that she is more of an academic than an artist she will become an art teacher in a minor public school and get sacked for smoking cannabis with her students.

Characteristics

Reading Material: NME, Julie Burchill, Arts Council grant rejection letters

Favourite TV Programmes and Films: Independent European movies involving an ambiguous sexual tension between a precocious twelve-year-old girl and Jean Reno

Heroes and Role Models: Tracey Emin, Andy Warhol, Frida Kahlo, Sylvia Plath

Most likely cause of death: Unknown

Favourite Music: The most obscure music she can find in the indie and art rock genres

Political Views: Feels that creation of art is more important than its consumption, but only because she couldn't sell any of her work

Ego Issues: She is attracted to older Europeans and thinks that anyone who conforms to any sort of cultural norms is boring and sad. She has strong opinions about politics and philosophy but little understanding of either

Fears: Seagulls, deckchairs, ice cream, candy floss, being ordinary

Likes: Talking about her work

Dislikes: The pill, contraception, getting her shit together and taking responsibility for her car crash of a life, thinks Grayson Perry is creepy but likes his pottery, Frida Kahlo's moustache.

Earnings: Rapidly increasing student loan

Offspring: Let's hope not

Drives: Motor scooter or parents' car

Most likely to say: "Yeah, but how do you define art?"

Cider Farmer

A bonkers West Country apple grower who makes his own cider but drinks too much of it. He makes money by selling overpriced bog standard cider to people who like to buy British and organic and his claim to fame is being on Rick Stein's Food Heroes.

All his ciders sound like death metal bands named by lobotomized medieval peasants, but in fact they have been carefully chosen to appeal to gullible middle class eco types who find them quaintly loutish and a little bit rude. These names always imply that the contents will give you diarrhoea or a cheeky dose of brain damage. His three most popular cyders – which he spells with a y to increase sales – are Bishop's Fistula, Brainstem and Comageddon. He claims his apples are the best because of the ley lines than run underneath his orchard.

His farm is verified by the English Tourist Board which means he can charge a family of four £52 to see some goats and ride through his orchard on a trailer. This is followed by a guided tour of a few tatty-looking apples being squashed, half a dozen barrels in a room, culminating in a bottling plant where a squirt of cider is poured with little precision into variously shaped and hygienically suspect bottles.

Characteristics

Reading Material: His bank statement, Farmers Guardian

Favourite TV Programmes and Films: Farming Today, The Archers, Countryfile

Heroes and Role Models: Adge Cutler (lead singer of The Wurzels, RIP)

Most likely cause of death: Alcohol poisoning (Twer suhn moin, one momun e wer alrigh, nex e wer gon)

Favourite Music: The Wurzels, Bryan Adams, Bon Jovi, Europe, Tina Turner

Political Views: Eye'm zorree, eye, doughn unnerstan. Cud e speek uh liddle zlower pleeze?

Ego Issues: Ah, noht too baahd.

Fears: Fire blight, scab, rust

Likes: Combination of heavy rain and sunny spells, cider, cyder

Dislikes: Incomers

Earnings: So much he uses a hayfork to count it

Offspring: Two

Drives: Old grey Fergie

Most likely to say: "That'll be £80 please"

Asian Genius Student

This young man showed extraordinary talent in maths at the age of three so his father, a college lecturer with a PhD in maths, gave up his job and home schooled him. Growing up he had no friends other than his parents, but by the time he was nine he could to do partial differential equations, recite Pi to 500 decimal places and play *Liszt's La Leggierezza* without a trace of emotional connection with the music.

A leading paediatrician, who also happens to be his mother, says that finding friends for this young whiz kid was difficult, but she is blind to how her vicarious ambition has turned her son into a robot who will quite probably be unremarkable in later life.

His parents have set up a website about him and he has appeared several times on TV and in the media, answering questions with a squeaky monotonous voice.

Characteristics

Reading Material: Books on mathematics, the digits of Pi

Favourite TV Programmes and Films: Not allowed

Heroes and Role Models: Terence Tao, Ainan Celeste Cawley

Most likely cause of death: Old age or suicide after murdering parents

Favourite Music: Liszt's La Leggierezza

Political Views: Doesn't have any

Ego Issues: He has no sense of himself as an autonomous being separate from his parents, so therefore no ego

Fears: Being locked in his room for playing a wrong note or getting Pi wrong

Likes: Fields Medal, Kakeya conjecture, wave maps, memorizing digits of Pi

Dislikes: Film crews

Earnings: A lot when he goes to work for Google

Offspring: n/a

Drives: Can not get to grips with clutch control

Most likely to say: "3.14159265358979323846264338327950288419716939937510582097494459230781640628620899862803482534211706798214808651328230664709384466"

Chelsea Pensioner

A British institution, he (or she, now there are a handful of women) is a retired non-commissioned officer or soldier of the British Army (or a Commissioned Officer who's served at least 12 years of non-commissioned service) over 65 years old (usually much older) with a War Disability Pension and no dependents.

After the death of his wife, he surrendered his army pension in return for free board (Grade I listed), clothing and medical care and occupies a 9 foot by 9 foot windowless wooden cabin at The Royal Hospital Chelsea with about 300 other Chelsea Pensioners. He has to walk a hundred yards to the toilet but he doesn't complain about living in this regimented Spartan environment described by some as a geriatric prep school, nor the £30 million that the government should be coughing up to bring his living conditions into the twenty-first century.

He spends his days in the bar reawakening old memories, watching visiting military bands, playing bowls or croquet and reading. Once a week he is a tour guide at the museum, because despite having given so much already for his country, he still believes in public service, health permitting. He is proud to attend ceremonies and Royal occasions in his scarlet uniform, service medals and tricorne hat. It takes him an hour to walk to the newsagent to buy his Buttermint Bon Bons because so many people want to talk and have their photo taken with him.

Characteristics

Reading Material: This England, Daily Telegraph, Puzzler Magazine, Popular fiction set in WWII

Favourite TV Programmes and Films: Tommy Handley, The World at War, The Price is Right, The Alan Titchmarsh Show, Strictly Come Dancing

Heroes and Role Models: Lord Mountbatten, Sir Winston Churchill, Field Marshal Bernard Montgomery, The Queen

Most likely cause of death: Old age, bonbon related choking

Favourite Music: Vera Lynn, The Andrews Sisters, Ella Fitzgerald, Katherine Jenkins, National Anthem, Last Post

Political Views: Tory, admired Margaret Thatcher's stand over the Falklands

Ego Issues: Quietly pleased that he is considered a war hero

Fears: Queers being allowed in the military

Likes: Monty's victory at El Alamein, Max Miller, Gracie Fields, Tommy Trinder, Joe Pasquale, Remembrance Sunday, Chelsea Flower Show, buttermint bonbons

Dislikes: Americans; being mistaken for a Beefeater by American tourists; The Graham Norton Show; being mistaken for a pillar box by dogs

Earnings: n/a

Offspring: Three grown up children, one in the military

Would like to drive but actually drives: Royal Enfield Scrambler/electric scooter

Most likely to say: "I say, would you be so kind…"

Young Farmer

Bovine, honest and cheerful but was often in trouble at school for being high spirited. Has dyslexia or ADHD, never properly diagnosed, so he can barely read or write, but he can give you all the specs for John Deere's entire product range. His parents aren't neglectful but the demands of a busy farm mean that he's had to grow up quickly and fend for himself. Has broken his arm three times, fallen in the slurry pit twice and is on a social services register. He is neither ugly not handsome, has pink ping-pong ball cheekbones, an unguarded superhero smile and looks overweight even though he's probably got a fairly low percentage of body fat. He has two modes of dress: blue jeans, white & brown twill check country shirt and green wellies, or a dinner suit. The female young farmer wears black jeans and rugby shirt/baggy sweat shirt or emerald ball gown.

He will pass his driving test the week of his 17th birthday because he's been on tractors since he was eight. He likes trials biking and has a quad bike too. Does not show an interest in girls until much late than your average teenager, then it's a heady whirl of Hookers and Haymakers discos and Spring Balls in village halls. Gets married in his early twenties. Always celebrates bonfire night with a huge fire concealing old tyres and scrap.

Characteristics

Reading Material: John Deere catalogues

Favourite TV Programmes and Films: Doesn't watch TV – he's too busy socialising, playing sports, and having tugs of war to raise money for charity

Heroes and Role Models: Angus MacAskill

Most likely cause of death: Tractor rollover, heart attack, suicide

Favourite Music: Knows what he likes but doesn't know the name of it

Political Views: Tory

Ego Issues: High self esteem and enjoys life

Fears: Phasing-out of the milk quota system, being priced out of the locality by shortage of affordable homes, paperwork and red tape

Likes: EU subsidies, is a member of the local drama group, drinking, getting up at 4.30am to milk the cows, hog roasts

Dislikes: People who are posh and stuck up, CAP reform, vegetarians, second home owners

Earnings: n/a

Offspring: n/a

Drives: Landrover 90

Most likely to say: "Tractor!"

Business Woman

Passive aggressive surly female executive in her early fifties who blames others for her own failings and thinks she has to copy the worst excesses of the male boardroom to succeed. Consequently she is rude, cuts off her staff in mid sentence then complains that they don't brief her properly. Her parents divorced when she was young and she grew up calling her step father dad. She hasn't seen her alcoholic real father since she was five. She has no children, a conscious decision based on her need to focus on work and the fact that she hates kids, fears dependents and dependency.

She made her millions by taking out bank loans to buy things and then sell them for more than they cost. So far she hasn't managed to screw things up too badly, so on paper she is a multi-millionaire. Obviously tens of thousands of other individuals fail trying the same trick, so inevitably there will be some successful ones. Rather than be thankful for her good luck she is defensive and aggressive about her ability and loves people to ask her advice. Despite her convoluted replies, her skill is limited to selling things for more than they cost. She likes to make her staff feel stressed out so she can appear to be the cool head at the centre of a crisis, when she's the sole cause of all office tension. She feels intellectually inferior so she always turns on other people when she can't understand an idea that is being pitched to her.

Characteristics

Reading Material: Anthony Robbins, Stephen Covey, Barbara Taylor Bradford, currently reading Overcoming Low Self-Esteem by Melanie Fennell

Favourite TV Programmes and Films: Dragons' Den, The Apprentice

Heroes and Role Models: Margaret Thatcher, Hillary Clinton, Angela Merkel, Cynthia Carroll

Most likely cause of death: Stress related

Favourite Music: Predictable classical and opera, which she doesn't enjoy but she has corporate seats

Political Views: Tory

Ego Issues: Hates that her wealth cannot really get her higher up the social order

Fears: Becoming an alcoholic and her PA resigning

Likes: Frowning because it makes her look thoughtful and incisive; partial facelift, entrepreneurs, living in Surrey

Dislikes: Men, children, women, her looks and the way she is ageing

Earnings: Has recorded losses for the last three years

Offspring: None

Drives: Regularly changes to whatever she has decided looks classy and powerful

Most likely to say: "You're insulting my intelligence"

Evangelical Preacher

Brought up by strong evangelical parents this handsome and self-confident alpha male gave up a lucrative career in sales and marketing with a large firm of medical equipment manufacturers for a more lucrative career with Jesus and the church.

"Praise God" and "Amen" trip indiscriminately from his mouth in a display of ostentatious holiness and he answers most questions with "Well, the Bible says . . .".

Whenever he's channelling the word of the Lord he does that weird wide-eyed smirk thing as if to suppress excitement at the continued gullibility of his flock.

He has recently been caught in a compromising position with a lap dancer but his unwavering insistence that the uploaded photographs were clever photoshop trickery and the work of the devil means that his congregation have not only forgiven him but are funding the lawsuit against the offending website. He of course has insisted that the matter be dropped and that the congregation move on and turn the other cheek as that is what Jesus would have done.

Characteristics

Reading Material: The Bible (mainly the Old Testament), pornography

Favourite TV Programmes and Films: The Passion of the Christ, the whipping scene in Flash Gordon, The Lovely Bones, Interview with a Vampire, Léon: The Professional, Skins

Heroes and Role Models: Michael Jackson, R. Kelly

Most likely cause of death: Immortal

Favourite Music: Soul, Gospel and a little bit of bump and grind

Political Views: Votes for the political party most likely to involve him

Ego Issues: Believes what he is saying most of the time. Considers his fear of death a sign that he is a great philosopher

Fears: That there really *is* a god

Likes: Conning people, money, Christian Voice

Dislikes: Jerry Springer: The Opera (although he hasn't seen it), homosexuals

Earnings: £100k

Offspring: Six children who will all rebel against their ridiculous fundamentalist upbringing by becoming pop singers and prostitutes

Drives: Specially converted motorhome

Most likely to say: "God will provide for us!"

Granny (Cuddly)

Fat Cuddly Granny wears a cardigan and beads and lives in a bungalow full of crap ornaments. You are the centre of her world. She's always baking or making trifle or giving you little presents that you put in a cupboard when you get home and never use. She has a cat and she does crochet and knits. She loves drinking tea and sitting in an electric armchair doing word search puzzles. Her hearing and eyesight are unreliable, and she gets your name wrong. She farts when she bends over and grunts like a wildebeest when she's climbing stairs.

Cuddly Grannies always have secrets. When she dies you discover that long ago she was a notorious Cold War spy or high-class Russian courtesan who single-handedly liberated Belsen. Cuddly Granny had her heart broken in her teens, either because her parents forbade the liaison or he got killed in a war. She married your grandfather on the rebound and then learned to love him. She can solve any problem with vinegar and bicarbonate of soda. Growing up you only ever saw Cuddly Granny get angry once and it scared the life out of you.

Characteristics

Reading Material: Puzzler magazine, Daily Mail, romance novels

Favourite TV Programmes and Films: Coronation Street, Jeremy Kyle, Bad daytime TV, Alan Carr Chatty Man, Midsomer Murders

Heroes and Role Models: Miss Marple

Most likely cause of death: MRSA, own cat opening her varicose veins

Favourite Music: Cliff Richard, Gareth Gates, Last Night of the Proms

Political Views: Votes for whichever politician she feels she trusts, regardless of politics

Ego Issues: She finds pleasure in the smallest things and always put others first, so she doesn't admit to loneliness

Fears: Cat dying, fuel bills, being completely immobile and dependent, dementia, loneliness, dying in hospital, Delroy Grant

Likes: Hoarding crap, buying lottery tickets, eating slowly, biscuits, cups of tea, opening a nice tin of salmon, handkerchiefs, coupons, overfeeding grandchildren, The Pope, telling you something she told you already, loud TV, driving on the pavement, Alan Titchmarsh, Noel Edmonds, Terry Wogan

Dislikes: Having a lie in, technology, loud music, being outside without a hat, throwing anything away, inflation

Earnings: Pension

Offspring: Three children, seven grandchildren

Drives: Old Nissan Micra

Most likely to say: "I'll go and put the kettle on."

Italian Restaurateur

77

He's worked six twelve hour shifts a week for the past thirty years since he left Napoli/Roma/Cardiff but the smile never leaves his face. He makes the lasagne just like Mamma, devotes hours to trickling candle wax down the side of Chianti bottles and when the mood is right can do a pretty impressive rendition of 'Mio Babbino Caro'.

He collects tea towels of Italy with which he adorns the walls and asks every minor celebrity who eats his pasta for a signed photo which he puts up in between the tea towels. Despite almost four decades living and working in Britain, his English is still fairly dodgy and he frequently baffles his customers with his bizarre menu explanations.

All his kitchen staff are from Italy and all take frequent breaks to smoke and shout "Ciao, bella" at passers by of either sex.

Three generations of his family eat at his restaurant every night and early diners are treated to a rousing display of a full-on Italian family dispute, complete with raised voices, a few bits of smashed crockery and the odd "Mamma Mia". That, along with Nonna's Tiramisu, keep the restaurant fully booked every night of the week.

Characteristics

Reading Material: Tea-towels from the Home Country

Favourite TV Programmes and Films: The Godfather for the nostalgia kick

Heroes and Role Models: He has no need of role models: he works hard and makes his own luck, his mother

Most likely cause of death: He'll pass peacefully in his bed, in the bosom of his family

Favourite Music: His passion is Verdi but he's also quite partial to Busted

Political Views: He opposed the smoking ban on that basis that everyone likes a little cigarette with their espresso

Ego Issues: Takes it personally if regular customers defect to the chain store pizza pasta restaurants

Fears: Angry women, that his sons won't want to take the business on from him

Likes: A full restaurant, melting candle wax onto chianti bottles

Dislikes: A dissatisfied customer

Earnings: Annual turnover £400k, but out of this he pays a staff of fourteen and supports a family of thirty-seven people

Offspring: Seven sons, three daughters and twenty-four grandchildren

Drives: In the old days, he rode a Vespa, but he never learned to drive a car because he always said they never made one big enough

Most likely to say: "Prego"

Clothing Designer

The most obvious sign of a decadent culture is when individuals start applying aesthetic principles to the rags that keep them warm and conceal their genitals. This usually emerges in post-agrarian tribes with excess leisure and more than one pair of shoes. In the modern world the fashion designer is king, not because he can commune with the spirit world or take out a mammoth with a well-aimed spear, but because he knows how to accessorize and cut on the bias. He creates oversized bows, tufted hems, lobster claw shoes and other ridiculous affectations so that self-loathing rich women can feel superior to the other self-loathing rich women in their social circle. He does this because he has an unhealthy relationship with his mother. He either hates her or is hopelessly devoted, so he turns his sadistic misogyny towards the rest of womankind.

He is trapped on his throne by sycophantic fashion editors, stylists, PR departments and celebrities like Posh Spice but deep down he knows that he spends a hundred hours a week doing something utterly pointless. Like the Celebrity Chef, his work is pretentious, he works the same antisocial hours and destroys his sanity to create so-called masterpieces, but rather than providing nourishment, his creations champion the demand for skeletal bulimics who have to risk their lives to fit into his clothes.

Characteristics

Reading Material: The life stories of history's most misunderstood – Lady Diana, Louis XIV, Napoleon, Genghis Khan; the fashion critics reviews of their latest collection

Favourite TV Programmes and Films: Anything that helps them gauge a turning zeitgeist: arthouse cinema, late night indie radio, GMTV

Heroes and Role Models: Coco Chanel, Marie Antoinette, Mother Nature

Most likely cause of death: Pretention

Favourite Music: Anything that isn't mainstream and that will not be recognized by anyone who may be pretentious enough to ask!

Political Views: Claims to use their art form to transcend party politics but they actually vote Lib Dem

Ego Issues: Depend on self-publicism, self-indulgence and self-aggrandisement in order to function

Fears: Losing their edge, being 'last year', getting fat

Likes: To shock, working 'outside of the box', being described as 'shy', 'humble', or 'understated', Buddhism

Dislikes: Being interviewed, being out of the spotlight

Earnings: Anywhere from £80k - £4bn

Offspring: "My collections are my children"

Drives: Always sends for a car

Most likely to say: "I don't make clothes, darling, I make magic"

Cricketer

Cricket (or "crick-eat" if you come from Yorkshire) is the most lacklustre sport ever devised. The occasional moment of mild drama punctuates an aeonian postponement of pleasure, the stupor of delivery after tedious delivery, no adrenaline required, just bowel control. So a cricketer has to be a special kind of boring, an automaton capable of several hours of inactivity with only the anticipation of Battenberg cake and cucumber sandwiches to stop the heart from flatlining.

He breathes in, he breathes out. He squints at the gathering clouds. Occasionally he polishes the ball earnestly on his crotch. In common with supporters of the most boring sports like golf and motor racing his eyes are too close together and his nose is the only obstacle preventing them from fusing into one beady little singularity.

In the evening he pours three pints of a carbonated alcoholic beverage into his mouth. He has no self awareness, no strong opinions, never questions humanity's vapid trudge from cradle to grave, so conversation is limited to the weather and a journey or meal he once had. He's hard work, but what else can you expect from someone whose main interest is standing in a field?

Characteristics

Reading Material: Novelty golfing books his kids buy him every Christmas and birthdays and nothing else

Favourite TV Programmes and Films: Cricket, Golf, Snooker, 5 Live Sport

Heroes and Role Models: John Arlott, W C Grace, Graham Gooch, Andrew Flintoff

Most likely cause of death: Struck in the chest by a fast ball

Favourite Music: Chris de Burgh, James Blunt, Dido

Political Views: Either doesn't vote or votes Tory

Ego Issues: He doesn't have an ego but neither does he have a personality

Fears: Ashes TV rights will never return to free-to-air; nightwatchman (sign that England has collapsed again)

Likes: Battenberg cake, scones, jam and cream, red stain on his crotch, standing still, bending over with his hands on his knees, Edgbaston, golf, snooker

Dislikes: Twenty20 (it's just not cricket), rain, googlies, left-arm leg-spinners, pigeons, newcomers to the team

Earnings: £35k

Offspring: Three children who are sporty bores

Drives: Ford or Vauxhall

Most likely to say: "Owzat!"

Real Ale Bore

He dresses in last season's Oxfam, sports out-of-control facial hair and always smells of pipe tobacco, even though he smokes roll-ups. He expects his beer to taste of something and searches hard to find the correct flavour without realising that most of the taste is created when the liquid passed through his matted beard. He has a bigger belly than lager drinkers because he doesn't drink to get drunk so he doesn't puke at the end of the evening.

He dyes his comb over and has worked in the same local government office for the past twenty-five years. His colleagues have yet to learn his name, let alone invite him out for a Friday night drink. None the less, he enjoys an active love life in the guise of his alter-ego and avatar, Achard the Dragon Slayer.

For real-world kicks, he is an enthusiastic member of the local Civil War re-enactment society and a stalwart of the local branch of the Campaign for Real Ale. He can list 87 separate English ales, and will tell you the keynotes of each, whether you ask him to or not. His rule of thumb for choosing a watering hole is that if it doesn't have a skittles alley and a shove halfpenny board it won't serve good ale. Other clues are thatched roofs, gloomy locals and a farting wolfhound.

Characteristics

Reading Material: The Good Beer Guide, 300 Beers to Try Before You Die, Beer Monthly

Favourite TV Programmes and Films: Time Team, Coronation Street, Al Murray's Happy Hour, Last of the Summer Wine

Heroes and Role Models: Graham Lees, Bill Mellor, Michael Hardman, and Jim Makin (founders of the Campaign for Real Ale in 1971)

Most likely cause of death: Cirrhosis of the liver

Favourite Music: Jazz, brass bands, Jethro Tull, Genesis, Progressive Rock

Political Views: Campaigns for the plight of the rural British pub

Ego Issues: His beer is naturally lively so he doesn't have to be

Fears: Dying before he's tasted all 300 Beers To Try Before You Die

Likes: Online "relationships", real ale, hand-pumping, secondary fermentation

Dislikes: Lager, keg beer, washing his cardigan, multinationals, showing he's an individual

Earnings: £26 - £30k

Offspring: None

Drives: Morris traveller or a motor bike with a side car

Most likely to say: "I'll have another go on Betty Stoggs, if you don't mind."

Butler

He's part of dying breed of men who devote their lives to running somebody else's household when it's too big to function without a small army of personnel. He spends four hours each day polishing silver, which for some reason he believes is time on this earth well spent.

Quiet, unassuming, happiest when he's busy and never voicing an opinion unless invited, his kind was once the cornerstone of polite society. The master of discretion, he has always known precisely what goes on behind the closed doors of the British elite, but would never be so self-serving as to 'kiss and tell'.

His knowledge of wine matches that of any sommelier, his grasp of etiquette is second nature to him and at the end of every long day he retires to his personal rooms where carpet slippers, a nice cup of tea and the newspaper await. He's been in service since the age of 14 and after decades of sedately mounting and descending stairs, he is fitter than a man half his age. He keeps his shoes polished to a military sheen and brushes his suit with a coarse horsehair brush for fifteen minutes every morning. His staff respect and revere him, and although Cook has been known to pat his shoulder occasionally, he has no close personal relationships.

Characteristics

Reading Material: Agatha Christie novels, The Times, Who's Who

Favourite TV Programmes and Films: The BBC news, the Archers, Book at Bedtime, The Remains of the Day

Heroes and Role Models: The first Butler he ever served under

Most likely cause of death: In his sleep

Favourite Music: Partial to a little Mantovani, that nice Desmond Carrington on Radio2

Political Views: Votes without fail, but his political bent is not for others to worry themselves about

Ego Issues: Uncomfortable with personal visits from his family

Fears: Damp problem in the drawing room, the increasing difficulty in securing reliable gardeners

Likes: Order, calm women, cook's steak and kidney pudding, a tight ship

Dislikes: Disobedience from junior staff, scandal, Paul Burrell

Earnings: £22,500

Offspring: None, though there was a chamber maid once, long ago, but now that ship has sailed

Drives: Actually doesn't drive but does dream of a run out in the Bentley

Most likely to say: "You rang, Sir?"

Computer Maintenance Bore (No. 80)

At school there is always that one kid in your class you want to go up to and say "Look Nicholas, we all think you're a dick". It's a mystery why racism is still popular while there's so many better reasons to hate computer geeks. He's got no friends and in his warped universe he's a maverick, and started writing null-free shellcode from the age of 6.

In common with babies and unmedicated schizophrenics, the computer nerd hasn't figured out when to go to sleep. His home PC is wildly overkilled with its titanium steel comp case, four times more RAM than necessary, a cooling system that uses the frozen tears of Orcs, more lights than a Pink Floyd concert and running a smug open source OS like Kolibri or OpenBSD.

He uses more proxies than Julian Assange, knows all the hacks and glitches for online shooters and has even built his own lag switch. You know when you're playing one of these cheating little gits because you get lag spikes every time his faggy ID appears which is always something like *{$"::[...] instead of a proper name. Even worse, you know he's making £100K a year flipping domains or teaching the Pentagon how to fend off DNS attacks from other little scum bags like him. When he owns you on Black Ops your only comfort is knowing that his diet of take away pizza, Nirvana and staying up all night is going to kill him long before he loses his virginity and breeds.

Characteristics

Reading Material: PC Advisor Magazine, The Silmarillion

Favourite TV Programmes and Films: N/A

Heroes and Role Models: Kevin Mitnick, Adrian Lamo, Richard D. James, Batman

Most likely cause of death: Assassination by CIA

Favourite Music: Nirvana

Political Views: Open Source Anarchist

Ego Issues: Will never agree with anything you say about computers because even if you are right you will have made a simple grammatical or syntactical error.

Fears: Dawn raid by Interpol

Likes: Being condescending and making other people feel stupid

Dislikes: Sleeping, giving a straight answer, Windows 7

Earnings: £100k

Offspring: None

Most likely to say: "I think you mean…"

Gay Snob

Narcissistic, cliquish and often single gay man who has never quite come to terms with his sexuality and compensates for his shyness, low self-esteem and self-loathing by being aloof and cold, especially to other gay men. Probably bisexual, he is holding out for the perfect guy, but he will never find true companionship because he protects himself from rejection by rejecting everyone else first. He ditched his last boyfriend on discovering he bought his underwear from H&M. He wears flamboyant clothes because he is a lapsed Catholic and preening attention-seeker.

His adult life has been dominated by the need to surround himself with the visible markers of superior taste. Misplaced apostrophes, regional accents, Kindles and iPods all cause him physical pain. He is staunchly anti-populist and hates anything he considers high art being appropriated by the sweating masses, who couldn't begin to appreciate the complexities of the final movement of Mahler's 9th. He has an acerbic view of the Turner Prize and sneers at British conceptual artists. He suffers from chronic insomnia and uses Latin phrases in everyday speech.

Characteristics

Reading Material: Andre Gide, Simulacra and Simulation (The Body, In Theory: Histories of Cultural Materialism) by Jean Baudrillard, Jean Genet

Favourite TV Programmes and Films: Un Chant d'Amour, pretentious foreign films that make you want to kick puppies for wasting your time

Heroes and Role Models: Brian Sewell, Judy Garland, Daniel Barenboim

Most likely cause of death: Unsavoury

Favourite Music: Mahler, Michael Tippett, Tchaikovsky, Poulenc, Britten, Puccini

Political Views: Tory; likes his Cabinet to be mainly composed of ex-Etonians

Ego Issues: Raised in a working-class family by a domineering father whom he hated and a put-upon mother he adored. Was kicked out of the house when he came out aged fifteen

Fears: Football supporters, single mothers, people with dirty fingernails

Likes: Excoriating the latest generation of everything, his two bald cats Tristan and Isolde, hoovering in his underpants

Dislikes: Pop music, Last Night at the Proms, Simon Rattle

Earnings: Independent means

Offspring: n/a

Drives: Saab convertible

Most likely to say: "Oh no dear, not me dear"

Manageress

She's worked her way up through the ranks to the dizzy heights of middle management in hotel and catering, retail or the NHS. She has the grey skin and the well-developed calf muscles of a woman who's spent twenty years under fluorescent lighting wearing stiletto heels.

She boasts of her high expectations for her staff and relishes corporate buzz words – they don't sell cosmetics, but 'beauty solutions' for instance. She likes to spring 'Quality Standards Inspection' on her staff's uniform and appearance, measuring skirt lengths with a ruler to ensure they conform to regulation stipulations and running a cotton-gloved finger over stubbled chins.

She motivates her staff with creative management speak, preferring, "That's an interesting viewpoint" when she really means, "I disagree" and selling an increase in hours to her overworked staff with phrases like, "we have to leverage our resources".

The truth is she couldn't function without the walkie-talkie, clipboard and staff rota, and over the years these have slipped into her private life, with an intercom installed in the shed and her teenagers' bedrooms, and an 'Executive Project Champion of the Week' photo display in the kitchen letting the household know who's in charge of emptying the dishwasher and taking the bins out this week

Characteristics

Reading Material: She keeps a stack of management how-to books by her bed, but rarely gets beyond the opening chapter.

Favourite TV Programmes and Films: The Devil Wears Prada, Glengarry Glen Ross, Swimming With Sharks, The Apprentice, Britain's Next Top Model

Heroes and Role Models: Meryl Streep in The Devil Wears Prada because she wants to be adored

Most likely cause of death: DVT in her calf muscle

Favourite Music: Billy Joel, Will Young, Boyzone

Political Views: Tends to gauge Senior Management's mood on issues of a political bent and tailor her comments to suit. She approaches election time in a similar way

Ego Issues: Driven by the misguided belief that she is a wise, effective and respected manager. In truth people refer to her as the Napkin

Fears: Redundancy

Likes: Clipboards, walkie-talkies, the fish pie at the staff canteen, delegating

Dislikes: Lunchtime meetings, missing lunch, getting to the staff canteen too late for the special

Earnings: £22 – £45k, depending in the sector she works in

Offspring: Brow-beaten teenaged son and daughter

Would like to drive but actually drives: BMW/Vauxhall

Most likely to say: "My door is always open"

BLENHEIM SUITE
VIKING WINDOWS CONFERENCE

LANCASTER SUITE
JAN AND SANDRAS WEDDING

CALORIE COUNTERS
IN THE FITNESS AREA

Office Bore

72

89

15

15

He's something in finance, IT or accounts, and he's the guy everyone avoids in the office canteen. He's a fast-talking bore who wears oversized novelty ties into the office at Christmas time and socks that play Jingle Bells every time he shakes a leg. He stands too close, laughs too loud at his own jokes and slaps the backsides of his co-workers as a gesture of friendly camaraderie which always backfires. He talks in an unedited stream of crass one-liners and uncomfortably crude jokes which he thinks make him more popular. He describes himself as the "life and soul" or "mad, me" and in twenty-odd years hasn't seemed to notice that no-one else is laughing.

Office parties make him more nervous than ever and so, to compensate for his social ineptitude, he invests in new comedy accessories every year. Easter bunny slippers, full-sized 'onesie' pyjamas with a reindeer motif, and a flat cap which created its own artificial snowfall were highlights. When that fails to raise the roof, he proceeds to get riotously drunk, in which state his delivery of one-liners borders on an anti-social personality disorder. He interrupts every conversation, dances like John Travolta and dishes out offensive nicknames to everyone he works with. And when he invariably fails to pull, he attempts to snog Derrick from reprographics.

Characteristics

Reading Material: Viz, Bumper Book of Office Humour, How to Win Friends and Influence People

Favourite TV Programmes and Films: Tries to watch The Office but doesn't get the irony

Heroes and Role Models: Dick Emery

Most likely cause of death: Choking on a peanut

Favourite Music: The Birdie Song, Oops Up Side Your Head, YMCA, Olivia 'Newtron Bomb'

Political Views: Once stood for the Monster Raving Loony Party

Ego Issues: Really thinks he's funny

Fears: Redundancy

Likes: Having a laugh, being one of the lads, donuts, karaoke

Dislikes: Being pranked, being ignored

Earnings: £23k

Offspring: None – his marriage failed before they'd managed to conceive

Drives: Ford Ka

Most likely to say: "Listen, right… there's an Englishman, a Welshman and a Scotch bloke…""

Mystic Meg Types

Flaky middle-aged woman a bit crazier than the usual new age types, who dyes her hair black and wears dramatic make up. She owns lots of books on witches and fairy spells, as well as a crystal ball on a cheap stained balsa wood base bought from a clearance toy and gift shop. It is a certainty that she will be making some money out of her beliefs, though not very much.

She wears long dark clothes, talks utter bollocks and hangs around with men who call themselves wizards, druids or shamen and is likely to believe that tsunamis are caused by the proximity of the moon, and that if your Sun, Pluto & Mars conjunct in Virgo you will be sceptical about astrology.

She claims to live her life according to the invalid and obsolete belief that the arrangement of the stars and planets at the moment of birth and thereafter are important. She can't tell you why that date is more significant than her moment of conception, or see a connection between her inability to keep a man with her refusal to date anyone who wasn't born between September 23rd and October 22nd. She also believes in ghosts but she draws the line at the Reptilian conspiracy theory because that's just plain daft.

Characteristics

Reading Material: Horoscopes, Crystal Ball Gazing: The Complete Guide, Working with Fairies, Magical Housekeeping, Predicting the Future with Dice, Everyday Magic: Spells & Rituals for Modern Living

Favourite TV Programmes and Films: Ghost Whisperer, Being Human, Ghost Hunters, Supernatural, Shopping Channel 'Healing Man'

Heroes and Role Models: Melinda Gordon, The Barefoot Doctor

Most likely cause of death: Robin flying into her room through an open window, clock which has not been working suddenly chimes, cow mooing after midnight, having only red and white flowers together in a vase, leaving a hat on the bed, but most probably house fire caused by sunlight shining through crystal ball

Favourite Music: Clannad, Enya, Sissel, Secret Garden

Political Views: Enviromysticism = Green

Ego Issues: Gains a lot of self esteem from knowing a lot about crystal healing, astrology, homeopathy and burning candles

Fears: Passing someone on the stairs, seeing one magpie, opening an umbrella indoors

Likes: Librans, candles, oil burners, stars, Cubic Zirconia Mystic Topaz jewellery, most forms of charlatanry and mystical nonsense, cats, talismans, amulets, the sound of running water

Dislikes: Mystic Meg

Earnings: £6720

Offspring: None

Would like to drive but actually drives: Magic carpet, Broomstick / Something belonging to and financed by someone else

Most likely to say: "No…Yes… I can see a person in your life…"

Hippy Couple

HIM

75

104

15

HER

78

104

15

He gave up life in the Home Office to move to the country. She abandoned her career in PR to learn to weave willow on the Somerset Levels. They bought a farmhouse together but sold it at the School Christmas Bazaar and built an eco-house out of straw-bales and horse manure in a plot of woodland. They soon embraced natural living, their hair growing more encrusted by the day, and became experts in edible fungi, preserving and bread making. Their vegetable plot flourished and they were soon trading organic celeriac and mung beans for holistic therapies in nearby Glastonbury.

After the first winter, they made the historic decision that living life encaged in clothing was unnatural. Dressed in nothing but a sunhat and walking boots, they strode out together, hand in hand, taking their message of love, harmony and free-range pubes the length and breadth of Britain. They ate from hedgerows and forest, and begged eggs and cups of tea from startled farmers, who went to put the kettle on while muttering something about 'city folk' and 'needing a good trim'.

They have been arrested one hundred and forty-two times for breach of the peace and indecent exposure.

Characteristics

Reading Material: Lord of the Rings, Naked Lunch, Jack Kerouac, New Age Vegetarian Cookbook, Carlos Castaneda

Favourite TV Programmes and Films: Although their naked travels will continue to keep them very much in the public eye, they shun all forms of media because of its interference with man's inate ability to tune in to nature.

Heroes and Role Models: Janis Joplin, Timothy Leary, Captain Beefheart,

Most likely cause of death: Mushroom poisoning or exposure

Favourite Music: John and Yoko, Carly Simon, Joni Mitchell, Bob Marley, Janis Joplin

Political Views: T-shirt slogans, always complaining about the government between bong hits

Ego Issues: None. When you're happy to free your genitals in the Scottish Highlands in December, you have to be pretty much without ego

Fears: Soap, man-made fibres, chafing, global warming, a dolphin somewhere might be having a bad day

Likes: The feel of the warm breeze running through their hair, not paying for stuff, tetrahydrocannabinol

Dislikes: Bras, deodorant, good music, nuclear energy, war, not having anywhere to keep a hankie, bad vibes, bad trips, being arrested, cruelty to animals, corporate greed

Earnings: Nil – although they both made a few sound property investments and a few high-yield bonds

Offspring: Three between them, all from previous relationships. They are not in regular contact with any of them

Would like to drive but actually drives: Converted Transit/VW Camper

Most likely to say: "Yeah, man"

Lesbian Activist

Fuming man hater who can't stop rubbing your face in her angry lesbianism. She manages to bring race, class, sexuality, feminist theory and gender conflict into any discussion. Now that every civilised person accepts that being gay or lesbian is normal she is even more focused on destroying existing relations of male power because all men have a penis so all men have the potential to become Martin Amis.

She has spent her whole life feeling discriminated against and raging against the urge to conform, but has just moved in with her son's birth father to give him a nuclear upbringing. Her actions are full of these kind of contradictions. She hates pretty women who like looking feminine, and you'd expect her to criticize someone like Jordan for objectifying herself and setting back feminism fifty years. Instead, she chooses to big up this witless attention seeker. She views her celebrity as a class/gender issue because she hates the rich snobby men who publicly denounce Jordan more than she hates glamour models.

Characteristics

Reading Material: Bitter beanflicker: Essays in Feminist Theory, DIVA magazine, Lesbilicious, Jeanette Winterson

Favourite TV Programmes and Films: Mulholland Drive, Desert Hearts, Better Than Chocolate, Sugar Rush, Bound, The Hunger

Heroes and Role Models: Ellen DeGeneres, Rosie O'Donnell, Hillary Clinton

Most likely cause of death: Anger

Favourite Music: K D Lang, Madonna, Beth Ditto, The Butchies, Tribe 8, Le Tigre, Joan Armatrading

Political Views: She votes Green because she likes Caroline Lucas's lesbian haircut

Ego Issues: Angry lesbian

Fears: Making eye contact with other lesbians, smiling

Likes: Complaining, moaning, lentils, dolphins, lesbian dolphins

Dislikes: All men, Jeremy Clarkson, the word 'lesbian'

Earnings: 15 percent less than a man in the same job

Offspring: One

Would like to drive but actually drives: Beetle or 2CV but that is too much of a cliche so she drives a diesel French hatchback

Most likely to say: Something whingy

Life Coach

 75
 T01
 10
 5
 28

Bald speccy fraud who hated his old job and just couldn't seem to attract wealth until one day a Life Coach convinced him to buy a self-published manual which explained a secret method for convincing people who hate their job how to attract wealth. So he quit his job and now sells people who hate their job a self-published manual which explains a secret method for convincing people who hate their job how to attract wealth. He also sells webinars, which make him money even while he's asleep. The webinars explain to clients how to make money while they sleep by selling webinars. He doesn't make much money yet but he says he's passionate to learn more about how to help people quit their job and attract wealth even while they sleep.

He spends all of his time and money on self-help manuals and expensive webinars run by more successful life coaches. He's also building a database of people he can flog stuff to, since he recognises that those at the top of the industry dung pile are merely the ones who can send their direct marketing spam out to the largest number of people. Ideally one day this whole despicable life coaching pyramid will collapse and he will have to go back to his job as a double glazing salesman in Nuneaton.

Characteristics

Reading Material: Ponzi scheme self-help books that claim that everyone in the world can attract riches to themselves

Favourite TV Programmes and Films: Webinars

Heroes and Role Models: Dale Carnegie, Anthony Robbins, Barefoot Doctor, Rhonda Byrne, Spencer Johnson, Deepak Chopra

Most likely cause of death: Abject poverty

Favourite Music: Self help CDs, whale music, binaural beats

Political Views: Pretends he's Liberal but votes Tory

Ego Issues: Tries very hard to be approachable and ordinary because in his industry it's the best way to fleece people

Fears: He hasn't read enough self help books or attended enough webinars

Likes: Money, self help books, webinars, making money while he sleeps

Dislikes: Direct questions about how much he earns

Earnings: Less than £5k

Offspring: Two children who he empowers with lots of family meetings

Drives: Old Renault

Most likely to say: "We all have within us the power to attract wealth . . . "

Male Dancer

The earliest origins of ballet may well lie in the methodology of reinterpreting a story through the medium of dance but some would have us believe that it stems from the patronage of bored, fat, wealthy Victorian gentlemen who would occupy a drizzly afternoon by sitting in the front row of the stalls at Sadler's Wells in order to ogle the thin, lithe pretty girls of the *corps de ballet*. This could all be done under the respectable guise of 'supporting the arts' and therefore avoiding the disapproval of their wives and mistresses.

However it was not long before the womenfolk became suspicious after one particularly inappropriate display made by a party of peers still giddy after a late night Giselle it was realised that a spouse-calming solution was required, and quick!

This was soon achieved by the introduction of the danseur or male lead whose testosterone filled physique and apparent state of semi-permanent arousal had the ladies flocking in. All audience genders were now happy, entertained and suitably self-righteous.

A stereotype was born and to this day the Male Dancer (gay or otherwise) likes to party hard and do hamstring exercises at every opportunity. He is focussed, single-minded and strong of body and will. He grew up in a mining town and had to fight against prejudice of his bullying father and the parochialism of his close-knit community to follow his dreams. His job is very important and demanding so he always carries a large bottle of mineral water to broadcast the fact that at any moment he could pass out from dehydration.

Characteristics

Reading Material: Call times, notices

Favourite TV Programmes and Films: Black Swan, Billy Elliot, The Red Shoes, An American in Paris

Heroes and Role Models: Kenneth MacMillan, Jonathan Cope, Roberto Bolle

Most likely cause of death: Combination of calorie restriction, coffee, cigarettes

Favourite Music: Classical repertoire

Political Views: Left wing

Ego Issues: Feels good when the reflection in the mirror looks good.

Fears: Injury, dehydration

Likes: Moving around beautifully in front of a paying audience, pointing his feet in opposite directions, leaping through the air, packing his jockstrap, ballet gossip, checking himself out in the mirror, miniature dog breeds

Dislikes: The pain, ballet gossip, white tights, wearing make up, Patrick Swayze, Fred Astaire, Jonathan Cope, arthritis

Earnings: £22k but spends a fortune on classes and shoes

Offspring: None

Drives: Walks and takes public transport

Most likely to say: "And then they ran out of mineral water! I was devastated . . . devastated."

School Teacher (Male)

75

118

9

6

He was never in the loop and has never had his finger on any pulse. He didn't understand youth culture when he was one himself: he has even less chance now that he's middle aged. He has always been so tragically unhip that it's a miracle his arse hasn't fallen off. He entered the teaching profession because of his love of Geography or Physics – it had nothing to do with a desire to work with children. In fact, he has never liked children particularly.

He dresses in the sedate grey tones of an unsuccessful lower-ranking civil servant, his only concession to comfort being a pair of unfashionable suede walking shoes on account of the fact that he spends most of his day on his feet. In fact, he spends most of his day locked in the store cupboard by the same pupil who locked him in the week before.

He experiences the world in 50 minute blocks and is never on top of his marking. He spends all year trying and failing to identify his students correctly by name and always has a long list of miscreant pupils in detention, punishing them for trying to enliven his God-awful teaching style with secret humming, note passing or paper ball flicking. He carries his tuna sandwich in a Tupperware box and his world in a brown leather briefcase that's seen better days.

Characteristics

Reading Material: Ian McEwan, The Times Educational Supplement Job Section, Steam Railway Magazines

Favourite TV Programmes and Films: The Sky at Night, Newsnight, anything with Fred Dibnah

Heroes and Role Models: Fred Dibnah, Sir Patrick Moore

Most likely cause of death: Mercury poisoning from too much tuna

Favourite Music: Last Night of the Proms

Political Views: Believes in single sex education, thinks the school leaving age should be lowered to 14

Ego Issues: Thinks himself intellectually superior to all his colleagues

Fears: Confined spaces, children

Likes: Steam trains, tuna

Dislikes: Teaching

Earnings: £31 – £35k

Offspring: 2 children who are desperately embarrassed by him

Drives: Vauxhall Chevette

Most likely to say: "Let me out"

Accountant (Junior, Exploited Young Assistant)

Despite eating more than Eamonn Holmes, the Junior Accountant is wraith-like and almost entirely without body fat. Pallid and grey from spending all daylight hours holed up in some dusty back office of a small-town firm of accountants, he speaks, moves and dresses for maximum obscurity. He sees figures the way Haley Joel Osment sees dead people and is prepared to quietly tolerate years of 14 hour days in exchange for the dim prospect of a partnership.

What little leisure time he has is devoted to following the cricket, catching up with latest financial news and popping vitamin D supplements. He is so boring and lacking in charisma that he could drive for the McLaren F1 team if he wasn't so busy number crunching to make his senior partners richer.

He has yet to identify a life partner, but has set his sights on marriage. Siring his first child is scheduled in for the fourth quarter of year three of his current five year plan, so he is overdue beginning the audit for a suitable mate.

Characteristics

Reading Material: Yann Martel, Jeffrey Archer, The Financial Times, TaxProf Blog, Practical Accountancy Magazine

Favourite TV Programmes and Films: Midsomer Murders, Moneybox, boring Jennifer Aniston films, anything with a David Attenborough voice over

Heroes and Role Models: Alvin Hall, Lewis Hamilton, Andy Dufresne

Most likely cause of death: Vitamin D deficiency

Favourite Music: An insipid mix of Paul McCartney Wings, Supertramp and The Corrs. However his secret guilty pleasure is an encoded playlist of 1980s hardcore US punk which he plays to celebrate the end of every tax year

Political Views: He is working hard to wean himself off his natural Liberal-Democrat tendencies

Ego Issues: Fears people see him as boring

Fears: Women, Top Man, dress-down Fridays

Likes: Tidy desk, the woman from the Corrs who played the tin whistle

Dislikes: Motorway service stations, being asked open questions, Davina McCall

Earnings: £18 – £25k

Offspring: Still entirely possible

Would like to drive but actually drives: Ferrari/ Five-year old Peugot 205

Most likely to say: "You're the first person I've spoken to in three days"

Old Ham Actor

Seventy-something old drama queen who trained in weekly rep, writing his lines on the scenery and making thirty costume changes per show. He did a voiceover for Stork SB in the seventies and his most notable screen credit was as a Time Lord (non-speaking) on Dr Who. He smokes forty a day, and talks like Patrick Stewart only he chews his words and the scenery more. Claims to have slept with Helen Mirren and Jeremy Irons when he was at the RSC.

He is an expert in applying prosthetic noses and make up, speaking verse, spraying the fifth row of the stalls with spittle and playing to the balcony, all skills which he laments have been lost by the latest generation of mumbling method actors.

He teaches once a week at a top London drama school, where he flirts with the female students and wastes most of the lesson telling anecdotes: "Ah, Dear old Larry. Such a dangerous actor – you never quite knew what he would be getting up to next! Dear old thing!"

Characteristics

Reading Material: Arden Shakespeare, The Stage, Radio Times

Favourite TV Programmes and Films: He can't bear to watch TV or films because of all the colleagues who are doing better than him

Heroes and Role Models: Donald Wolfit, Larry, John and dear, dear Ralphie

Most likely cause of death: Smoking or Drinking

Favourite Music: Show tunes, especially Rent and Judy Garland

Political Views: Left wing

Ego Issues: Cannot function without applause

Fears: Never working again

Likes: Circling the names of actors he knows in the Radio Times, drinking, smoking.

Dislikes: Fellow Thespians who are more successful than he is

Earnings: £6k

Offspring: Divorced, one girl who is a bonkers actress and doing better than him

Drives: Old Jag

Most likely to say: : "Of course, when I was at RADA"

Sex Tourist

If you know any 56-year-old divorced history teachers who wear tinted glasses and return from their summer holidays as white-skinned as when they left, you can be sure they are sex Tourists. It's the one time every year they can forget about irritations such as the National Curriculum and UK law and jet off to soak up some fluorescent lighting in a windowless room. Sex Tourists are all balding and/or bearded and obese, a sign that they can't control their urges, but also for the practical reason of having some fat reserves when they get arrested; Gary Glitter always loses stacks of weight when he's doing time in a Vietnamese prison.

He believes his money provides employment and boosts the local economy, the airline, taxi, restaurants and hotel industries. Instead of offering handouts he pays for a service which gives impoverished foreigners dignity and the prospect of a better life. He also helps to improve education since illiteracy and poverty go hand in hand.

He lives somewhere bland and anonymous like Milton Keynes but owns a specially converted motorhome which he uses during half terms to explore isolated beauty spots around the British Isles. He wears slip-ons with bare feet or Birkenstocks with socks. His hobbies include video editing, Chatroulette and playing cricket (see page 249).

Characteristics

Reading Material: The Guardian, National Geographic,

Favourite TV Programmes and Films: The Lovely Bones, Bugsy Malone, Olsen twins movies, Interview with a Vampire,

Heroes and Role Models: Gary Glitter, Michael Jackson, R. Kelly

Most likely cause of death: Death penalty in Vietnam

Favourite Music: Gary Glitter, The Who, Michael Jackson, R. Kelly, The Scratch Perverts (disappointing), Pornucopia

Political Views: Votes for the political party most likely to legalise man/boy love, which is UKIP

Ego Issues: He is a whingeing little twonk who will blame anyone but himself when he eventually gets put away for an eight year stretch

Fears: AIDS, arrest

Likes: Young girls, Thai food

Dislikes: Pubic hair

Earnings: Public sector pension

Offspring: Two estranged children

Would like to drive but actually drives: Riley motorbike; specially converted motorhome

Most likely to say: "Are you working, luv?"

Maths Teacher

In a recent survey in Bliss magazine 2,000 teenage boys and girls were asked who were the most "evil" teachers. Twenty-five percent said Maths, but they were beaten into second place by Science Teachers as the most "boring".

He is passionate about his subject, but has such a repertoire of tics, speech impediments and repeated phrases that most of his students spend the lesson counting them rather than paying attention. A spittle ball dances around his lips at all times so you can't concentrate on what he's saying or look him in the eye when he's talking to you.

He worries about his brood of seven fat children (who all have Old Testament names) because they are turning into smaller obese versions of him, so he has just invested in a large climbing frame for the back garden to encourage them to be more active. He has a flatulent King Charles Spaniel called Gauss which he brings into lessons and which sits and farts under his desk.

Characteristics

Reading Material: Fermat's Last Theorem, The Man Who Loved Only Numbers, The Phone Book, Daily Telegraph

Favourite TV Programmes and Films: Countdown, Money Box, Snooker, A Beautiful Mind, Drowning by Numbers

Heroes and Role Models: Gottfried Leibniz, Carol Vorderman

Most likely cause of death: e2 = cos Z + i sin Z, complications from long-term chalk dust inhallation

Favourite Music: Bach, Mozart, Philip Glass, Michael Nyman, John Cage

Political Views: Liberal

Ego Issues: His high opinion of his own intelligence and thinks less of society for not appreciating it

Fears: Any situation or problem where there isn't a method to follow resulting in a right answer.

Likes: Reciting calendrical facts, railway timetables and remembering Pi to 20 decimal places. bad puns

Dislikes: Students, untidiness, not showing workings out, students finding his lessons easy

Earnings: £39k

Offspring: Seven children

Drives: Old Renault Espace

Most likely to say: "That bell is for me not for you"

Property Developer

 81

 125

 5

 2

Raised in London and the Home Counties, he started his career as a student borrowing a few grand from his dad to do up the two-up-two-down terraced house his grandmother left him in her will. When his three months of sweat and his dad's money made him a twelve thousand pound profit, he realised that he had found a way to buy himself an early retirement.

Twenty years on and he's worth several millions. He changes his car every year and keeps his beard trimmed into a youthfully quirky goatee. He has established good working partnerships with local builders, plumbers and electricians and is on first name terms with all of them. His design specs have improved significantly since he's started watching Kevin McCloud and his newly honed eye for the aesthetic has prompted him to ditch his wife and look for a newer model. However, he prides himself that he can still make a B&Q kitchen look like a million dollars with clever lighting.

He believes that poverty is a choice and has already warned his kids they will be getting none of his money. He expects them to make their own fortune in life, although he is prepared to give them favourable rates on a start-up loan.

Characteristics

Reading Material: The property sections of local rags, online estate agents

Favourite TV Programmes and Films: Grand Designs, A Place in the Sun, Location, Location, Location, A Place in the Country

Heroes and Role Models: Nick and Christian Candy, Kevin McCloud

Most likely cause of death: Falling off a ladder

Favourite Music: Queen, Dire Straits

Political Views: Poverty is a choice, votes Tory to avoid High Rate Tax

Ego Issues: Believes he is a self-made man – despite that fact that it was his Grandmother's house and his father's savings that helped him get started

Fears: Double-dip recession

Likes: Getting a good price, telling people how much he's worth

Dislikes: Building Regs inspectors, Listed properties, Sarah Beeny

Earnings: Net worth £1.5 – 2million

Offspring: Two or three who live with their mother

Drives: Lamborghini

Most likely to say: "Have a guess how much I'm worth? Go on, have a guess . . ."

Gents Outfitter

Polite old-fashioned chap of indeterminate age who has spent a lifetime measuring inside legs and demonstrating exhaustive knowledge of his stock (which has always been decades out of date or 'classic', depending on your viewpoint). He's not an upmarket outfitters; his stock is more middle of the road – but he is one of the few remaining retailers who actually knows what he is talking about. He can recommend the right combination of cufflinks, bow ties, studs and collar stiffeners and gently steer you away from that shiny vermillion cummerbund that you think adds elegance to your tuxedo but actually makes you look like every other clueless hair gelled twit at a wedding.

The only time young people today get to meet these types is before their end of school party (which they incorrectly call a 'prom') when they go to hire the only suit they are likely to wear except for when they get married. They will then revisit the nice gentleman in the gents outfitters who will still look exactly as he always has. This chap is a dying breed along with all his good customers.

Anyone in their forties and above will remember making the yearly pilgrimage to his long thin shop at the end of every summer holiday to glean items of school uniform that didn't have St Michael on the care label, such as ties, caps, crested blazers, cricket whites or some monogrammed handkerchiefs for Dad's birthday.

Characteristics

Reading Material: Daily Telegraph, books on golf, tape measure

Favourite TV Programmes and Films: Gosford Park, Cranford, Antiques Roadshow, Gardeners' World, Question Time

Heroes and Role Models: Eric Clapton, the guardian angel of gentleman's outfitters

Most likely cause of death: Neglect

Favourite Music: Anything really as long as he can hum the tune

Political Views: Liberal Democrat

Ego Issues: Feels cross when people ask questions that are not appropriate, as he feels they don't appreciate his expertise

Fears: Calling in the receivers, high street closures

Likes: Viyella country shirts, Polo shirts and Melka casuals, Jockey underwear, being expert, polite and courteous, mahogany display units he hand-built himself

Dislikes: Being talked down to by people with new money, local Chamber of Commerce, wholesale reps

Earnings: £9,850

Offspring: Never married, no kids

Drives: Never been spotted driving

Most likely to say: "Suits you, Sir."

Hippy Single Bloke

Free Love has never quite worked out for this part-time Free Lover, but he's determined to keep the faith, although he feels deflated with the reality that being a stoner doesn't pay the bills. More than three decades on, he works nine-to-five as an archivist for the National Trust or local records office, wearing suit trousers and a v-neck pullover and inhaling centuries-old dust mites from the crumbling tomes of lunatic asylum records and workhouse diaries.

Thirty years of 'tuning out' with a bedtime spliff have left him with considerable paranoia issues – he's a regular in HR, lodging repeated workplace bullying complaints and will talk conspiracy theories for hours if given the opportunity.

At weekends, he sheds the rags of convention, dusts down his kaftan and beads and pitches a tent on a nearby hillside. In the glory days he would spend whole summers living in a hassle-free canvas community, sharing spliffs, love and lentil soup. These days it's usually just him and a couple of librarians from Warrington, but they don't dress up any more. They go foraging for woodland mushrooms and berries, open up a few tins of beans they've brought just in case foraging doesn't work out and spend the weekend getting maudlin and not washing.

Characteristics

Reading Material: He treasures his prized collection of vintage '70s Robert Crumb's Keep On Truckin comics, and a few Gandalf's Garden magazines from his days hanging out on the King's Road. He makes a lot of late-night visits to conspiracy theory websites

Favourite TV Programmes and Films: He talks a lot about TV being the main weapon 'They' use to brainwash the people and therefore claims he rejects all that. But he cant resist Glee and Strictly Come Dancing

Heroes and Role Models: John Lennon, Bob Dylan, Jerry Garcia

Most likely cause of death: Mushroom poisoning, or something smoking related

Favourite Music: The Grateful Dead, Jefferson Airplane, early Pink Floyd, Neil Young, Jimi Hendrix

Political Views: Hardline counter-culturalist, still angry about Vietnam, wants to ban the bomb and save the whale. Lost track of politics after Nixon was impeached

Ego Issues: Despises the conventionality he sees in his colleagues; sees their conformity as cowardice; secretly envious of their shed/family saloon/wife

Fears: The six most powerful men who rule the world, selling-out, global warming, bad vibes

Likes: Smelling bad, drum circles, wearing stupid bracelets, daisy chains, vegetarianism, running naked in the bushes, reading, trees and birds and rocks, good vibes, reading some more, playing shitty riffs on his guitar

Dislikes: Archivists, his brother's success, washing, bad vibes, war

Earnings: £24,782

Offspring: One estranged daughter who works for KPMG

Would like to drive but actually drives: Mini Metro/Old Beetle

Most likely to say: "Yeah man, nice one, let's knock up a number…nice one!"

Latin Teacher (Old)

The Lady Latin teacher can be found in every girls' boarding school in the land. Buried away in a Classroom That Time Forgot, she is as ancient as the institution itself and just as feared. Deep lines are etched into the fabric of her face, keeping her mouth perpetually poised to conjugate.

She has spent her professional life walking the halls of the very same school she first entered as a young boarder. She has worn the same wardrobe for at least four decades and leaves the stench of disappointment in her wake. In recent years the introduction of male members of staff has thrown her a little off-kilter so that she has become prone to spontaneous lapses in self-control and a mild form of Tourette's.

Her career has been marked by a sustained failure to inspire and her classes are noted for their tangible air of mutual abhorrence. She no longer attempts to disguise the fact that she resents her pupils for their youth, their optimism and their ability to talk to the opposite sex without having to battle a nervous gag-reflex. For their part, successive generations of her pupils have sensed that verbs are the only thing this gnarly spinster has ever successfully conjugated.

Characteristics

Reading Material: The love poetry of Catullus in the original, Ovid's Metamorphoses

Favourite TV Programmes and Films: Tunes in to the Archers and the Radio Four news daily, but hasn't owned a TV since Angela Rippon started reading the news in 1974

Heroes and Role Models: She once dreamt of being Miss Jean Brodie, but those days are a murky memory now

Most likely cause of death: Dehydration

Favourite Music: Britten's Requiem and the Schubert liede

Political Views: Victorian laissez-faire

Ego Issues: She knows she is too good for the girls she teaches, of superior intellect to her colleagues, perhaps with the exception of the Head of Music, and world's apart from the jumped-up nouveaux who sit before her at Parents' Evenings.

Fears: Men, sex and the unshakeable feeling that nothing will ever change.

Likes: Her cats, broth and the smell of moth balls

Dislikes: Co-educational schooling, pop music and OFSTED

Earnings: Around £45k, most of which sits unused and unloved and will most likely be passed on to a home for abandoned cats after she dies.

Offspring: Highly unlikely

Drives: Fiat Panda

Most likely to say: *Abutebaris modo subjunctivo denuo.* (You've been misusing the subjunctive again.)

Alternative Therapist

 79

 90

 5

 9

 20

Bored menopausal vegetarian seeking an easy second income. She is called Sue and lives in a seventies bungalow with husband Dave, a recently-vasectomized civil engineer.

She suffers from a variety of niggling ailments which stubbornly persist despite her extensive alternative healing knowledge. These include irritable bowel syndrome, eczema and migraines. Consequently her kitchen cupboards are fit to burst with castor oil enemas, benwa balls and Tamoxifen. Even the small family dog has an impressive repertoire of health issues necessitating bi-weekly visits to the Canine Herbalist and lying to her husband about the cost. She doesn't perceive any conflict of interest between peddling flower remedies to her gullible clients while personally propping up the share price of the larger drug companies.

She's attended half-day courses in Reiki, Colour Therapy, Rolfing, Vegetable Juicing and Craniosacral something-or-other so her smudged business card (produced with a cheap inkjet printer) correctly announces her as an expert in all these fields.

Characteristics

Reading Material: Rainbow World, Nuts & Seeds, Chakra Monthly, Magazine, The Secret, Nutrition labels

Favourite TV Programmes and Films: Free Willy, Taylor Camp, Animal Park: Wild in Africa, Woman's Hour

Heroes and Role Models: Gillian McKeith, Anita Roddick, Kate Humble, Derek Acorah, The Barefoot Doctor, Dr Bach

Most likely cause of death: One of the illnesses that can't be healed by diluting a gallon of water with a nasturtium and then placing two drops on your tongue

Favourite Music: Enya, Whale Music, binaural beats, anything if the cover features rainbows, mushrooms, wolves, red Indian sunrises, and silhouettes of people doing Yoga

Political Views: The world's destroyed by men, all men are rapists, except Druids (see page 134)

Ego Issues: She derives a feeling of superiority from maintaining good posture and talking quietly in modulated tones but suffers an inferiority complex about being professionally qualified

Fears: Her son might be gay, illness, taxation

Likes: Organic quinoa and buckwheat soba

Dislikes: Capitalism, third runway at Heathrow, Ben Goldacre, anything that isn't fair trade

Earnings: £8-12k per year, the rest being subsidised by handouts from husbands or fathers

Offspring: One

Drives: A really old polluting banger

Most likely to say: " We need to balance your shakras"

Antique Dealer
(Junk Stall On Portobello Road Selling Junk To Toursits)

Condescending twit who sells nothing but repro and crap with just enough of a mark up to sustain his snobbish delusion that he is a "true" dealer, and scorns all the newcomers and rogues. He clucks moodily at all the auctions he attends because he thinks people are stupid to pay such high prices, but really he is just resentful that he can no longer treble his money as easily as he could in the seventies. Nowadays he'd make more cash selling jam jars decorated with sea shells at craft fairs.

He is rude to anyone who dares to browse at his stall and interrupt his reading which is either something with pose value like The Anthology of Rap, or more likely the latest novel by Jonathan Franzen. He sighs at any questions and bizarrely only tolerates nerds who wish to gas about great gains they once made in the trade whereupon he tries to outdo them by name dropping and boasting about the incredibly valuable things he has made fortunes on. Most of his stories turn out to be amazing near misses that he failed to secure.

Characteristics

Reading Material: Independent, Jonathan Franzen

Favourite TV Programmes and Films: Eyes Wide Shut, Eraserhead and similar tedious self-indulgent toss

Heroes and Role Models: James Harries

Most likely cause of death: Stall backed into by transit van

Favourite Music: Jazz, opera, ballet and other such tumid pursuits

Political Views: He votes Labour or Lib Dem, but he has the elitist sensibilities and cruel heart of a Tory

Ego Issues: He knows he lacks a chin so he has grown a faggy little goatee to make up for it

Fears: Failing to recognize a genuine rare antique and selling it for 50p

Likes: Gitanes, fake French food markets, smelly cheese, sandals, wearing wussy artistic scarves, having an earring

Dislikes: Customers, browsers, children, haggling, competition from charity shops

Earnings: £18k

Offspring: One daughter aged 38 who he has not seen since 1985

Drives: Old burgundy Citroen.

Most likely to say: "Yap. I run an antiques business. Yap."

Celebrity Chef

The celebrity chef owes his perfectionism and relentless drive to an abusive childhood. The middle child in a family of four boys, he was raised in poverty by an alcoholic father who night after night would stagger home raging drunk from the working man's club, drag the terrified child out of bed and demand Escalope de Foie Gras Chaud et Pastilla à la Cannelle followed by Mille-Feuille aux Poires, Sauce Caramel au Beurre Salé. He had to think on his feet to avoid a good belting, and often had to improvise if his Béarnaise sauce separated or if the tyrant wanted ingredients that were out of season.

This blighted upbringing has made him a culinary tour de force but also an angry coward who only picks on contestants he can beat in a fight; he never dares to get chippy with guys who could lay him out with one punch. His simian chest beating attracts cute women with self-esteem issues and he is currently in a protracted divorce with his fourth doormat. He is a serial adulterer who defends frequent accusations of chauvinism with the woman-hating mantra: "But I love women, they are beautiful".

The three Michelin stars of softly-spoken French chef Anne-Sophie Pic prove that you don't have to throw tantrums and be aggressive to achieve excellence. Despite this the male Celebrity Chef uses his kitchen to explore how colossal a twat it is possible to be.

Characteristics

Reading Material: Anything in which he features

Favourite TV Programmes and Films: His own TV programmes, interviews, gets his PA to record and catalogue all his appearances

Heroes and Role Models: Himself; is publicly estranged from his former mentors

Most likely cause of death: Vanity

Favourite Music: Rock

Political Views: He donates large amounts to the Tory party in hope of a knighthood

Ego Issues: Underneath the bravado he's still a frightened little boy who wets the bed. Real life is confusing and he is most comfortable on TV. Fears fading out of the limelight so much he will do adverts for boil in the bag products

Fears: Metrosexual males; real tough guys

Likes: Swearing, smashing plates, bullying staff, being on TV, money, flash cars, Michelin stars

Dislikes: Women, vegetarians. the French, all other celebrity chefs especially Jamie Oliver, kitchen porters

Earnings: Loads, but mostly at other people's expense - he will have folded several limited companies

Offspring: Six kids because he is God's gift to the gene pool

Would like to drive but actually drives: Ferarri 599/chauffeur-driven BMW 7-series

Most likely to say: "If I want your opinion I'll give it to you"

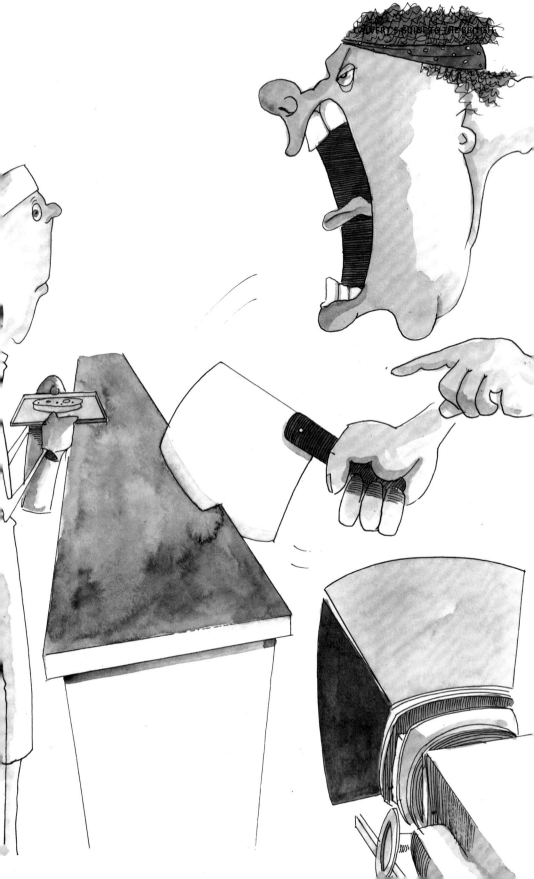

Gay Vicar

The gay vicar is a force for good in the world, put on earth by God to expose the hypocrisy and bigotry of the homophobic evangelicals who call him an abomination. Twice a year a gay vicar pops up in the media because he's decided to marry his long-term partner, and predictably this always puts him in conflict with his bishop who won't allow a blessing in the church and insists he remain celibate.

He is popular with the vast majority of his parishioners, apart from the sour-faced ones who like to equate homosexuality with social chaos and moral degeneration, failing to see that all man-made suffering on this planet bar none is caused either by inequality or intolerance. While the Anglican Church tears itself asunder with this long-overdue schism, the gay vicar gets on with doing what human beings are meant to, loving his fellow man and trying to live a good life; the only mystery is his continued attachment to a church which clearly abhors him.

Characteristics

Reading Material: The Bible, Alan Hollinghurst, James Baldwin, Colm Toibin, Jean Genet, Pink Paper, Attitude, Gay Christian 101

Favourite TV Programmes and Films: Songs of Praise, Radio 4, Stonewall, Strawberry and Chocolate, Brokeback Mountain, Glee

Heroes and Role Models: Jesus Christ, Gene Robinson, Kylie Minogue

Most likely cause of death: Impaled by a church spire

Favourite Music: Hymns, Diana Ross, Kylie Minogue, Ricky Martin

Political Views: Liberal Democrat

Ego Issues: Doesn't like the thought of being thought of as straight just because he is a vicar.

Fears: Religious homophobia

Likes: Jerry Springer: The Opera, tarts and vicars charity events

Dislikes: Christian Voice, Christian Fundamentalists – The Official Bigots of the Anti-Gay Movement, St Paul

Earnings: £25k

Offspring: One son from first marriage

Drives: Daewoo

Most likely to say: "Dearly Beloved, we are gathered together here in the sight of God – and in the face of this company – to join together this man and this man in holy matrimony"

Motto: God is an Equal Opportunity Lover

Lesbian (Greenham Common Type)

Raised in a privileged but loveless household by an alcoholic actress and an absentee father in the Home Office, this eco-warrior has a whole lot of love to give but has never been able to persuade anyone to take her on. Consequently she pours her heart into Causes and often bursts into tears about the desperate need for mankind to save the planet, the whale, the trees and now the icebergs and polar bears.

She's been a fully paid up member of Greenpeace and CND since the early eighties and spent weeks of her life chained to the gates of the Greenham Common cruise missile site. She's been charged by riot police, trampled by mounted police and warned off by transport police. Though she doesn't know for sure, she suspects that she was on an MOD Watch List throughout the Thatcher years.

She lives alone in a rented studio flat in a bleak corner of North London with three cats called Cuddles, Swampy and Rainbow and earns her living writing freelance articles for the Big Issue, Earth First Magazine and Your Cat Monthly. At night, she despairs about the political apathy of the modern youth as she seeks comfort in Green and Black's Hazelnut Chocolate spread and Banana Cake.

Characteristics

Reading Material: She subscribes to a host of tax-deductable environmental and socialist publications which she reads cover to cover, before snipping out significant articles for her Save the Planet and Conspiracy scrap books and cutting the rest up for loo paper

Favourite TV Programmes and Films: Though she knows she shouldn't let herself succumb to the government-funded opiate of American pulp drama, she can't get enough of One Tree Hill

Heroes and Role Models: Chico Mendes and Ken Saro-Wiwa

Most likely cause of death: Savaged by a dolphin

Favourite Music: Joni Mitchell, Emerson Lake & Palmer, John Denver

Political Views: Green/socialist, unilateral disarmament

Ego Issues: Needs the camaraderie of the protest march in order to feel she belongs to something

Fears: Global nuclear holocaust, that she is being followed, the disappointment in her mother's eyes

Likes: Brushing up against people on public transport

Dislikes: Tony Blair, America, her bosom

Earnings: £14 - £17k

Offspring: Cats

Most likely to say: "God, that bloke is such an arsehole"

Size Zero Model

Despite claiming to have always been naturally thin, this moving coat hanger lives on Diet Coke, cocaine and lettuce leaves. She hasn't been to the toilet for three weeks or had a period for a year. Her waist is the size of an average eight year old girl's. She is six feet tall and her vital statistics are bust 31.5", waist 23" and hips 34". She totters around on her gimlet thin legs and pukes after meals because she has been told by her model agency that she will be a huge star if she can just lose another two stone.

This deluded ironing board is starving herself to the brink of death because a clique of women-hating male designers claim their ranges sit better on models who look like ET. She is dating a man in his late thirties who is probably cheating on her but she can forget having babies and look forward to osteoporosis, ovarian cysts and teeth like Shane McGowan.

At least she doesn't have to do the exaggerated runway strut that was fashionable in the eighties and nineties, and is encouraged to walk more naturally but that's only after several fashion journalists were poked in the eye by wayward hip bones.

Characteristics

Reading Material: Vogue, Elle, Harper's Bazaar, i-D

Favourite TV Programmes and Films: Ugly Betty, Desperate Housewives, Malcolm in the Middle

Heroes and Role Models: Lily Cole, Erin O'Connor, Kate Bosworth

Most likely cause of death: Heart failure

Favourite Music: Drowned out by the sound of her stomach eating itself

Political Views: Hates fur or wears it, depending on the current fashion; John Galliano shouldn't have said those mean things

Ego Issues: Never feels pretty or thin enough even though she is creating the illusion of perfection and foisting it onto other women

Fears: Putting on a pound, being sent home from a shoot for being too fat

Likes: Laxatives, slimming pills, vomiting, speed, cocaine

Dislikes: Eating, feeling hungry all the time, having no energy, having no libido

Earnings: £60k

Offspring: Not a chance

Drives: Black 4 x 4

Most likely to say: "I'm so fat and ugly"

Business Woman (Young)

This exceptionally selfish young woman models herself on one of those unattractively ambitious and aggressive females from The Apprentice. She attended a minor public school a long way from civilization, either in Devon or tucked away at the top of Scotland, and she had a spell in the Officer Cadets but failed the medical for Sandhurst. Despite this she claims to have had a career in the military.

Unfortunately she brings her brief military 'training', and on-your-bike political beliefs into the world of business. She has never had a proper job but has done plenty of PR consultancy for several blue chip companies with too much money and too many incompetent managers to realise that she doesn't know her arse from someone else's elbow.

When her career stalls she will try to get on a reality TV programme or have an affair with her rich married boss who is twenty years her senior, thus embarking on a series of adulterous relationships. Despite only ever really exceeding at lying to get sales she considers herself a rounded business woman and potential MP.

Characteristics

Reading Material: Her own blog, Facebook or Twitter

Favourite TV Programmes and Films: The Apprentice, Dragon's Den, Wall St

Heroes and Role Models: Darth Vader, Deborah Meaden

Most likely cause of death: Ambition

Favourite Music: She says Elgar (if anyone asks)

Political Views: Thatcherite Tory; she thinks that gender equality has gone far enough and that women need to just stand up for themselves

Ego Issues: Always looks with envy at what others have, especially husbands. She is deeply insecure but has buried it so deep that she would needs years of therapy to stop her from being competitive and aggressive

Fears: Being found out

Likes: Attracting attention, lying about her salary, exaggeration, men's attention

Dislikes: Women with fake tans, women who take maternity leave, overweight women, all pretty women

Earnings: One third of what she claims to earn

Offspring: "None, but God, I am only 34 for Christ's sake"

Would like to drive but actually drives: 1 series BMW/Mercedes SLK

Most likely to say: "People just don't, like, 'get' me. I think, I like, threaten them"

Horsey Mum and Daughter

Their 4 x 4 is full of mud, dogs and hair, their house full of cats, their land full of neat wooden fencing, and their lives very much full of Horse !

Every working minute is filled with point to point, hunting, dressage, country shows, mucking out, grooming, vets bills, purchasing tack , clothing, magazines, winter feed, stables, horse boxes, farriers and general horse maintenance.

They have more boxes of potions, brushes, waxes, ointments and specialist tools than the local hospital and they are as happy picking up poo as they are settling down to read Horse Monthly.

They are blissfully unaware of how much it all costs, poor old daddy has to earn £5000 a month just to keep up with on-going horse overheads and that is over and above the £250,000 capital he had to sink into stables, vehicles and equipment.

As is so often the case when women spend an unhealthy amount of time together they are starting to dress, look and intonate identically. They smell disconcertingly of horse but are very jolly and will only want to stop to talk to you for 20 seconds before making it clear that they are too busy to stop and talk to you.

Opportunities for daughter to find a suitable partner are diminishing rapidly as finances and breeding dictate that choices are limited to wealthy farmer, wealthy vet or wealthy landowner. Eventually she will find a suitable partner who will be something horse or farming related but who is unlikely to arrive with sufficient wealth, so will end up living in a bungalow on the farm where he will be committed to a life of running errands for the family.

Characteristics

Reading Material: Horse & Rider, Horse Monthly, Horsing Today

Favourite TV Programmes and Films: Dick Francis, Jilly Cooper, Black Beauty

Heroes and Role Models: Horsey Royals, Harvey Smith and Sea Biscuit

Most likely cause of death: Horse or old age

Favourite Music: Radio 2

Political Views: Tory

Ego Issues: None, They only think about horses. Ill-fitting jodhpurs prove no signs of self-consciousness

Fears: Poorly Horses

Likes: Riding horses, talking about horses, kissing horses' noses, riding side by side on tarmac and holding up traffic

Dislikes: Cars that don't slow down, ragwort, bad weather and the French

Earnings: Daddy sees to all that, but it is a lot

Offspring: 3 horses, 2 donkeys, 4 dogs three cats and crow with a broken wing

Drives: Landrover, horseboxes

Most likely to say: "The Horses"

Ladies' Golf Captain

She took up golf more than two decades ago and over the years it has risen to the level of obsession. Since retirement, her life is one long round of golfing ladies' lunches, golf club fundraisers, golf club quiz nights, golf club charity auctions and golf. She even blogs about it.

She likes to lighten the mood on even the most blustery of days, taking genteel bets for the number of balls which will end up being blown off-course and into the pond, which all her ladies find jolly good fun. She hates to walk, however, and always takes the cart which ensures that she gains minimal health benefits from her hobby. Still, the clubhouse serve a generous lunch which always finishes the morning off nicely.

She ends the year buoyant with the news that her Winter Trophy triumph has brought her handicap down to 11 and that her ladies have raised £208.57 for the Gladys Harington Home for Abused Donkeys. She celebrates by arranging a ladies weekend away and is sure to post riotous photographs of her ladies having fun on the blogsite.

Characteristics

Reading Material: The Times, Women & Golf Magazines

Favourite TV Programmes and Films: The afternoon movie, though she generally has a snooze and misses the end, Countdown, the golf

Heroes and Role Models: The outgoing Ladies Golf Captain, Anne Murray

Most likely cause of death: Stroke

Favourite Music: Celine Dion, Harry Secombe

Political Views: Tory, fought to overturn the neighbouring Golf Club's antiquated 'Men Only' policy

Ego Issues: A smug sense of superior gamesmanship, which she fails to disguise

Fears: Having to give up the captaincy

Likes: Being captain, charity quiz nights, golf

Dislikes: Walking, the cold, women who are noticeably better players than her

Earnings: Her husband is a retired army officer and they live comfortably off his pension

Offspring: Two grown daughters, who also play golf

Drives: Always drives a Mercedes

Most likely to say: "Stableford, par, foursomes and lunch"

Walker (Female)

Sixty-eight-year-old retired English teacher who likes walking around in a big circle with thirty other pensioners, with a break for lunch in the middle to paint an inept watercolour and eat egg sandwiches that smell of ointment.

She regularly pops up on some dull programme on Radio 4 accompanied by a breathless Clare Balding or an annoyingly chipper Matt Baker as they walk the entire length of Saint Oswald's Arsecrack or some other dreary swathe of Northumberland. She always trots out the same five facts: she only discovered walking in the last two years since her husband died; it keeps her active; she's met lots of nice people; everyone goes at their own pace and finally she has to point out that in their group (of which she is the self-appointed leader) there is one gentleman who is ninety-three and they have some babies in their late fifties, ha ha ha.

Like farmers, walkers have a high opinion of their importance to the countryside. They feel that their walking all over it contributes to sustainability and other important issues like keeping the riff-raff out. They tend to get a little over excited at the prospect of a walk. This is not the only characteristic they share with dogs.

Characteristics

Reading Material: 1001 Walks in Britain, compass, OS maps, Wainwright guides

Favourite TV Programmes and Films: Ramblings, Rivers, programmes in which Griff Rhys Jones feigns interest in the landscape

Heroes and Role Models: Alfred Wainwright

Most likely cause of death: Trampled by cows, shot by farmer

Favourite Music: Elgar, Vaughan Williams, Holst, Dvořák Hovis advert, George Butterworth

Political Views: Tory, despite policies often at odds with a love of the countryside viz selling off forests, building wind farms

Ego Issues: For her walking is definitely a class issue and a sign that she is middle class.

Fears: Cows, walking routes cut, wind turbines, gamekeepers, trespass laws

Likes: The Ramblers' Association, pretty landscape, pretty buildings, cream teas, tucking trousers into socks, keeping stuff in transparent cases, peering into Jeremy Clarkson's lighthouse holiday home and taking photographs

Dislikes: Madonna, blisters, Nicholas Van Hoogstraten, Jeremy Clarkson, Ffyona Campbell, mountain bikers

Earnings: State pension plus big life assurance payout after husband died

Offspring: Several children, all of whom apparently claim she has a more active social life than them, ha ha ha

Drives: Honda CRV

Most likely to say: "Right-to-roam . . . stop at the pub . . . access battles . . . oh look there's the Devil's Garlic Press . . . etc."

Walker (Male)

A know it all pedant called Derek who "organises" his local walking society outings in the Peak District. He is full of his own self importance and briefs everybody with a detailed health and safety analysis prior to each week's ramble. He claims to like the fact that rambling is accessible and something everyone can do but what he enjoys most is believing he knows more about the local countryside and its features than anyone else, and he's always offering unwelcome tips on how to enhance the walking experience. Before he was made redundant and took early retirement he was a middle manager for an engineering company but spent most of his time micromanaging the tea and biscuit rota.

National Park wardens avoid him because once cornered he can drone on for ages about footpaths that need resurfacing, stone walls that need repairing, stiles and paths where vegetation needs cutting back, biodiversity, the extreme vulnerability of the moorland in this dry weather, complaining about mountain bikers or some litter that he discovered last weekend but didn't pick up, or asking why he hasn't received a reply yet to his complaint about a 4x4 owner.

Characteristics

Reading Material: 1001 Walks in Britain, compass, OS maps, Wainwright guides

Favourite TV Programmes and Films: Ramblings, Rivers, programmes in which Griff Rhys Jones feigns interest in canals

Heroes and Role Models: William Hague, Wainwright, Chris Bonnington

Most likely cause of death: Trampled by cows

Favourite Music: Elgar, Vaughan Williams, Holst, Dvořák Hovis advert, George Butterworth

Political Views: Tory, he supports tighter immigration because he thinks ethnic minorities look out of place in the landscape

Ego Issues: Walking combines his two favourite things: walking and showing off his local knowledge.

Fears: Cows, walking routes cut, wind turbines, gamekeepers, trespass laws

Likes: Ffyona Campbell, The Ramblers' Association, points of interest on the hike (proof that the walking bits in between are boring), tucking trousers into socks, keeping stuff in transparent cases

Dislikes: Madonna, blisters, Nicholas Van Hoogstraten, Jeremy Clarkson, mountain bikers, Yorkshire Water

Earnings: State pension

Offspring: One son who is a leading bore in fertilizer developments

Drives: Ford Focus

Most likely to say: "…Of course being secretary for the local ramblers association, I have objected"

Cornish Artist

White-haired inbred old pederast who wears a fisherman's smock and clogs, deliberately gets paint on his clothes and drinks beer or cider with bits in. Taciturn and suspicious of strangers, he lives alone in a ramshackle Georgian town house in Falmouth overlooking the sea which he bought in the late fifties for pennies and is now worth millions. Rocks from side to side as he walks because of joint problems. Claims he trained at The Slade. Nicknamed Pervy Mike by local schoolchildren.

He likes nothing better than painting *en plein air*: sitting on the quayside smoking his pipe while ogling twelve-year-old boys in their swimming trunks under the pretext of attempting to capture the unique qualities of maritime light (as it bounces off their alabaster flesh). He usually has his lunch in The Seven Stars, where he bores the bar staff with his two abiding memories – watching the ships leave for D-Day during the war and designing an album cover in the seventies for misunderstood singer-songwriter Paul Gadd.

Heavily influenced by the Newlyn School, he sells watercolours of local scenes featuring naked adolescent boys in boats or frolicking on rocks. These hang fading and unsold on the walls of various deathly quiet gift shops and cafés that mainly make their money from selling snorkels and small ceramic lighthouses.

Characteristics

Reading Material: Lewis Carroll, J M Barrie, biographies of Richard Trevithick

Favourite TV Programmes and Films: Brokeback Mountain, Maurice, anything featuring Hugh Grant, Rupert Graves, James Wilby

Heroes and Role Models: Henry Scott Tuke, Baden Powell

Most likely cause of death: Old age

Favourite Music: Local Cornish bands, fiddle music, sea shanties

Political Views: Paid up member of the Cornish Nationalist movement Mebyon Kernow; believes whatever washes up on the shore is fair pickings

Ego Issues: Can trace his roots to the ancient Britons

Fears: What exactly can be traced from the deleted history on his PC

Likes: Dramatic skies, windswept beaches and stormy seas, figurative painting, Falmouth Municipal Art gallery, Wilhelm von Gloeden, Gugleilmo Pluschow, Cornish wrestling

Dislikes: Dame Ellen MacArthur, the A39, people who call Cornwall a county rather than a Duchy

Earnings: State pension

Offspring: Has two grown-up estranged children in their forties whom he hasn't seen for twenty-five years

Drives: N/A - Walks

Most likely to say: "Ow hanow yw Michal, a wre ta kewsel kerngwt?" (My name is Michael, can you speak Cornish?)

Jazz Lover

This sixty-something with lank Grecian Formula hair spends his days smoking and memorizing sleeve notes and his evenings smoking and listening to hours of weird free form shit on a pair of headphones that cost more than your car, occasionally twitching, although it is hard to tell whether he does so with approval or disapproval. He gets excited whenever he hears Miles and John playing together. He takes his music very seriously, so he can tell you who's playing on each track and which cocktail of drugs they inhaled beforehand. He's the one at the next table at the jazz club wearing a beret and shushing you for whispering to your friend if she wants the last slice of pizza.

He likes all of Miles Davis' albums, especially the crap ones and the more contorted and indulgent the instrumental the better. His all time favourites sound like a bunch of sugar rush toddlers blowing plastic trumpets at a birthday party, or a honking ten-mile tailback on the M25. His one saving grace is that like the rest of humanity he hates jazz fusion because even he concedes that jazz should not be allowed to fuse with anything.

Characteristics

Reading Material: Guardian, books on jazz, sleeve notes

Favourite TV Programmes and Films: Anything by David Lynch, The Coen brothers, Wes Anderson, Charlie Kauffman

Heroes and Role Models: Miles Davis

Most likely cause of death: Lung/liver cancer

Favourite Music: Jazz, especially Ornette Coleman, Don Cherry, Cecil Taylor, John Coltrane, Miles Davies

Political Views: Cross about the nannying state

Ego Issues: He can't play but wants to be as cool as a jazz musician.

Fears: Killing himself through drink and smoke

Likes: Cigarettes and jazz, posting adverts on craigslist asking for women who share a genuine interest in jazz for companionship

Dislikes: Anything that isn't jazz

Earnings: He's probably a school teacher, a lecturer or something in the publishing or music industry, so between £25k - £35k

Offspring: Single or divorced, one fat grown-up son who wears leather waistcoats and is a jazz drummer

Drives: Volkswagen

Most likely to say: "Cannonball is definitely listed as "Ronnie Peters" on Milt Jackson's Plenty, Plenty Soul LP, Atlantic 1269, 1957"

Lady Vicar

In her opinion, something that she holds dear, the greatest day in the history of contemporary Christian religion was on 11th November 1992 when the General Synod of The Church of England passed the legislation permitting the ordination of women priests. From earliest childhood that was all she ever craved and this single historic proclamation may have fleetingly cast a warm glow in the vicinity of her soul. Displays of emotion are, again in her opinion, the outward manifestation of a rancid and corrupt spirit.

The one thing that she failed to take into consideration when about to enter the priesthood was that the very essence of the job was to broadcast the love of God and cast a light into the darkest recesses of men's hearts and minds. She is not, sadly, one of life's natural communicators and what is sometimes known as the 'common touch' has always managed to elude her. It has been mooted, some might say deservedly so, that a place in an enclosed order may be more appropriate.

Characteristics

Reading Material: Serious Call To a Devout Life, William Law 1729, The Christians Greatest Interest, William Guthrie (c1650), The Bible (King James version only)

Favourite TV Programmes and Films: The TV is a frivolous tool created by Satan to promote his evil works

Heroes and Role Models: John Calvin, Martin Luther, the Protestant Martyrs and Jesus Christ the only begotten son of our Lord

Most likely cause of death: Infection brought on through excessive wearing of a hair shirt

Favourite Music: Unaccompanied Church Music (early) musical instruments are an affliction and will inevitably lead to impure thoughts

Political Views: The Church (once lead by a strong woman) is the only hope of salvation in this profane world.

Ego Issues: Ego does not come into it, she is right and she knows it

Fears: Nothing

Likes: The absolute cast iron, 110% certainty that God exists

Dislikes: The irritating behaviour of parishioners

Earnings: A pittance, certainly less than £20k a year but she stills manages to spend less than half of it

Offspring: "How DARE you!"

Drives: Hyundai

Most likely to say: "I won't marry sinners in this church"

School Run Mum

She may have been captain of the school lacrosse team, Head Girl (see page 367), an Oxbridge Graduate and the youngest (possibly even the first) female ever to be fast-tracked through the graduate programme at the largest financial institution in the city, but her dream of a house in the country, three adoring kids and life with the gymkhana set, came horribly true and soon brought an end to all that ever made her feel good about herself.

Having denounced the scumbags from the local comp on account of their local accents, cheap shoes and unattractive uniform, she packs her precocious Harrys, Charlies, Annabelles and Caledonias into her 4 x 4 to make the fifty-mile round trip to the better, expensive schools. The hour and a half or so a day she has free in between her mammoth school runs, is hers to do with as she pleases.

She embarks on a perpetual cycle of redecorating, devotes hours to finding good private tutors to give her kids the edge, and renews her gym membership – and her resolve – on a regular basis. Generally, however, she fills the lonely daylight hours with gin, and bores her chocolate Labradors with memories of her season as a chalet girl at Klosters, rants about her absentee-husband and his 18-hour days, and wonders out loud where it all went wrong.

Characteristics

Reading Material: Nigella Lawson, Rick Stein, Jamie Oliver and whatever's Booker nominated this year

Favourite TV Programmes and Films: The Today Programme, Woman's Hour, The Archers, Waking the Dead, and anything featuring Nigella, Jamie or Rick

Heroes and Role Models: Nigella Lawson, for juggling family, career and a second marriage to a business icon

Most likely cause of death: Stress

Favourite Music: Beautiful South, Suzanne Vega, Prefab Sprout, Deacon Blue

Political Views: Liberal

Ego Issues: Her inferiority complex drives her vicious social climbing ambitions

Fears: Having one of her offspring get into body art, piercing or Catholicism

Likes: Boiler catalogues, having her husband home for the weekend

Dislikes: Regional accents, friends who Facebook, having her husband home for the weekend

Earnings: Her husband sees to all that now, but she never seems to run short

Offspring: Privileged, buck-toothed and bland

Would like to drive but actually drives: Mercedes SLK/4x4 full of kids

Most likely to say: "I'd love to, but Caledonia/Charlie has pony club/rowing/chess tournament that day"

Vet (Female)

81

140

5

8

16

Invariably blonde and attractive, these girls did well at school, enjoyed sport and enjoyed the company of their friends and parents. She will have been brought up in a rural environment surrounded by lots of horses, cats and dogs and tennis courts. She will be descended from a well-bred stock of tall lean attractive humans all of whom were afforded a private education.

She is posh without being superior and controls social interaction with all classes. When it comes to home visits, she is equally at home sewing the torn ear of a pit bull terrier as she is removing lead shot from the ear of a spaniel.

It is hard to imagine her wearing a dress on any other day but her wedding, not because she wouldn't look stunning in it, but because she's too practical. She has a neat centre parting bob or keeps her hair tied in a no-nonsense pony tail. She runs a busy practice, will produce several children, keep a well-kept smallholding and several animals, but will never seem flustered or out of time.

She is so attractive that local men have been known to buy dogs and break their legs just to get into her surgery. She does not wear makeup, because it is tested on animals but mainly because she does not want to blow away the competition completely.

Characteristics

Reading Material: Veterinary Times, Guardian or Independent,

Favourite TV Programmes and Films: Radio 4, Human Planet,

Heroes and Role Models: James Herriot, Cesar Millan

Most likely cause of death: Old age or trampled by cattle

Favourite Music: Radio 2

Political Views: Liberal Democrat or Green Party

Ego Issues: Despite being perfect, she worries that she is not attractive and smells of dog

Fears: Defra funding cuts, BSE, bird flu, tetanus

Likes: Ray Mears, winter sports

Dislikes: Kate Humble, Bill Oddie, urinary-tract infections, unneutered males

Earnings: £30k - £60k

Offspring: No children but a menagerie of chocolate brown Labradors, cats, poultry and other feathered and furry friends

Drives: Subaru Forester

Most likely to say: "How often do you walk him?"

Doctors (Friendly Great Bloke GP)

Over-worked and forced to withstand an inhuman degree of work-related stress, he has an impressive repertoire of medically-damaging habits of his own. Alcohol is almost certainly his chemical relaxant of choice but the occasional pack of Benson & Hedges and a few late-night byrianis come in a close second. He's been known to match the crowd pint for pint up the Horse and Hounds. He knows better than to preach healthy diet and lifestyle in his consulting room. Instead he gently advises caution with a practiced and well-received humility.

He is your archetypal Great Bloke. He is an integral member of the local community and his patients know him by his first name. They meet him at the school playground, on the golf course or with the Sunday league football team. A few of them arrange the occasional lads' cycling weekend away with him. Makes people feel better as soon as they sit down in his surgery.

Characteristics

Reading Material: Douglas Adams, Issac Asimov, Ray Bradbury and Arthur C Clarke

Favourite TV Programmes and Films: Star Trek, Dune, Avatar, Stargate

Heroes and Role Models: Leonard Nimmoy

Most likely cause of death: Coronary heart disease

Favourite Music: Ska

Political Views: Kept very close to his chest

Ego Issues: None that you'd notice, unless you play golf with him

Fears: Screwing up and being struck off, examining breasts

Likes: Being popular, being one of the lads

Dislikes: Being on call, supercilious consultants, judgemental nurse practitioners

Earnings: In excess of £100k, allegedly

Offspring: Yes – and most likely cute, sporty and privately educated

Drives: German estate car

Most likely to say: "That's fine, what can I do for you?"

Entrepreneur

The entrepreneur knew instinctively at an early age that the educational system is designed to churn out identical docile wage slaves who will sacrifice forty years of their lives working to make entrepreneurs like him super rich in exchange for a guaranteed take home wage. He figured out years ago that working conscientiously for someone else is not the way to make money; he makes money work for him while he sleeps. He also has the irritating ability to defer gratification so while the rest of us blow our extra cash on pointless status symbols, he invests his surplus so that in five years' time he can drive a car that cost more than your house.

Like all successful people he recognises other people bound for success and forms alliances with them. He doesn't have friendships because he doesn't need people – he has a curious detachment and self-reliance. Annoyingly, when he has the £5 million mansion and material wealth that you can only dream of, it doesn't ever seem to excite him. Now that he's reached the upper echelons of society he has a vested interest in maintaining the status quo so he can continue to employ a workforce to make his widgets for the masses, so when he's invited back to his school to give a speech, he will roll out the same old platitudes about following your dreams before posing for a photo for the local paper with a hand-picked group of the most compliant and photogenic pupils..

Characteristics

Reading Material: Newspapers, avoids books about being an entrepreneur, which are written to make the author rich

Favourite TV Programmes and Films: Stock market, Reuters, eclectic mix of programmes when he gets the chance, The Big Lebowski

Heroes and Role Models: Van Morrison

Most likely cause of death: Helicopter or old age

Favourite Music: Rap music, the only musical genre that's about mass market appeal, making money and then spending it

Political Views: Tory, but he can't vote because he officially lives in Switzerland and the Cayman Islands; despite this he will probably become Tory party treasurer in near future.

Ego Issues: Supremely confident; he's motivated by ideas and being creative rather than making money

Fears: Labour government and high taxation

Likes: Taking responsibility for his own success, taking calculated risks

Dislikes: Blaming others, whining, procrastination

Earnings: £10 million

Offspring: Two kids (he's a responsible breeder)

Drives: Bentley

Most likely to say: "I am interested in your opinion"

Lady Organiser

Since her retirement ten years ago, this is the woman who has never quite been able to let go of her long and much-celebrated career supervising a team of three in electrical homeware at her local department store. Management and organisational skills are her raison d'être and retirement would have been intolerable had she been unable to find a new outlet for her passions.

The Women's Institute, Village Hall Management Committees, Parish Council Social Committees and village whist drives fill the void for thousands of women like this every year. They provide a vehicle with which the Lady Organiser can continue to function, reassured by the knowledge that she can continue to give the local community the benefit of her expertise. The Lady Organiser forms the bedrock of the Village Hall Crockery and Cutlery sub-committee, for example, which she steers through the complex procurement of plastic teaspoons for the village fete. This takes six months of fortnightly meetings at which she delegates, collates and feeds back on a monthly basis to the Management Committee, with all the precision and professionalism of a Parliamentary Commission. Without the Lady Organiser's rigorous procedural maps and whist drives, everywhere would remain in disarray and WI cake sales would be in chaos.

Characteristics

Reading Material: Reader's Digest, Woman's Weekly, W.I. Life Magazine, Saga Magazine

Favourite TV Programmes and Films: Calendar Girls, Shirley Valentine, Mamma Mia, As Time Goes By, Keeping Up Appearances

Heroes and Role Models: The Queen Mother, Patricia Routledge

Most likely cause of death: Extreme old age – she'll go on and on

Favourite Music: Frankie Valli, Val Doonican, Peggy Lee

Political Views: Right wing to the extent that she'll organise a bring and buy for the local Conservative candidate's campaign fund

Ego Issues: She's a seething mass of frustration when it comes to having to watch anyone else take the lead on a social committee

Fears: Being ousted from every Committee within a ten mile radius

Likes: Aled Jones, talking about the importance of ecumenicalism

Dislikes: Change, lack of order, photocopiers

Earnings: £16k and as much tea as she can drink

Offspring: Two

Drives: Dhiatsu, Daewoo or Honda Jazz in a bad colour

Most likely to say: "And, thank you to the ladies in the kitchen"

Pilot (Helicopter)

This stalwart, level-headed guy is the first person you would turn to in a crisis, especially one requiring a helicopter. As a kid, he was forever rescuing other kids from trees and calling 999 when their Gran fell down the stairs. All he ever wanted to do was fly.

With 2,000 flying hours under his belt, he performs with consummate skill and courage and never takes uncalculated risks, because when something goes wrong with a helicopter you can't glide your way our of trouble like you can in a plane. That's why helicopter pilots tend to be introspective anticipators of danger. Even climbing in and out of the cockpit they can get their heads cut off.

Well built, with the flush of the outdoors on his cheeks and well-oiled spiked hair, he is ruggedly sensible and everyone's slightly boring friend. He's called Jonsey, Becko or Ian and he's engaged to a pert young thing from Berkshire. He studied at a red brick university, learned to fly with the RAF and has probably seen Prince William naked in the shower.

Characteristics

Reading Material: Biggles adventure books, The Times

Favourite TV Programmes and Films: Those Magnificent Men in Their Flying Machines, The Red Baron, Star Wars, Reach for the Sky, Apocalypse Now

Heroes and Role Models: Air Vice-Marshall James Edgar "Johnnie" Johnson, Douglas Bader

Most likely cause of death: Old age

Favourite Music: Wings, The Flying Pickets, often hums the Dambusters Theme

Political Views: Conservative

Ego Issues: Secretly gets a kick out of playing the hero

Fears: You would think he fears nothing, but he is always on high alert for possible mechanical failure

Likes: Helicopters, taking off and landing vertically, hovering, flying backwards and laterally

Dislikes: Antis, yobs, lefties

Earnings: £65k

Offspring: None

Drives: Sporty Audi

Most likely to say: "When I was at Cranwell"

Head Mistress

 77
 109
 12
 10

She was educated at a private girls boarding school and a female Oxbridge college and has taught in girls' schools all her life. Her emphasis on good diction and deportment may have fallen out of fashion, but she is one of a dying breed of private school teachers who believe that manners, good tailoring and a perfect *Boeuf en Croute* are all a girl needs to land the perfect husband. She will not be thrown off course by the fact that this ethos is yet to work out for her.

In spite of her every effort, she churns out reliably over-sexed girls who have no intention of bagging themselves a husband any time soon, unless he's someone else's. While she's busy getting them reciting Shakespeare and teaching them how to climb out of a Porsche without showing too much leg, they're sexting the school groundsman and stealing condoms from the village pharmacy.

Nonetheless, her twice-termly 'Champagne and Chat' sessions have proved sufficiently sophisticated to fool the Essex New Money/Footballers Wives' brigade who are the only ones who can still afford the thirty grand a year it costs to send their precious Paris, Victoria or Chlamydia to school there. She consoles herself with the idea that she is raising her girls out of the gutter; the Mother Teresa of Essex.

Characteristics

Reading Material: Intercepted letters home

Favourite TV Programmes and Films: Secret Diary of a Call Girl, anything with Colin Firth in it

Heroes and Role Models: Mother Teresa and her Latin teacher

Most likely cause of death: Osteoporosis from decades of dieting

Favourite Music: Luther Van Dross

Political Views: She believes a woman should leave that sort of thing to the men

Ego Issues: Struggles with being surrounded by mothers with fake tan who say things like, "Oh my days", or, "We did have a proper giggle, though"

Fears: That class really is dead

Likes: Champagne, a clean twin-set, school holidays

Dislikes: People who holiday in Marbella

Earnings: £75k

Offspring: None

Drives: VW Polo

Most likely to say: "Stop running, girls, do not run!"

Undiscovered Genius (Unemployed Musician)

This classically trained 3rd violinist is frustrated by never having made a living from classical music and feels (like the many brilliant composers before him) that the world does not appreciate his offering.

He spends his days dressed as a suitably wind-swept-and-interesting cliché, teaching musical theory at a dull concrete, suburban, technical college which he keenly refers to as a 'University' as do the students and the Government.

Despite being currently out of work as a paid musician, he uses his career choice for social elevation. He spends his evenings dressed in concert attire, to inspire work on his latest important contribution to the modern interpretation of the meaning of classical music, a 3 hour piece composed of the detailed arrangement of a violin concerto layered with the digitally sampled sounds omitted by a variety of modern home appliances.

He believes the work 'beautifully highlights the juxtaposition of the freedom brought about by the tools of classical music and the imprisonment of ones soul by domestic routine'.

He lives on his own somewhere in London and feels that it is the only place that offers him the culture that he knows he deserves. He dare not leave the city despite living in poverty, but takes comfort that at least he lives in area well known for its musical residents.

Characteristics

Reading Material: The more unfathomable the better - James Joyce , Jack Kerouac and Alan Ginsberg a bit too accessible

Favourite TV Programmes and Films: Doesn't own a TV, detests cinema, occasionally tunes in to obscure Radio 3 programs

Heroes and Role Models: John Cage and Brian Eno at a push - more impressed with himself to be honest

Most likely cause of death: Malnutrition

Favourite Music: Hair dryer - setting number three

Political Views: Extreme left verging on extreme right - potentially dangerous though too confused to do much about it

Ego Issues: Considers himself more intelligent than the people who do not like his music

Fears: Losing his hearing (already has tinnitus but assumes it a permanent wave of inspiration for his next masterpiece)

Likes: Being alone and misunderstood

Dislikes: Anything given the chance

Earnings: Low

Offspring: Not even considered it

Drives: Prefers to walk

Most likely to say: "No, Yes, it really is a remarkable piece"

Family Man

He's a well-raised middle class professional with a healthy respect for traditional family values. His parents worked hard to give him a public school education, and he grew up believing that hard work was the answer to everything. Sadly, this led him to a career in the Civil Service; no matter how hard he worked, the public school education he cherished was out of the question for his own children.

Deeply troubled by his children's barely adequate schooling at the local comprehensive, he has compensated with lots of healthy outdoor pursuits and educational family outings. He is proud that with a little persuasion, family cycling trips now cover more than ten miles and that his children have been exposed to theatre and the fine arts from an early age.

Unfortunately, no amount of mountain-biking across the Fells, or excursions to see the latest Rodin exhibition can combat the irresistible pull of an eight hour stretch playing Call of Duty which is all his sons actually want to be doing with their leisure time. His sense of disappointment is all the greater when he says, "Shakespeare" and they reply, "He's well gay".

Characteristics

Reading Material: Parenting manuals with titles such as How to Raise Boys, Why Boys Are Different, Siblings Without Rivalry

Favourite TV Programmes and Films: Question Time, Newsnight, South Bank Show

Heroes and Role Models: Steven Biddulph

Most likely cause of death: Old age

Favourite Music: Highbrow classical, Telemann, Janáček, Scriabin

Political Views: New Labour/Lib Dem

Ego Issues: Driven by deep-rooted sibling rivalry with his elder brother who went into Merchant Banking and who therefore can afford a top-notch education for his children

Fears: The yobs his sons go to school with

Likes: Seeing his sons cook dinner, read a book or play the piano without being asked

Dislikes: Battling to get his sons off the X-Box

Earnings: £35 – 45k a year

Offspring: Three sons, who talk like they've been raised in Tottenham, despite growing up in Leamington Spa

Drives: Nine-year-old Volvo estate

Most likely to say: "Please, turn that off!"

Head Boy

Mr Perfect Timmy Boy has a natural tidiness and has spent his entire school career with his top button done up and his tie knot pressing hard against his Adam's apple. Years of this mindless conformity has restricted blood flow to the higher brain but his brainstem is functional so he excels at sport and can perform basic duties such as breathing, blinking and sitting on the governing body every Wednesday afternoon behind the gym.

He is a bovine ambassador and public face of the school so he must be able to shake hands with visiting parents and inspectors without dribbling or swallowing his tongue, and once a year at Speech Day he is called upon to make a fawning State of the School Address of which the main focus is the performance of the rugby and cricket teams.

He probably dates the Head Girl (see page 367) in a souless parody of heterosexual coupling. His main function is maintaining school discipline, which he achieves, like all cynical oligarchies, by confiscating cigarettes and magazines and sharing them among the junta of prefects under his command. When he leaves school he will join the army or church or some other organisation that requires him to obey orders and be a repressive puppet of the state.

Characteristics

Reading Material: Porn mags confiscated from fourth formers

Favourite TV Programmes and Films: Sport

Heroes and Role Models: Ben Fogle, Ghandi and Gladstone

Most likely cause of death: Conformity

Favourite Music: Boring repetitive predictable music like The Killers, Leona Lewis

Political Views: Tory

Ego Issues: He thinks he is a natural leader, but he will never be an iconoclast, and will realise too late that his conventionality and lack of imagination are a hindrance in the real world so he'll grow a stupid goatee

Fears: Things can only go downhill from here so he doesn't want this perfect year to end, price of car insurance.

Likes: Debating Society, playing rugby, exemplifying good behaviour, leading by example, showing school spirit, serving on various committees, covering up bullying

Dislikes: School holidays, forming his own opinions, baseball cap wearing youths, people who eat with their mouth open, men who work in fairgrounds

Earnings: n/a

Offspring: n/a

Would like to drive but actually drives: Dad's car (passed at 17, first time, only had 7 lessons)

Most likely to say: "Past experiences have made me a better person today, blah blah blah . . ."

Barrister

Super cerebral Brummie with a huge ego who can argue that black is white. She works 12 hours a day, takes herself very seriously and is always right; she has had to be to fight the discrimination of her profession. On her first day of mini-pupillage in a stuffy London chambers she was told she only won a bar school scholarship because of her premium booty cleavage, but that doesn't explain how she took a double First from Oxford. On another occasion two senior male barristers took her to one side and suggested she change her name to Simon Heathcote-Forbes.

She left London after the birth of her first child and now works in one of the provincial superchambers where she practises family law and child protection. Her entry in Chambers UK says, "capacity for punching well above her weight, which is considerable". She is married to a policeman, votes Liberal Democrat and on a matter of principle she sends her three super bright kids to an inner-city comprehensive, where they have learned to smoke and try to avoid being robbed.

Characteristics

Reading Material: The Guardian, briefs, Law Society Gazette

Favourite TV Programmes and Films: There is no TV in the house (another reason the children get bullied); they are encouraged to practise a musical instrument instead

Heroes and Role Models: Lord Bingham, Martin Luther King

Most likely cause of death: Heart disease/stroke

Favourite Music: Earth, Wind & Fire, Gladys Knight and the Pips

Political Views: Liberal Democrat, but will vote Labour in the next election

Ego Issues: She has a natural empathy with the underdog and a passionate sense of justice

Fears: Present management of legal aid by the LSC, ever more statutory guidelines and interference from politicians on sentencing

Likes: The intellectual challenge; passionate supporter of the jury system

Dislikes: Cherie Blair, all-night preparation sessions and early-morning travel, thick policeman she encounters every day in her work

Earnings: £80k

Offspring: Three school age children

Drives: Black Audi TT

Most likely to say: "Objection"

BBC Correspondent

This super-high-flyer and all round top bloke risks his life on a daily basis to bring us the latest footage and as much gory detail as possible from the latest country that America has decided to bomb.

His parents were diplomats, so he spent his formative years in six different countries before being packed off to a top independent school in the UK. He read PPE at Oxford, where he twice coxed the Isis crew to victory. He speaks four languages, could have been an Olympic skier and spent several years in the Territorial Army. Insight, wit and analysis are his watchwords as well as the common touch and ability to explain complex issues to the average stupid viewer.

He is prepared to stick his neck out to badger a politician and many remember the famous episode of Panorama when he repeated the word "Bollocks" twenty-seven times in response to Tony Blair's assurances that "Hand on heart, I did what I thought was right".

Characteristics

Reading Material: Leaked documents and emails from politicians, all the newspapers, Reuters

Favourite TV Programmes and Films: Reuters, Sky News

Heroes and Role Models: Kate Adie

Most likely cause of death: Friendly fire while stationed with US troops in yet another Middle Eastern/North African conflict

Favourite Music: Dubstep

Political Views: He votes Tory but keeps his political views secret in the name of impartial reporting

Ego Issues: One of his elder siblings is a human rights lawyer; they are fiercely competitive.

Fears: Missing out on a big story, breaching BBC rules on accuracy and impartiality

Likes: Being famous and being recognised

Dislikes: Female news presenters tarting themselves up

Earnings: £80k

Offspring: Lives in Chiswick with his three children

Drives: Volvo Estate

Most likely to say: "I'll hand you back to the studio"

Wine Bore

Tedious twit who displays his premier cru cockitude every time he takes a sip of fermented grape juice. He furrows his brow, slurps and gargles and then proceeds to compare it to every other wine he's ever tasted. He has perfect recall about the typical weather patterns of the major wine regions, he bemoans the homogeneity of New World offerings and sneers at people who only buy merlot or chardonnay.

He always complains about the glasses in restaurants (he has been known to bring his own) and takes twenty minutes to study the wine list, smell the cork and interrogate the sommelier with rhetorical questions that begin with "Of course" designed only to show off his knowledge. Anything you've drunk he's had better and he will even insist on telling you what his wine tastes like while you're drinking it too.

The more expensive the wine the more he intellectualises the joy from what should be a sensual experience, clearing tables with his sermons on micro-oxygenation and Ban de Vendange. The baffling obsessiveness with which he puts away a glass of Petrus is on a par with David Beckham tidying his sock drawer.

Characteristics

Reading Material: Cataldo Uncorked: All You Really Need to Know About Wine To Be Pretentious As Well As Obnoxious and More, Pamela Vandyke Price, Daily Telegraph crossword

Favourite TV Programmes and Films: Nigella Swallows, The Delicious Miss Dahl, snotty art-films

Heroes and Role Models: Andrew Jefford, Frasier Crane, Pamela Vandyke Price, Robert Parker

Most likely cause of death: Old age

Favourite Music: Classical of course, and Philip Glass

Political Views: As well as wine he is also obsessive about the state of the property market, and can tell you the most desirable properties in his area, as this is the next best thing to being able to actually afford one: so, Tory

Ego Issues: He's part of the 'squeezed middle' but likes to think he's upper middle because he has a few ISAs and possesses the special knowledge required to enjoy wine

Fears: Falling house prices, declining living standards of middle earners, repeating the time he mistook a Mouton Cadet for a Grand Chateau d'armailhac three times its price

Likes: Supports uncapping of university tuition fees, market-based public sector reforms and all the other Tory policies that make him poorer

Dislikes: Ed Miliband, chardonnay, his final salary pension under threat

Earnings: £42K

Offspring: Two

Drives: Very old XJS V12 he can't afford to run

Most likely to say: "Mmmmmng, an impudently sacchariferous little Trockenbeerenauslese."

Vet (Male)

85

140

5

3

75

The male vet is taller and smarter than a doctor, and as a breed more popular and sociable. (There are far more socially inept doctors than vets, because you can get away with being an idiot in the NHS, but vets have to work with farmers, who can smell inauthenticity a mile off.)

He's quite the ladies man, despite his young Jeremy Clarkson hair and body frame and the fact that he spends most of his time up to his elbows in a cow's back bits (he keeps his Tattersall shirt sleeves rolled up just in case he's called on to rescue a breached calf at short notice) but he's off limits because he will already have married a pretty, slim, middle class girl who has his dinner on the table every evening and plops out children biennially.

He is never judgmental but his slight inscrutability can make pet owners feel a bit paranoid and judged. He won't answer a question directly, and uses it as an opportunity to glean more information. "Is my dog too fat?" would meet the tactful reply "Well, hmmm he's quite a chunky fella. How often do you exercise him?" Cue intangible feelings of incompetence and intellectual inferiority. You feel sure he's on the phone to the RSPCA as soon as you've left his consulting room, although when the receptionist prints out your bill you reflect that he's probably just ordering another Breitling.

Characteristics

Reading Material: Veterinary Times, The New Statesman, Guardian or Independent, literary fiction, Malcolm Gladwell

Favourite TV Programmes and Films: Radio 4, Human Planet, eclectic range of films from Synecdoche, New York to Adam Sandler, but mainly the latter

Heroes and Role Models: James Herriot, Cesar Millan, Jeremy Clarkson

Most likely cause of death: Old age or trampled by cattle

Favourite Music: Norah Jones, James Blunt

Political Views: Conservative

Ego Issues: He has high self esteem, gained from his work and intellectual achievements, but sometimes wakes up in the middle of the night in a cold sweat worrying he should have chosen brain surgery as his contribution to society rather than saving the lives of hamsters

Fears: Defra funding cuts, BSE, bird flu

Likes: Spaying and periodontal disease which pays the bills

Dislikes: Aggressive dogs with pushover owners, breeders, grieving clients, PETA, hamsters

Earnings: £80K

Offspring: Four children and a menagerie of dogs, cats, poultry and other feathered and furry friends

Drives: Subaru Forester

Most likely to say: "How often do you walk him?"

Tory Politician

Stupid shiny-cheeked ex-public schoolboy, or clever shiny-cheeked ex-comprehensive schoolboy who ought to know better. He was an active member of Conservative Future, joined the Tory party aged sixteen and campaigned even though he was too young to vote.

In his short career he has twice managed to get in The Mirror for making crass remarks like Italians are all wops, or that homosexuals ought to see a psychiatrist. He loudly espouses family values and silencing the press so they can't report his extra-marital affairs. He looks back to a fictional golden age when immigration controls, competitive individual enterprise, personal responsibility and drip-down wealth made us all happy and productive and there was no sex before marriage. He supports the war on drugs but snorts meow meow in his hotel room at the Party Conference. The only drug-taking he wants to stamp out takes place on squalid council estates with stairwells that wreak of urine. Pretends to believe in God and that problems like education, housing and health can be solved by making efficiency savings.

Characteristics

Reading Material: Daily Telegraph, Daily Mail, New Statesman, Spanking Bi-Weekly

Favourite TV Programmes and Films: The Today Programme, The Archers, Last of the Summer Wine, Yes Minister

Heroes and Role Models: His father, Margaret Thatcher, George Osborne

Most likely cause of death: Something posh

Favourite Music: Predictable classical like Bach, Mozart, Beethoven & bland MOR stadium bands like Dire Straits, Coldplay, U2

Political Views: Rolling back the state, family values, Big Society, strong law & order, swingeing cuts in public services, blah blah blah

Ego Issues: Judges himself and others on wealth and social niceties

Fears: People who shop at Asda, people with tattoos, poverty – not in others, just the shocking thought of himself being poor

Likes: The Westminster bubble, rolling back the state, family values, public service, strong law & order, Waitrose

Dislikes: Political correctness, David Cameron, homosexuals, women MPs

Earnings: £65k + £200k expenses, even under the new system + £200k other business interests

Offspring: Two young children he will one day exploit for political gain by feeding them BSE-ridden beefburgers, or get to stand next to him outside his house while he apologises to the Press over an adulterous affair

Drives: Jaguar

Most likely to say: "I am a man of the people. Vox populi, vox dei."

Motto: "I'm alright Jack"

Conceptual Artist

75

This post-structuralist pillock claims the ideas contained within his "installations" – plus the hours of chin stroking prior to paying someone else to flick some paint at a canvas or brush gold leaf onto his stools – are more important than traditional aesthetic considerations, like having any talent. Late in his career he will finally exhibit some works he actually painted himself, but since they will lack the imagination and technique of a first-year art student they will get unanimously slated by the press.

All he does is sit and question the nature of art instead of creating some and before he became rich and famous he even managed to get an Arts Council Grant to disappear up his own arse. He is a firm believer in getting everyone else to do all the work, so once his assistants have nailed some self-indulgent craft-less tat to a wall, it's the viewer's job to scrape some meaning from it or demand a refund.

In what other arena could you get away with this pretentious rubbish? A bricklayer doesn't spend all day deconstructing houses and when a scaffolder whistles at someone's tits you can be sure he isn't pondering the observer-observed pair within a context of viewing and the nature of duality, so why do we tolerate this nonsense at Tate Modern and the ICA?

Characteristics

Reading Material: Roland Barthes, pretentious art blogs, Strangeland, biological supply company catalogues, The Guardian

Favourite TV Programmes and Films: He will tell you he doesn't watch TV

Heroes and Role Models: Georg Baselitz, Joseph Beuys, Carl Andre

Most likely cause of death: Drowned while attempting to float a shed down the Rhine

Favourite Music: Whatever he thinks sounds suitably arty, depending on who is asking

Political Views: The Arts are underfunded

Ego Issues: Can't deal with the lack of fame and is consumed with being recognised as an artist

Fears: Death, Billy Childish and Charles Thomson, clowns, being egged by Stuckists dressed as clowns outside Tate Modern

Likes: Money and recognition

Dislikes: Tracy Emin, Damien Hirst, Prince Charles

Earnings: £600k

Offspring: None, thankfully

Drives: Volvo P1800 or VW Karmen Ghia

Most likely to say: "It's not about money or recognition"

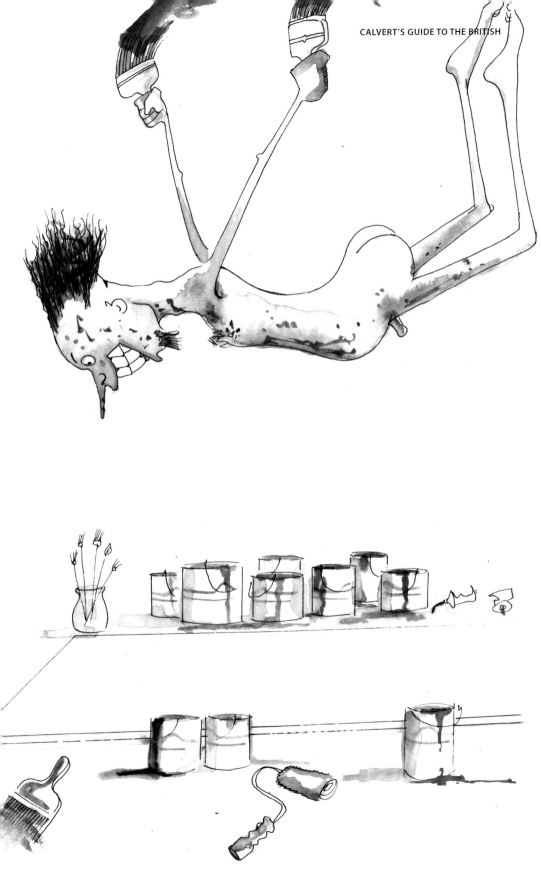

Farmer (Wealthy)

Rich red-faced porker who has inherited his mother's chins and his father's breasts along with 4,000 acres of prime farmland. He can trace his ancestry back to the Doomsday book and one of his ancestors was advisor to Elizabeth I. His family has eaten gargantuan quantities of meat over centuries and has clearly prioritised breeding themselves for sheer size rather than looks because he is six foot eight. His Amazonian wife is posher than Kirstie Allsopp and their grown up children are all so tall and barrel chested they look like they've swallowed a fleet of Landrovers.

They own several black Labradors, but they couldn't tell you precisely how many. Being a super rich farmer with lots of land he is jolly pleased to also receive the lion's share of CAP grants from the EU. He bores women to tears in the local pub before copping a feel and then gives them free meat to keep quiet. He likes to whinge about the weather and forecast food shortages and higher prices in the shops while in the same season your allotment has managed to produce enough tomatoes and runner beans to feed the world.

Characteristics

Reading Material: Farmers Guardian, John Deere catalogue, Dick Francis

Favourite TV Programmes and Films: Farming Today, The Archers, South Riding

Heroes and Role Models: Duke of Westminster

Most likely cause of death: Tractor rollover, heart attack

Favourite Music: Classical if asked, but prefers Elton John, Queen

Political Views: Tory

Ego Issues: He sings loudly in the shower; if he wasn't so busy counting his guns he fancies he might have a career as an opera singer

Fears: Having to split income from Saxon hoards discovered on his land with metal detectorists

Likes: Meat, money, social climbing

Dislikes: farmsubsidy.org, metal detectorists

Earnings: £400k

Offspring: Four grown up children who are politicians or vetox.

Drives: Landrovers

Most likely to say: "They should be made to buy bloody British"

Oxbridge Boy

Most Oxbridge boys aren't stinking rich, but many of them try to emulate the lifestyle that they saw on Brideshead Revisited, and almost bankrupt their parents in the process before graduating with a third. Before his transformation into a punting half-wit, Oxbridge boy was a hard-working and conscientious comprehensive kid who was always top of the class but lacking in social development. In short, he was a swotty lower middle class soft lad.

Once he got to uni he quickly realised that he was surrounded by effortlessly brilliant minds and decided that it was futile to try to compete intellectually. Where the normal teen strategy of wooing a girlfriend consists of getting drunk and doing burn-outs in a Peugeot 106. In Oxbridge this translates to dressing in a stripey blazer and using a long wooden pole to propel a flat-bottomed boat along the Cam or the Cherwell and mooring under the shade of a convenient willow tree for a nervous snog and a glass of champagne.

Characteristics

Reading Material: Wikipedia, YouTube, Facebook, Project Gutenberg, HowStuffWorks, How to Chat-Up Posh Totty

Favourite TV Programmes and Films: TV is for losers with no life; by third year he'll stay in more and more watching TV

Heroes and Role Models: Boris Johnson, an accomplished alumnus who you won't have heard of

Most likely cause of death: Leptospirosis, diving off the punt

Favourite Music: Now's the time to ponce about with some classical music – that should impress the girls

Political Views: Green

Ego Issues: He feels intellectually inferior to everyone at his Uni and superior to everyone not at his uni

Fears: Climate change, debt, tuition fees, bridge-hopping, not getting laid

Likes: Lazy summer days, champagne picnics, Pimm's

Dislikes: Losing the pole, low bridges and branches, soggy feet

Earnings: Minus £9,000

Offspring: None

Drives: Bike

Most likely to say: "Shall we eat our sandwiches now?"

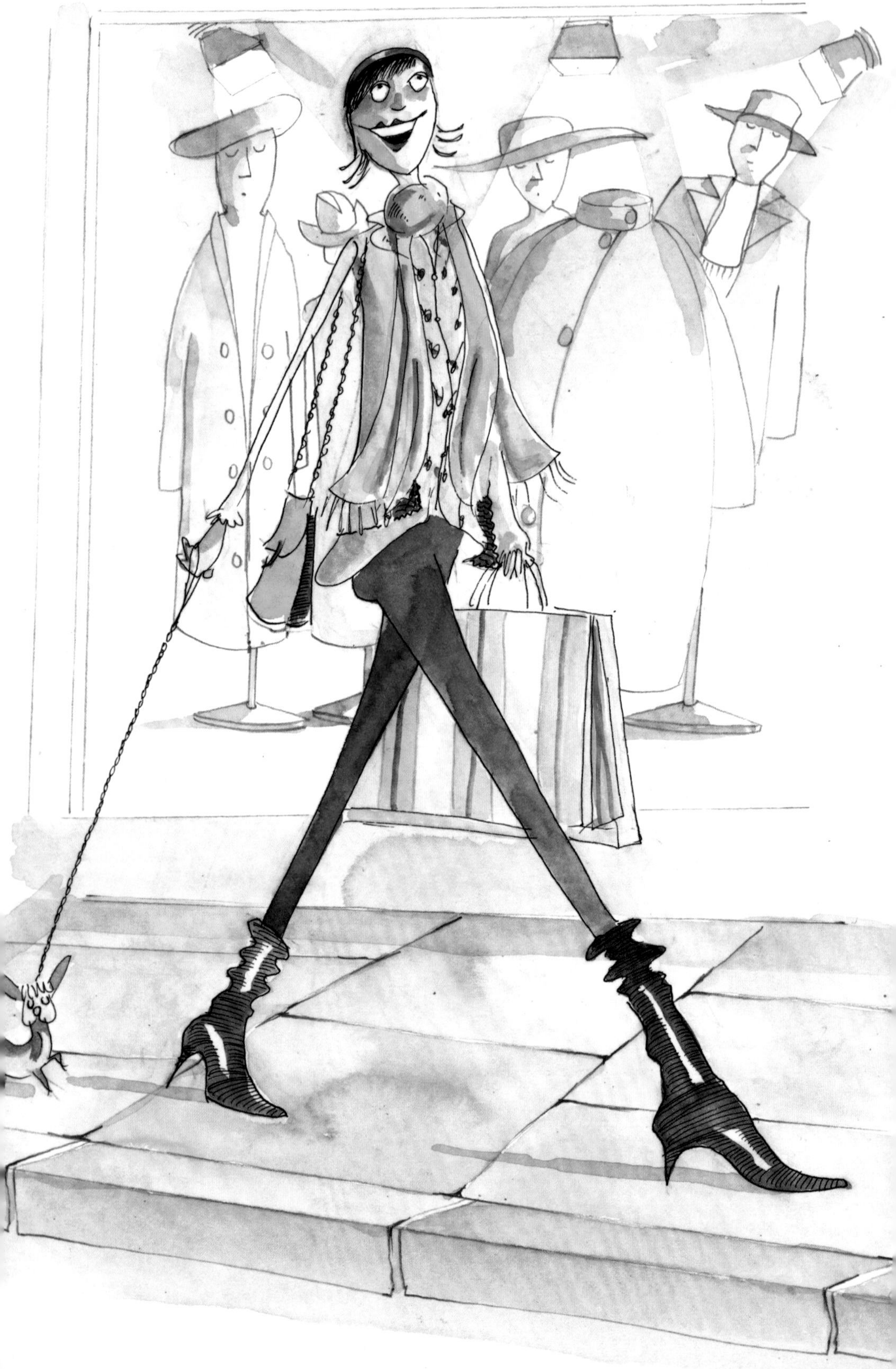

Celebutante

Witlessly shallow and always female (on the rare occasion that rich men break the pattern of siring yet another daughter, the male ones never seem to attract much media attention), the Celebutante is a spoiled attention-seeking twenty-something billionaire heiress. She lives in a £50 million seven floor house in Chelsea which she claims her father only bought because it has a large garden for her twelve dogs, although she always carries five of them around in her handbag and the rest of her collection of Chihuahuas, Shih Tzus, Pomerarians, Papillons and Pugs could easily fit into a brick-weighted sack. She claims she's not spoiled because she only has two walk-in wardrobes.

She has dabbled in just about everything from writing and acting to modelling and fashion design, and has displayed no discernible talents apart from tweeting, snorting cocaine, collecting traffic violations, making sex tapes and being photographed falling out of limos without any knickers.

Characteristics

Reading Material: She is proud to admit that she has never read an entire book

Favourite TV Programmes and Films: She doesn't watch TV, she's on it

Heroes and Role Models: Her mother (an alcoholic ex-fashion model), any heiress with more money than her or Victoria Silvstedt

Most likely cause of death: Attention seeking behavior

Favourite Music: Whatever is playing at Tramp or Annabels

Political Views: Poor people choose to be poor because they have no vision or imagination

Ego Issues: She can't understand why people don't like her and don't take her seriously

Fears: Kate Moss, Naomi Campbell, losing her nasal septum, being kidnapped, never being able to make her parents proud

Likes: Cocaine, Manolo Blahniks, Hermès Birkin bags, dating chubby Chelsea playboys with Lamborghinis, champagne wars in swanky nightclubs

Dislikes: The hangover she wakes to every morning, her older sister

Earnings: Has done some modelling and has published an autobiography, netting her more than most people earn in a lifetime

Offspring: Far too busy

Drives: Mercedes G Wagon, Red Ferrari

Most likely to say: "It isn't easy being me"

Investment Banker

Louche well-educated wunderkind who knew he was "going into finance" ever since his premature baldness started at puberty. This venal twenty-something deals in wealth management (more commonly known as toxic futures) and brays loudly over champagne brunch about the unfairness of back-end loaded bonuses since the global financial crisis, which couldn't have been his fault because he was on a yacht snorting coke off a Singaporean hooker's back at the time.

When he isn't on the phone to Turnbull and Asser barking an order for another dozen contrast-collared shirts, or firing off emails to his chums about his sexual conquests, he drunkenly jiggles numbers on a computer that don't really exist. A solid platinum Swiss watch pokes brazenly from his cuff as a constant reminder to everyone how much bigger it is than his wrist. He lives in a loft-style shag-pad in a converted factory in the East End surrounded by strangers who hate him. He affects a conspicuously fake posh accent and enjoys reading the FT and then peering into the middle distance like an alopecic underwear model with a James Dean squint.

He doesn't really understand what he's doing but fortunately for him his superiors know even less and so long as his greedy bungling continues to marginally out-perform a monkey pooing on a stock-chart, they can justify his earnings to the shareholders.

Characteristics

Reading Material: Pretends to read the FT but just carries it around. Actually looks at the adverts in FHM and GQ

Favourite TV Programmes and Films: His long irregular hours leave little time for TV, but he regularly, A sneaky free preview on pornography channels

Heroes and Role Models: Dick Fuld, Bernie Madoff, Vlad the Impaler

Most likely cause of death: Greed

Favourite Music: Bland MOR stadium bands like Dire Straits, Coldplay, U2

Political Views: He's dimly aware that understanding politics would allow him to make better investment decisions, but he prefers to occupy his mind with more immediate concerns

Ego Issues: Sneers at people with less money than him and hates being sneered at by people with more money than him

Fears: World economic meltdown, bank regulation, margin calls, being asked to explain a complicated derivative instrument

Likes: High-octane champagne quoffing

Dislikes: Minus signs, the colour red, other bankers

Earnings: £200k bonus

Offspring: Two

Drives: Black or silver Audi , BMW or Porsche

Most likely to say: "F****g get in! It's not about the money, it's the exit opps"

Rugby Union Lad

Professional Rugby Union players are bred in public schools. They will have shown a talent from an early age and have had their skills nurtured by over attentive school masters hell bent on producing an 'international'. They will have captained their school, played for their county and looked 30 at the age of 17. Professional Rugby will offer them a measly salary for the first 10 years of their working lives but then they will have to fall back on their public school accent and manners to secure a well paid job in Sales. Most will have slept with a high number of pretty young things before marrying one and turning out the next generation of rugby internationals. In most cases their children will not reach the potential of their father and unfortunately their offspring will never overcome a feeling of guilt and inadequacy bought about by Daddy's ambition for them to walk in his shoes/boots.

Characteristics

Reading Material: Ian McEwan, great sporting biographies, The Times

Favourite TV Programmes and Films: Michael McIntyre, Armstrong & Miller, Mock the Week, Have I Got News For You, Live at the Apollo

Heroes and Role Models: Rory Underwood, Andy Irvine, Barry John, JPR Williams, Willie John McBride

Most likely cause of death: Old age

Favourite Music: Tom Jones, The Sterophonics, Tina Turner, Coldplay

Political Views: Tory

Ego Issues: Worries that he is perceived as arrogant

Fears: Being injured out of the Championship, life after rugby, Charlotte Church

Likes: Winning, communal showers, celebrating, singing, curry, lager, being arrogant

Dislikes: Losing, being teased

Earnings: £70 - £200k

Offspring: Of course, nothing blank about his little swimmers

Drives: Whatever the sponsors offer

Most likely to say: "What are you girls drinking?"

Dysfunctional Daughter

Her father is a brilliant astro-physicist and her mother a Nobel laureate in genetics. Their decision to mate was based entirely in the interests of humanity rather than any purely socio-anthropological desire to celebrate their union.

Despite her superior genetic inheritance and the atmosphere of intellectual excess within which she has been raised, she is a ceaseless disappointment to her progenitors. Her six-figure education, exposure to a cross-section of Russian chess masters and cello prodigies from the earliest age have amounted to nothing.

She demonstrates neither flare nor enthusiasm for pure maths, quantum physics or molecular biology. Even if she had, she lacks the bone structure or the sense of style which her parents know would help compensate for intellect and enable her to secure a mate through the conventional release of pheromones.

She is socially inept, has shown no interest in socialising with any of her contemporaries. She spends her days skulking around the house between the piano and her bedroom.

Characteristics

Reading Material: Nineteenth century gothic novels

Favourite TV Programmes and Films: Lorenzo's Oil, Dead Man Walking, Flatliners, In Cold Blood, Girl, Interrupted

Heroes and Role Models: Mary Shelley

Most likely cause of death: Found dead in old age half-eaten by her cats

Favourite Music: Discordant obscure classical

Political Views: Right wing

Ego Issues: She believes herself without worth and thinks causing damage to herself, or others, is the only way she will ever persuade her parents to value her.

Fears: Disappointing her parents

Likes: Very little

Dislikes: Family holidays, girls who wear pink, smiling

Earnings: None

Offspring: None

Drives: Too young to have a licence

Most likely to say: Nothing

Head Girl

The Head Girl is more academic than her male counterpart, but she is still a perfect conformist called Lucinda or Olivia, with exemplary attendance, behaviour and appearance. She has been selected as much for her looks as her achievements, but looks that a middle-aged head teacher hopes will appeal to parents, not her contemporaries. She is proud to be a responsible representative of her school and she aims to develop her organisation and communication skills and is excited to face any challenges that may present themselves during her tenure. She could bore a hole in your face with an endless stock of these shrill platitudes.

She wants to go to Cambridge University and she may even pass the entrance exam but at interview she will fail to distinguish herself from all the other hopefuls by spouting what she thinks the tutors want to hear, rather than having interesting opinions of her own. (She admits to liking Coldplay, for God's sake). She may scrape into Nottingham Uni if she's lucky, where she will study modern languages and enjoy a brief spell as a female sailor. She will eventually join the BBC, where after fifteen years of social climbing and bullying she will become Head of Regional & Local Programmes and marry a sensible silver-haired chap called Tim.

Characteristics

Reading Material: Jane Austen, Emily Bronte, Charlotte Bronte, Stephenie Meyer

Favourite TV Programmes and Films: True Blood, One Tree Hill, Glee, The OC, The Vampire Diaries, Waterloo Road, Scrubs

Heroes and Role Models: Ellen MacArthur, Dame Kiri Te Kanawa, Jane Austin, her dad

Most likely cause of death: Old age

Favourite Music: Rihanna, Jessie J, Lady Gaga, Adele, Bruno Mars, Coldplay

Political Views: If she goes to a public school she will vote Tory when she turns 18, if she goes to a comprehensive she won't know enough about politics and will probably copy her parents

Ego Issues: She feels pressure to be perfect and sometimes she makes herself sick after meals

Fears: Global warming, tuition fees

Likes: Hiking, debating society, Edward Cullen, giving people more human rights

Dislikes: Injustice, poverty, famine, global warming

Earnings: £130k after 18 years of being underpaid

Offspring: No children. Career comes first and her husband had the snip in his twenties

Drives: VW - something funded by her parents

Most likely to say: "Yup. I can't wait to go skiing again"

Top Surgeon

Surgeons are the fighter pilots of the medical profession. Medicine has a healthy share of the world's egomaniacs but he is best of the best. He needs to have unshakeable self-belief to shoulder immense responsibility while relying on a team of OR staff to support him (he can't even scratch an itch or adjust his face mask himself) but when things go wrong he's the one who has to pass the blame.

He cuts people apart and puts them back together for a living, which would give anyone a God complex. He's arrogant, decisive, organised, practical, very driven and still predominantly male. All ambitious workaholics in performance-driven fields share these traits, especially those who have seen their contemporaries become rich corporate lawyers and bankers, while they are still training. He has a slim wife and can hold his bladder for eight hours.

He values self-sufficiency, discipline and motivation above people skills, so he is either a poor communicator or has a carefully cultivated detachment. This doesn't really matter since if the anaesthetist is any good the vast majority of his patients will be unconscious when the surgeon gets up close and personal with the scalpel.

Characteristics

Reading Material: Historical mysteries, Robert Ludlum, The Times, The Lancet

Favourite TV Programmes and Films: Likes to get in touch with his artistic side by watching the Time Team and BBC4 documentaries about Tolstoy and biblical archaeology

Heroes and Role Models: Hillary, Scott, Shackleton

Most likely cause of death: Immortal

Favourite Music: Likes to work to Bob Marley

Political Views: Old school Conservative

Ego Issues: Arrogant, self-assured and self-reliant

Fears: He doesn't have as good a second home as his Oxbridge peers who went into corporate law or finance

Likes: A run before breakfast, a hearty dinner, something interesting on the operating table

Dislikes: ER doctors, anaesthesiologists, radiologists; inappropriate consult requests from ER, missing lunch, appendectomies, tonsillectomies, fat people

Earnings: £200k+

Offspring: Two daughters with three-syllable Christian names and a pony each

Drives: Porsche or Aston Martin

Most likely to say: "Swab"

CHOLMONDELY-SMYTHE

S COLLEGE CAM

University Challenge Boffin

These mild-mannered British eccentrics live in a serene pencil-necked world of their own completely untarnished by modern influences. Despite shopping at the same high street outlets as the rest of us their enduring ability to combine dark lilac shirts with geo patterned knitwear shows astonishing resilience in the face of twenty-first century popular culture.

Hair also plays a key role in their boffin time bubble, with Jeffrey Dahmer side partings for the boys, wiry fringes for the girls and David Mellor glasses for both. Their fact retention inspires awe and pity in equal measure. The arrogant self-pretentious exasperation when they answer incorrectly is a bit creepy, but their nervous glee at a mispronunciation of a 17th century scientist is quite endearing and reveals a need for urgent remedial dental work.

They are the only students in the country with positive bank balances and carefully reconciled statements. They don't smoke and are virtually teetotal. When they do drink they go very red, get scared and go home early vowing never to do it again. They are one of the last branches of British human with any chance of saving sexual intercourse for marriage. They are likely to have only a couple of intimate partners in their lives and one of those may be a cuddly toy.

Characteristics

Reading Material: Everything

Favourite TV Programmes and Films: Wasn't allowed a TV growing up but listened to lots of Radio 4 and World Service

Heroes and Role Models: Gail Trimble, Alex Guttenplan, Magnus LaDue

Most likely cause of death: Old age

Favourite Music: Bach, Chopin's "Double Thirds" Etude, Scriabin

Political Views: Tory

Ego Issues: Desperately concerned that they should never give an incorrect answer

Fears: Being wrong, drunk girls

Likes: Does lots of things for fun like maths programmes on the computer and manipulating prime numbers.

Dislikes: Making eye contact, cuddling (toys are OK), fractals

Earnings: 0.1% interest on student bank account

Offspring: Carefully planned for the future

Most likely to say: "I can't I'm afraid, I'll be in the library"

Accountant (Senior Partner)

The Accountant occupies both extremes of the Body Mass Index: lean and grey when young, he quickly succumbs to pink-faced obesity caused by rich food and too many hours spent wearing brogues and a stripey shirt.

Emotionally stable and reactionary to the point of autism, the only things that make him raise a sweat are his first, second and third heart attacks, which he likes to get under his Gant classic leather belt before turning fifty. When he isn't commuting First Class or fantasizing about his homely secretary, he enjoys a wide range of non-thrill-seeking hobbies – mowing the lawn, collecting Rugby Union memorabilia and memorising the Michelin Guide (to bore blue chip clients with opinions about meals he hasn't eaten).

A family man, he is an extremely conscientious though often absent parent, even when home. He appreciates single malt whisky, pretends to like real ale and looks forward to his twice-monthly bout of efficiently plodding sex with a socially climbing wife chosen for her competence at making jam and small talk but primarily to reduce his capital gains liability.

Characteristics

Reading Material: Financial Times, Michelin Guide, Ernest Hemingway, Simon Singh, Robert Ludlum

Favourite TV Programmes and Films: Top Gear, Masterchef, My Family, The Shawshank Redemption

Heroes and Role Models: John Harvey Jones, Gordon Ramsay, Andy Dufresne

Most likely cause of death: Gout

Favourite Music: Piano Concertos, Last Night of the Proms CD, and some 'pop' music, probably Cream, Dire Straits, or Katie Melua

Political Views: Creative types are dangerous subversives, poor people are stupid and lazy, Thatcher was right all along, anyone who doesn't own a Stilton spoon isn't worth the effort

Ego Issues: Overcompensates for social awkwardness and a life spent adding up numbers in accordance with Generally Accepted Accounting Principles by standing too close to other people, making clumsy jokes and holding eye contact a tad too long.

Fears: The Russians, burgeoning debt crises, attractive self-actualized women

Likes: The Cricket, Tasmin Little

Dislikes: Accountancy, investment bankers and lawyers (jealousy), queues, queers and the French

Earnings: £80-£200k

Offspring: Fergus (ginger) and Candice (chubby freckly bulimic), both at a boring campus university (usually Loughborough), excruciatingly dull but destined for financial security and cheery marriages to people with glasses and split ends who enjoy rambling

Drives: Grey or dark blue 7 series BMW

Most likely to say: "Get the man a whisky, dear, there's a good girl"

Antique Dealer (Old School)

79

129

4

8

12

The old school antique dealer (not the ones with an orange tan or the charlatans who sell junk on the Portobello Road – see page 284) is your pukka aesthete and as close as someone can be to a Buddhist without actually being one. He is a lover of beauty, rarity, functionality and uniqueness, and during his forty years of honest dealing he has seen prices go up and down as fashions change so he knows that time makes fools of us all. His brusqueness when faced by a customer who thinks he is being ripped off, masks a deep sadness that his values have fallen out of fashion as eBay and greedy little worms who want to get rich quick have turned his passion into a sleazy game.

Margins have always been small but recently his two biggest overheads, shop rental and petrol have doubled so he will soon be out of business. He has a sharp eye and a core of real knowledge. He is in it for the long haul not a fast buck and he is humble enough to acknowledge that he is still learning. In the future when popular culture has grown weary of the quick and easy profit mentality of TVs appalling antiques programmes, we will realise too late that knowledge and trust are priceless, but by then his skills and expertise will be long dead.

Characteristics

Reading Material: Daily Telegraph, reference books on antiques

Favourite TV Programmes and Films: Inspector Morse, Cricket

Heroes and Role Models: Walter Scott, Winston Churchill, Robert Adam, Thomas Chippendale, René Lalique

Most likely cause of death: Stroke

Favourite Music: Beethoven, Haydn, Schumann

Political Views: Centre-right Tory

Ego Issues: Is so keen not to be pigeon-holed with the likes of David Dickinson that he misses out on fulfilling his potential

Fears: Moving big mirrors, creepy ceramic dolls

Likes: Patina, true collectors, finding wonderful things, the buzz of doing the research

Dislikes: Dealers calling junk designed in the fifties and seventies 'antique'; Antiques Roadshow, Cash in the Attic, Lovejoy, repairs and restorations, David Dickinson

Earnings: £25k

Offspring: Two grown up children who have well paid creative jobs outside of antiques

Would like to drive but actually drives: Rover 75

Most likely to say: "Where did you get this?"

County Set

Retirement has meant that they can finally settle full-time into what was once the family's weekend home in the country, with their three Labradors and their freshly waxed Barbours. They fill their days with pretty bone china, jam making and a spot of gardening and attend the occasional course at the village hall on bread-making or genealogy. Their wardrobe is a mixed assortment of baggy tweed, crisp cotton shirts and dusty evening wear.

Their lives are ordered and sedate, their Land Rovers smell of wet dog, they own a sturdy pair of walking boots and their heads are always covered in appropriate head gear. They are probably on the Church Flower Rota, and say things like, "Just off for my constitutional" and, "Shan't be a tick".

They display their upper middle class proclivities with pro-hunting car stickers, but in truth don't really participate. Likewise, they have cellars and garages full of fly-fishing gear, but it's been a long while now since any of it has seen the light of day.

Their children are all appropriately successful so that they can boast over supper in their drawling-yet-also-clipped English about their son's latest career triumph, or his new holiday property in Gstaad.

Characteristics

Reading Material: The Times, Country Life, Tatler, Margaret Fraser, C.S Forester, Margaret Atwood, Antonia Fraser

Favourite TV Programmes and Films: Inspector Morse, Midsomer Murders, Woman's Hour, Book of the Week, Desert Island Discs

Heroes and Role Models: The Duke of Edinburgh, Joan Bakewell, The Queen Mother

Most likely cause of death: Old age

Favourite Music: Music doesn't feature in their lives any more, but occasionally you will hear them humming a bit of Vera Lyn or Glenn Miller

Political Views: Conservatism, though they don't believe the country will ever be the same without Mrs Thatcher

Ego Issues: Upper middle class to a fault, will take a long route if it means avoiding the more unsightly rural towns in the County

Fears: The group of travellers who are camping horribly close to the village outskirts

Likes: Home-made marmalade, their gravel drive, a well-clipped box

Dislikes: Townsfolk, regional accents, unpruned roses, poverty

Earnings: Very comfortable pension and a property in the city/Scotland/the Lakes

Offspring: Three, all something big in the law, medicine or the UN

Drives: Anything Landrover

Most likely to say: "Toodle-pip", "Jolly good" or "Cheerio"

Huntsman

Six generations of his family have hunted this corner of East Sussex, each of them initiated into the hunt as a young boy with the blood of the kill smeared on their faces. It's character building, an institution, a birthright. And now it's illegal.

He's been haughty and aloof all his life, and for the last twenty-odd years has added a sizeable dose of anger into the mix. Animal rights activists have been top of his hate list for some years now, and over a large brandy with friends, he often boasts of the time he beat a protestor into Intensive Care with his riding whip.

After the ban, his run-ins with the anti-hunting lobby intensified as they camped out in woodlands collecting video evidence of his hunt's flagrant disregard of the law. He retaliated by having the lead protestor's photograph posted in every village shop and pub in the area. It makes him feel warm inside to know that he has defended his birthright so successfully.

Since the ban he has turned to man-hunting, setting the hounds on the trail of an athletic bunch of willing locals. The lack of slashing and daubing makes it entirely unsatisfactory, however, and he's working on a plan to chase the local activists. He's been collecting fabric scraps to lay the scent for a while now and knows it's only a matter of time.

Characteristics

Reading Material: Horse and Hound, the Telegraph

Favourite TV Programmes and Films: Radio Four, Countryfile, BBC News

Heroes and Role Models: Duke of Edinburgh, Harvey Smith

Most likely cause of death: Horse

Favourite Music: Foxhunting horn calls, anything else is pointless clatter

Political Views: Tory, although he thinks his grandfather was probably right to mourn the demise of the Whigs

Ego Issues: Still worries that people think he is not as competent as his predecessor

Fears: English Heritage, outgrowing his ability to keep a mistress, being charged with criminal assault for whipping a protestor and forced to undertake two hundred hours community service with inner city teenagers

Likes: Dogs, horses, pretending hunting brings people from all walks of life together, killing foxes, shooting badgers, drowning kittens, pest control

Dislikes: Foxes, hunt saboteurs, hippies, Burns Inquiry, League Against Cruel Sports

Earnings: Unknown

Offspring: Three sons and a daughter, all aristocratically born in the saddle

Drives: A big horse or a big horse box

Most likely to say: "Tally Ho"

Huntswoman

Born into privilege and married into even more, life has been one long round of doing what is expected of one and learning to like it. Some of those duties have proved difficult to grow fond of: marriage and motherhood, for example. Others, like charity work and entertaining have on occasion provided a small degree of personal satisfaction. And smiling throughout it all has become second nature to her.

But in the hunt, she has found her outlet. The 'hunting pink' riding jackets and prized mares, the terriermen and houndsmen, the horn blowers and the crystal champagne flutes: she is set apart, raised up and in her element. From up there she can look even further down her nose at the tatty locals with their lost consonants and scruffy children. And once the hounds find the scent and the hunt is on, with the wind in her hairnet and the horse-power between her thighs, something ancient and primordial is unleashed.

These days, of course, that ghastly New Labour lot put an end to real hunting. Instead she indulges in the local 'Man-Hunt'. She finds something very Lawerentian about a woman of her breeding chasing an athletic young man from the local village through the countryside, sweat dripping from his forelock and hounds following the scent of his testosterone. Entirely satisfactory.

Characteristics

Reading Material: D H Lawrence, Jilly Cooper, The Lady, Black Lace

Favourite TV Programmes and Films: The Queen, Brideshead Revisted, Desert Island Discs, Miss Marple Mysteries, Secret Diaries of a Call Girl

Heroes and Role Models: Boudicca, Agatha Christie, Angela Rippon

Most likely cause of death: Alzheimer's

Favourite Music: Wagner, Classic FM

Political Views: She votes Tory every election, but with the exception of her vehement opposition to the 2004 Hunting Act, she generally leaves politics to the men

Ego Issues: Her social superiority is a given; specifically, her bouillabaisse and tarte tatin are unparalleled, as far she's concerned.

Fears: Public toilets, public transport, public address systems, the public

Likes: Henley Regatta, a good cup of tea from Mother's bone china tea set, gentlemen's relish, Country Life

Dislikes: The anti-hunt lobby, vegetarians, common behaviour

Earnings: She has no idea

Offspring: Two daughters

Drives: C Class Mercedes

Most likely to say: "Good heavans, how ghastly"

Old School Boss

The CBI would like you to believe that the Old School Boss is an extinct dinosaur but there are still plenty of his type in the Civil Service, BBC, local government, sports governing bodies like FIFA and the ECB, and the investment banking sector. He's the old fashioned dopey conservative sitcom boss who still wears a tie, takes long lunches, drinks whisky in the morning and would never been seen dead eating sushi or having his chest hair removed to raise money for Comic Relief.

In the old days his conservatism ensured that his organisation enjoyed either stagnation or steady slow growth, but now he's a barrier to much needed modernisation, or so clueless about the complex financial products the young whizz kids beneath him are cooking up that he exposes the entire company to risky strategies that few understand, least of all him.

He still enjoys his golf and business trips abroad. Whenever he's in Germany he visits his usual S&M dungeon for a good spanking. When a Sunday newspaper breaches his privacy he will criticise the media for embarrassing his wife rather than taking moral responsibility for his own conduct. He will then retire on a full final salary pension leaving the younger generation to make a right mess of it.

Characteristics

Reading Material: Red tape

Favourite TV Programmes and Films: Panorama, The News, The Weather, Foyles War

Heroes and Role Models: Tony Hayward, Jeffrey Skilling

Most likely cause of death: Heart attack

Favourite Music: Whatever the wife listens to

Political Views: Tory

Ego Issues: Terrible bore who thinks that a topic is worth talking about because he's talking about it

Fears: China, India

Likes: Rejecting anything new, ditching the old for the sake of looking decisive, final salary pension

Dislikes: Chinese, Indians

Earnings: £300k

Offspring: Three children, stay at home wife

Drives: Jaguar

Most likely to say: "No, no, we have people to see to that "

Rugby Girlfriend

She's skinny, sleek and slender and as posh as they come. She describes her years at a top Girls' Boarding School as "hell on earth" and has considerable personal issues which prohibit her from befriending another woman and dropping her guard enough to laugh like she means it. She doesn't 'do' emotion and abhors shopping for anything other than Marlborough Lights which over the years have conspired with her regular bellowing of rugby anthems to lower her voice by at least an octave.

She lives in Southwest London, most likely Richmond, Chiswick or Fulham, and likes her men tank-like, with unnecessarily large shoulders, able to take their drink without resorting to violence and just a little bit posh. Which pretty much narrows it down to rugby union players. She lusts after the sturdy thighs of players like Gordon d'Arcy, Mike Phillips and Florian Fritz and would ditch her man for any one of them.

In the years since leaving school, she has turned being 'one of the lads' into a lifestyle choice although she doesn't like being called a ladette. She can match the rugger team pint for pint, is on the guest list for every one of their stag do's, but none of the hens, and fills in the dull daylight hours with a job in PR or marketing which supplements her allowance from Daddy.

Characteristics

Reading Material: The sports section of the Sunday Times, the Six Nations Fixtures Lists

Favourite TV Programmes and Films: Rarely watches TV except when the rugby's on in the pub. Has 5 Live on at home for company

Heroes and Role Models: Zara Phillips

Most likely cause of death: Sclerosis of the liver

Favourite Music: Bland soft rock, The Eagles, Foreigner, Joan Armatrading

Political Views: Hopelessly ill-informed, thinks David Cameron's probably the 'Right Sort', gets hacked off about increased duties on booze and fags.

Ego Issues: Torn between being accepted by the boys and liked by the girls

Fears: Womens' Rugby, Charlotte Church, the moment on her Wedding Day that the Vicar asks the congregation "If any of you know cause or just impediment…"

Likes: The mood in the pub after the lads have had a win, the feel of a freshly washed rugby jersey, Twickenham

Dislikes: Footballers, footballers' wives, being alone, female company, hair salons

Earnings: £25k a year from her 'little job' and a £40k a year allowance from her landowning parents

Offspring: Not yet, but she dreams of a house full of boys

Drives: Golf GTI

Most likely to say: "Swing low, sweet chariot"

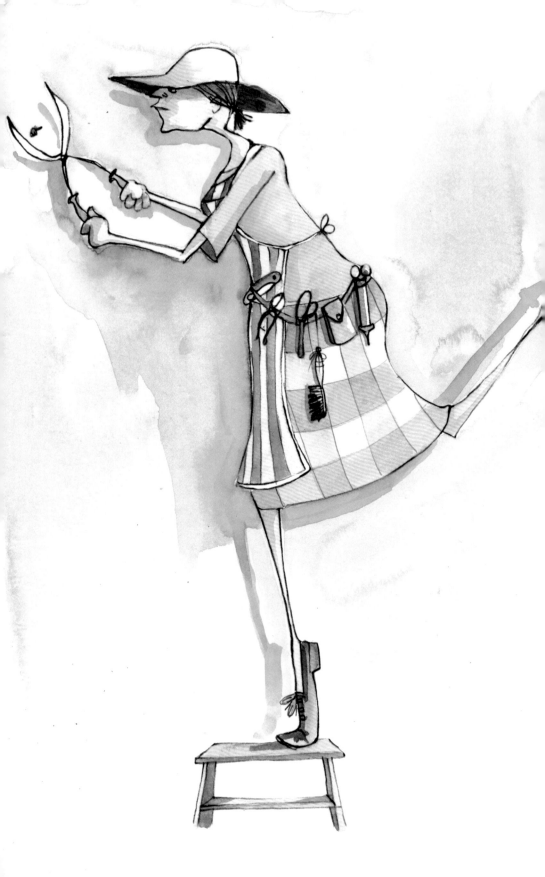

Lady Gardener

Charming posh woman who uses the word *Rancunculus* a lot and can spend six hours weeding without getting dirty. She has the stamina of a mountain goat and will live well into her nineties. She is married to a smugly retired gentleman with no neck who has made lots of money doing something boring, while she has spent her life playing host and propagating. She has had the leisure to look after herself, so she is still quite slim and well kept.

Her type regularly pops up on Gardeners' Question Time asking a question designed to show how wealthy she is. "Margaret Foxton-Smythe, Sunningdale Ladies Horticultural Guild. I have a sizeable garden with light sandy soil. Can the panel offer some planting suggestions to fill a south-facing border between the parterre and the Palladian Tea House?"

She wears a wide-brimmed hat because it reminds her of her formative years in colonial Kenya before she was sent to a convent school in Britain. This was the last time she talked to a black person. Gardening's main appeal is that it allows her to discreetly demonstrate her wealth, social standing and good taste, without resorting to the vulgar displays of the lower classes. In her social circle a camomile lawn serves the same function as a 52" plasma telly.

Characteristics

Reading Material: The Accidental Gardener, RHS Publications, seed catalogues, BBC Gardeners' Magazine

Favourite TV Programmes and Films: Gardeners' World, Gardeners' Question Time

Heroes and Role Models: Alan Titchmarsh, Monty Don, Gertrude Jekyll

Most likely cause of death: Infected rose wound

Favourite Music: Mozart, Vivaldi (Four Seasons), Tchaikovsky

Political Views: Tory

Ego Issues: Feels that her plant selection is very much a reflection of who she is

Fears: Aphids, black spot on her roses, slugs and snails in her brassicas, black people in her neighbourhood

Likes: Gardening, wedding, planting, rooting, Chelsea Flower Show, bacon grease as a rabbit deterrent

Dislikes: Pervasive weeds, pruning, taking stuff to the tip, moles, cutting the grass

Earnings: Husband earns six figures

Offspring: She has kept her figure despite three grown up children

Would like to drive but actually drives: Morgan/Mercedes

Most likely to say: "One simply never has enough time, does one?"

Trendy Rich Ski Girl

She has her own chalet in Gstaad which Daddy bought for her 21st birthday, complete with a Lady Who Does. She has been able to ski and snowboard since the age of five and takes to the slopes with the grace and poise of a pro. But being seen to ski well takes a firm second place: in the Alps, it's all about the look.

She wears ski goggles by Versace, mittens by Chanel and high-performance gilet and jacket by Dolce et Gabbana. She loves Chanel for the cute factor and Prada for the skin-tight fit and sleek silhouette. She brings with her an extensive range of luggage and never has to wear the same outfit twice. Every year, she replaces her entire ski-wardrobe: one year monochrome, the next high-impact pattern, the year after, metallics.

Her half-season as a chalet girl has left deep psychological scars: burnt shepherd's pies, vomit-filled bathrooms and rolls of bank notes left on pillows for which she discovered the hard way that she was expected to pay in kind. Cooking eggs and bacon on two hours sleep and a raging hangover for a bunch of monkey-suited telephone engineers on a stag do is simply beneath her. Consequently she is even more vile to her own chalet girl.

Characteristics

Reading Material: Harpers, Vogue, The Telegraph

Favourite TV Programmes and Films: She is too busy to watch TV but tries to make as many movie premieres as she can

Heroes and Role Models: Claudia Schiffer, because she has always looked divine *en piste*

Most likely cause of death: Falling from a chair lift

Favourite Music: Coldplay, U2: Gwyneth and Chris are best pals of their's and Bono's just a sweetheart

Political Views: Generally without an opinion and in any case, isn't the Polling Station generally in some god-awful comprehensive school? There's no way they're going inside one of those places

Ego Issues: Doesn't understand why the poor don't at least get their nails done, everyone's got £20 to spare, surely? There's just no excuse

Fears: Missing a trend, missing a party, not getting onto the right guest lists

Likes: Being seen in the right places, getting drunk, Switzerland, Harvey Nick's

Dislikes: Chapped lips, breakfast, the poor

Earnings: Has a trust fund and a flat in Mayfair or Chelsea

Offspring: None

Drives: Aston Martin DB9

Most likely to say: "I hear the Princes are here this season."

Climber

We've all been to school with one of these: he looked a bit like the actor Owen Wilson, was called Ben or Steve, did Biology, Physics and Chemistry A Levels, then studied pharmacy at Uni. Intelligent and calm, but slightly old before his time because he wore a navy blue fleece and talked about carabiners and pitons when all you could think about was hair gel and sneaking vodka into the school disco. Discreetly lost his virginity aged fifteen without really trying or boasting.

He enjoys an enviably active lifestyle. While everyone else burns themselves out working 9-5 under fluorescent lighting he works at an outdoor pursuit centre where he gets paid to do what he loves – teaching adventure sports.

He is probably a born again Christian, but doesn't make a big deal about it and it doesn't stop him being ruggedly cool and a bit nerdy at the same time. He is super fit and strong, even though he looks like a skinny beardy vicar. His dream is to live on a remote island in the Hebrides tending a lighthouse and some sheep, where for five months of every year he and his family are the only inhabitants, but he would miss the mountains. His girlfriend is slim, posh and outdoorsy and would be pretty if it she didn't remind you a little too much of David Cameron in a blonde wig.

Characteristics

Reading Material: The Guardian, Climber magazine

Favourite TV Programmes and Films: Doesn't own a TV; sometimes listens to Radio 4

Heroes and Role Models: Reinhold Messner, Alex Lowe, Jerzy Kukuczka, Don Whillans

Most likely cause of death: Hypothermia just before the push to the summit

Favourite Music: He has very eclectic musical tastes and can get equal enjoyment from Chris de Burgh and Jimi Hendrix.

Political Views: Quietly Tory, surprisingly, probably something to do with a belief in self-sufficiency, getting on your bike etc, you'd have to ask him

Ego Issues: Longs to name an unconquered peak after himself

Fears: Parental disapproval

Likes: Climbing, mountain biking, canoeing, caving, skiing, white-water rafting, hacking his hand off with a penknife when required

Dislikes: People stepping on his rope

Earnings: £30k

Offspring: Three honey-haired children, all of the same sex

Drives: Old Volvo

Most likely to say: 'If you don't let go, you can't fall off'

Opera Goer

These days the dignified British Opera Goer, dressed in all the slick understatement of the British elite is a dying breed. With a perfectly coiffured wife draped on his arm he is forced to battle his way to his box through two distinct opera-going hoards. The first are comprised entirely of crowd-watching gay aficionados who simply can't keep away. The second, are uneasy clusters of young, straight city professionals who park their pin-striped backsides on freebie corporate seats a couple of times a month to impress a client – the Arts equivalent of the prawn sandwich brigade at Old Trafford.

The Opera Goer despises the gay aficionados, with their animated chatter about Glyndebourne and La Scala. He sees no reason to hide his contempt for the other sort, the city boys who couldn't tell their Rigolettos from their Gilbert and Sullivans, and who depend on the subtitles to know what the ruddy hell is going on. He indulges in derisory thoughts about these comprehensive school spawn all the way home, resenting them for playing some ghastly corporate game in the vain hope that a little class might inadvertently rub off on them.

These die-hard few cling to their gold-stencilled opera-glasses for dear life and huddle together over a glass of bubbly at the interval to mourn the passing of prohibitive ticket prices.

Characteristics

Reading Material: The Telegraph, The Spectator

Favourite TV Programmes and Films: Radio Three and Four. They do own a TV somewhere in the house but it's in a wing they no longer inhabit

Heroes and Role Models: Tito Gobbi, Dame Joan Sutherland, Maria Callas, Earl of Harewood

Most likely cause of death: Gout

Favourite Music: Rossini, Verdi, Handel, Puccini

Political Views: Conservative, vehemently opposed to any efforts to eradicate the hereditary peerage

Ego Issues: Still smarting from an early dose of second-son syndrome. However his elder brother died heirless of AIDS in 1987, leaving him with the family seat and a hefty guilt problem.

Fears: The discovery of a gay gene, the operas of Engelburt Humperdink

Likes: A good pair of brogues, summers in Tuscany, subservient women

Dislikes: Non-hereditary peers, foreigners, Mozart

Earnings: Enough to keep the East Wing habitable

Offspring: Three sons – one in politics, another Barrister at Law, the youngest does something unthinkable in the music industry

Would like to drive but actually drives: Used to be driven/now drives

Most likely to say: "Absolutely ghastly"

Posth Students

They are dull, clumsy and pasty, with none of the energy or vibrancy typical of their generation and no clue as to how to style their hair beyond a side parting. They come from intelligent stock which their parents spent £300k nurturing at top public schools and where they learned that bland invisibility was the only way to survive if you couldn't play rugby. They favour corduroy and tweed and are the only undergraduates to purchase the University scarf, and they think the ensemble lends them an ironic retro charm.

After school, they won a place to read History or Philosophy at a red brick university where they gravitated naturally towards others of their kind and gave themselves quirky Latin nicknames. They stay in most nights making toast against the gas fire and eating Patum Peperium. They join the debating society or the orienteering society but never go to any of the socials. Occasionally they venture into the student union, where they order mild or port.

During university vacations they return home and get a holiday job with the local accountancy firm, or litter collecting for the council and lie awake at night fretting that their parents want them to try out for the University Challenge team. (see page 359).

Characteristics

Reading Material: The full reading list

Favourite TV Programmes and Films: I'm sorry I Haven't A Clue, University Challenge, Countdown

Heroes and Role Models: Bamber Gascoigne, Stephen Fry

Most likely cause of death: Alzheimer's

Favourite Music: Mike Oldfield, Julian Lloyd Weber, Kate Bush

Political Views: Lib Dem

Ego Issues: Suffer from very poor self-esteem which makes them giggle outrageously whenever they're in the vicinity of women

Fears: Being spotted, standing out from the crowd, a recurring nightmare about being on University Challenge

Likes: Lectures, French cheese, wearing humorous badges and comfortable slacks

Dislikes: Having to contribute to a seminar, students

Earnings: Father gives them a generous allowance and has bought a flat in their University town, so they have no need to call upon a student loan company

Offspring: It seems unlikely, but stranger things have happened

Would like to drive but actually drives: Golf

Most likely to say: "My name's Gerard, but chums call me Doctor Abstractionum, snort!"

Estate Agent (Posh)

Dull and avuncular land economy graduate who also managed to qualify as a chartered surveyor, despite the several square feet of vacant space between his ears. He walks with one hand behind his back like a butler which makes him lean forward at the waist and he points backwards when speaking about something that just happened to lend immediacy and interest to a tedious anecdote punctuated by one of those unnecessary posh speech impediments like saying "wuh" instead of "r".

He earns a packet selling top-end rural property to second home owners and foreigners. All he has to do is unlock the front door and lie to the buyer for ten minutes, job done. He has a firm handshake and loves using meaningless jargon and estate agent clichés. He will pretend to like you but will have forgotten who you are by the next time you call to chase him for being slow. Despite being loathed by his customers, British class culture dictates that whilst in his company we do as he says and do not question his over-inflated commission rates.

Characteristics

Reading Material: Country Life, The Negotiator, Private Eye, The Times

Favourite TV Programmes and Films: Location, Location, Location; Relocation, Relocation; The Property Chain, Brideshead Revisited, March of the Penguins

Heroes and Role Models: Boris Johnson, Kirstie Allsopp

Most likely cause of death: Stroke

Favourite Music: Elgar, Robbie Williams, Genesis, Coldplay, Classic FM compilations

Political Views: Tory

Ego Issues: He has the confidence, bluster and connections to muddle along in most social and business environments despite his lack of intelligence

Fears: Lack of posh housing stock; double-dip recession, lack of finance

Likes: Money, lying, lying for money, flyboarding, the fact that in the UK you have greater consumer protection when buying a tin of beans than a house

Dislikes: Other estate agents

Earnings: £75k

Offspring: One girl who is not very attractive but is posh so will marry well

Drives: BMW 7 series

Most likely to say: "Convenient for motorway access; incredible potential; delightfully secluded; needs some renovation; Look! There's the Aga"

Granny (Posh)

Impeccably dressed older lady with poise and grace and several grand's worth of precious stones on her fingers. Her soft white-blonde locks frame the remains of great bone structure and the beauty she once was is still clearly evident.

She knows how to break the ice, feign interest in your life and discreetly bring the conversation to an end when she's bored of you. She can hold a plate of canapés and a glass of Prosecco in the same hand and gesticulate, flirt and attract the waiter's attention with the other. She has a house in the Home Counties and another in Tuscany and still talks about going 'up' to London, even though it's due South.

Her sons are a source of great pride and she never misses an opportunity to drop their career highlights into the conversation. She rarely mentions her daughter-in-laws, who don't parent the way she did and therefore don't do it right. She is nonplussed by the formless art work her daughters-in-law send her through the post: frankly, she couldn't care less whether it is little Olivia's first go at finger painting or not. Her grandchildren's photographs are framed neatly on the grand piano, but secretly make her anxious until they're safely settled into Oxbridge and can talk civilly about the cabinet re-shuffle, the falling value of the dollar and their latest Rowing Blue.

Characteristics

Reading Material: Margaret Atwood, Ian McEwan and whatever's on her Book Club Reading list

Favourite TV Programmes and Films: Radio 4, Woman's Hour, Desert Island Discs, The Archers, Lark Rise to Candleford and anything with Colin Firth.

Heroes and Role Models: Dowager Duchess of Devonshire

Most likely cause of death: Old age

Favourite Music: Has no favourites, but likes to have a little Classic FM on in the background

Political Views: Thinks children should be privately educated from the age of two, should board as early as possible, shouldn't wear coats in cold weather nor be molly-coddled with centrally heated houses. She thinks boiled egg and toast soldiers is never acceptable at lunch time, and that an infant should never sleep in the same room as its parents, let alone the same bed

Ego Issues: Is in a permanent state of frustration that none of her off-spring or their spouses will acknowledge her superiority when it comes to parenting choices

Fears: Close contact with an unclean nose, vomit, having to respond to the words, "I love you Granny", being called "Granny"

Likes: Celebrating her grandchildren's birthdays by post

Dislikes: Her grandchildren associating with children with regional accents, shaved heads or football strips

Earnings: Her husband's healthy pension and investment portfolio keeps them very secure

Offspring: Two sons

Drives: Mercedes or Volvo

Most likely to say: "Very nice darling, but don't touch Grandma's frock. It's new"

Fighter Pilot (Retired, 80+)

George "Chalky" White was born just before WWI, in which his father fought and died from his wounds a few years afterwards. During his school days he was a skilled boxer, captained the rugby team and nearly got into the national squad.

When war broke out again he flew Hurricanes with Douglas Bader at Dunkirk and in the Battle of Britain, clocking up nineteen credited Jerrys before being hit by flak on a sweep over France in '41. Bailing out he picked up a back injury which always remained with him.

After being shot down he spent the rest of the war in Colditz where he was recaptured three times having tried to escape. After the war he became a test pilot, was awarded the CBE and vowed never to forgive the Germans and Japanese. Until recently he was a familiar sight at RAF social gatherings.

Characteristics

Reading Material: Books about Spitfires, the war and Colditz which he keeps getting bought by his grandchildren, Radio Times, Daily Telegraph

Favourite TV Programmes and Films: Cricket, Rugby, The Boat Race, Grand National, Queen's Speech

Heroes and Role Models: Sir Keith Park, Douglas Bader, von Richthofen, Barnes Wallis

Most likely cause of death: Old age

Favourite Music: Vera Lynn

Political Views: Won't vote Tory again after Liam Fox's decision to cut two Tornado squadrons and almost half our trainee airmen

Ego Issues: None

Fears: Defence cuts

Likes: Air shows, his two Distinguished Service Orders and Distinguished Flying Crosses

Dislikes: Kids today who don't know what the Battle of Britain is or who Rommel was

Earnings: Tiny war pension, state pension

Offspring: Grown up children and grandchildren

Drives: Fraser Nash – dangerously

Most likely to say: "I'm sorry, I can't hear you!"

Young Toff

Braying hooray called Peregrine with more money than sense of sneering entitlement and tendency to judge others on how they eat their soup, whether they buy or make marmalade and what they call their settee. His manner makes most people want to kick or shoot him in his ruddy face, so it's a miracle this hasn't happened yet, despite him spending so much time around horses and guns. He has the permanent look of bemusement that usually accompanies having no chin.

He says "what" instead of "pardon" and calls his parents "Mummy and Daddy". A strict upholder of the status quo, his snobbery and inbreeding are so extensive that he can claim the Queen as a several-times-removed relative and can't close his mouth over his teeth. After a childhood spent dressed as a girl, surrounded by nannies and private tutors, prep and public school, Daddy the diplomat got him a job as a public relations executive, which consists of loudly expressing his opinions over the phone in a plummy voice and spraying Moet during lunch. He sticks his finger in his ear when he's on his mobile even when there's no noise and would probably do the same on a deserted glacier.

Characteristics

Reading Material: Tatler, Country Life, Harpers and Queen, The Times, Evelyn Waugh

Favourite TV Programmes and Films: Gosford Park, Downton Abbey

Heroes and Role Models: Michael Gove, George Osborne, Lord Young, Julian Fellowes

Most likely cause of death: Kicked or shot in the face

Favourite Music: Predictable classical like Mozart, Bach (Brandenburg Concertos), Beethoven

Political Views: Unemployment is a price worth paying for low inflation; the fox hunting ban should be lifted

Ego Issues: Is only 4,389th in line to the British throne

Fears: Council-houses, people with regional accents, women

Likes: Killing animals with guns, killing animals by chasing them on horseback, primogeniture

Dislikes: Scruffy people (who must be lefties)

Earnings: £75-£100k

Offspring: Despite his own unfortunate features, when he is older his inherited wealth will enable him to marry well out of his league and sire five future fashion models called Olivia, Octavia, Gabriella, Arabella and Georgiana

Drives: Landrover 90

Most likely to say: "Now look here"

Matriach

A difficult, unhappy and vastly wealthy harriden who is scathing and judgemental about everyone in her life. Her staff are reduced to tears on a daily basis, her children have been in therapy for decades and her husband is either a mute depressive who confines himself to the East Wing where he contemplates suicide every moment of his waking hours, or has had the gumption to bugger off to Argentina long ago, where he's shacked up with a thirty-something cabaret dancer called Raquel.

She is never seen around the house until perfectly coiffured and dressed in a frock, pearls and heels. She nibbles on her food at mealtimes without enthusiasm, and weighs herself twice a day.

She tolerates visits from her children, and spends the duration of her time with them berating them for their poor choice of university, inappropriate career paths and intolerable spouses. Her grandchildren offer her no comfort but are simply a further focus for her disapproval: they are ill-educated, improperly dressed and talk like comprehensive school riff-raff.

Their childhood insecurities have condemned all her offspring to pitifully unsuccessful careers, and it is only their mounting debt problems that keep them coming back. Naturally, she is sharp enough to realise this, and the knowledge only makes her hate them even more.

Characteristics

Reading Material: The Telegraph, particularly the Obits

Favourite TV Programmes and Films: Radio 4, The Today Programme, only has the TV on for the Queen's Speech at Christmas

Heroes and Role Models: The Queen

Most likely cause of death: she will almost certainly come to a violent end and the police will have a tough time deciding which of her close family members they should regard as their chief suspect

Favourite Music: She tolerates organ music at the parish Church on Sundays, at any other time she finds music distasteful

Political Views: Bigotry

Ego Issues: She is untouchable: no-one has ever had the courage to stand up to her. No-one challenges her opinions to her face, and she has yet to find any source of satisfaction in the actions, choices and achievements of her closest family members

Fears: That one of her children or grandchildren might become homosexual, Roman Catholic or an alcoholic. Worse, that one of them may want to become a teacher, a nurse or a dental assistant

Likes: A weekend without guests

Dislikes: Journalists, the Scots, dining in company

Earnings: No one but her and her accountant know for sure

Offspring: Four, tortured, anxious and with considerable commitment issues

Drives: Is driven

Most likely to say: "Are you still seeing that hideous woman? That colour drains you. Your hair makes you look common"

English Eccentric

Over the years this chap has compensated for his shocking lack of social skills by a combination of extreme intelligence, mild Obsessive Compulsive Disorder and a growing array of bizarre inventions and anti-social dining habits.

He lives with an extensive collection of taxidermy and can chart the sexual history of Britain using stuffed woodland animals. Pride of his collection is a diorama of carefully posed grey squirrels depicting the execution of King Edward II. However, his intellectual pursuits extend beyond the history of British bestiality. His technological genius enables him to reproduce the weaponry of medieval siege warfare and his full scale Trebuchet has attracted the attention of the press after he used it to lob dead cattle into neighbouring farmland during the Foot and Mouth crisis.

His wife and children have grown accustomed to his extended periods of nudity, his political protests involving monkey nuts and cartwheels, and no longer complain about sharing the dinner table with his pet skunk.

Characteristics

Reading Material: The Complete Works of Darwin, Guardian, Encyclopedia Brittanica, Practical Reptile Keeping

Favourite TV Programmes and Films: Anything with Bill Oddie, Godzilla, Travels With My Aunt

Heroes and Role Models: Brunel, Wagner, Moses

Most likely cause of death: Something horrible and extremely rare

Favourite Music: Pre-war rolling stock of the LNER

Political Views: He is paranoid about genetically modified crops, thinks vegans are aliens and believes the local Post Office to be bugged

Ego Issues: Too tight to pay for first class rail travel but takes his temperature at regular intervals with an anal thermometer in order to clear the carriage because he hates to travel with strangers

Fears: Dairylea cheese triangles, bathing, GM Foods, the six reptilian aliens who rule the world

Likes: Bill Oddie, Indian food, short trousers

Dislikes: His wife's company, working for a living, small talk, social conventions

Earnings: Currently nil

Offspring: His sons are both in Merchant Banking and have long suspected that their father is just putting it on

Drives: 1970s Mercedes estate

Most likely to say: "Would you mind taking my temperature"

Landowner

78

105

8

2

30

Like an angry storm cloud he appears when you least expect it and then ruins your day with a list of reasons why you are damaging his land/hedges/fences/gates, scaring his sheep, destroying his livelihood and giving him the legal imperative to shoot your dog. Reasoning with him is futile because he is completely inflexible. If, for example, you are crossing a clearly empty field and your dog is roaming free, the landowner will suddenly appear and gruffly shout at you to keep your dog under control because there might have been sheep or horses in the field next week. He does this with an urgency that almost convinces you that you're in the wrong, so you comply apologetically, and it's only five minutes later that you realise what an angry unreasonable man he is. If you try to answer back: "I thought that—" he will cut you short and jab a craggy finger in the direction of a hand-painted sign clearly stating his right to fill your dog with lead if it is FOUND AMONG SHEEP, whatever the hell that means. Apparently this includes "in the same county".

Characteristics

Reading Material: Sporting Gun, Shooting Gazette, Country Life, Horse & Hound, Countryside and Rights of Way Act 2000

Favourite TV Programmes and Films: The Archers, Farming Today, Countryfile

Heroes and Role Models: Nicholas van Hoogstraten, Tony Martin

Most likely cause of death: Heart attack

Favourite Music: n/a

Political Views: Tory from cradle to grave, frequently bribes the parish council to support his appeals to reroute footpaths and bridleways

Ego Issues: Does not like being teased by gamekeepers

Fears: Ramblers, dog walkers, Ramblers' Association

Likes: Shooting and social climbing, selling large quantities of lamb and beef to supermarket chains

Dislikes: Trespassers, Right to Roam

Earnings: £150k, +£100k for having a few wind turbines

Offspring: Three daughters, all posy and wayward

Drives: Anything Land Rover

Most likely to say: "What the bloody hell do you think you are doing"

Minor Royals

He's a pleasantly charming, red-cheeked, jovial sort, great at small talk and capable of surprisingly funny one-liners when the situation calls for humour. With his full face, side parting and tight vowels, there's no mistaking his Teutonic pedigree although most people need a nudge to know precisely how he's connected to the Monarchy.

He ranks highly enough to enjoy a life of gentle privilege in a crumbling, bijou 100-acre corner of Gloucestershire where his carefully chosen wife helped raise their four fresh-faced gymkhana-loving offspring by investing in a sound, boarding school education from the age of three. He complains constantly of lack of funds needed for the conservation of the house.

Freed from the restrictions of life as First-In-Line, he has been able to enjoy all the perks of royalty without too much of the fuss. His hand-shaking, hospital-opening, medal-wearing days are kept to an absolute minimum, which leaves him plenty of time to fly helicopters, play polo and garden.

However on ceremonial occasions he's as happy as the next man to buff up his military sash and stand to attention, although he has no idea what his various military honours are actually.

He likes to give back to the country by taking an active interest in organic farming methods, the plight of inner city strays and the Rugger.

Characteristics

Reading Material: Rudyard Kipling, Enid Blyton, Arthur Ransom, Arthur Conan Doyle

Favourite TV Programmes and Films: Anything featuring Willie Rushton, Spike Milligan, Peter Sellers, Tony Hancock

Heroes and Role Models: Lord Mountbatten, Duke of Windsor

Most likely cause of death: Helicopter crash, complications following a riding accident, gout, embolism

Favourite Music: The Three Degrees

Political Views: Wanted to talk to the CIA about getting Tony Blair bumped off

Ego Issues: Feels hard-done by because primogeniture's given his elder brother the better title, the bigger pad and the better looking wife

Fears: Republicans, Paul Burrell, The Rise of Asia

Likes: Running a discrete little pad in Chelsea, shooting, tweed, having a jolly good laugh, fancy dress parties

Dislikes: Italians, New Labour

Earnings: Most of his earnings come from rent from his country pad

Offspring: Yes, he's sure he has three or four, somewhere around the house, ha, ha, snort!

Drives: a Jaguar, a Landrover, a Volvo estate for the Labradors, and a helicopter

Most likely to say: "One does, doesn't one"

Tim Bulmer

He was born into a comfortable, privileged and well appointed middle class family that was dysfunctional well before he appeared. His father went up the aisle reluctantly and by the time his older brother appeared the atmosphere was one of loathing and hostility wrapped in a blanket of repressed denial. He was neither particularly academic nor athletic but rest assured the small amount of confidence he did possess was soon kicked out of him at expensive and loveless establishments that have left him pathetically craving approval ever since. He found salvation at Art College where he met a kind, well adjusted girl from a perfectly functioning working class background and they had two brilliant children together who went to wonderful, perfectly functioning state schools. His career path, if plotted on a graph, would flawlessly represent that of a man undergoing the rigours of defibrillation whilst trying desperately to avoid permanent demise.